Peugeot 309 Owners Workshop Manual

I M Coomber

Models covered
All Peugeot 309 models with petrol engines, including GTI and special/limited edition models
1118 cc, 1294 cc, 1580 cc & 1905 cc

Does not cover revised range introduced October 1989
For information on Diesel engines see OWM No 1379

(1266-8R2)

ABCDE
FGHIJ
KLMNO

THE BOOK

Haynes Publishing Group
Sparkford Nr Yeovil
Somerset BA22 7JJ England

Haynes Publications, Inc
861 Lawrence Drive
Newbury Park
California 91320 USA

Acknowledgements

Thanks are due to the Champion Sparking Company Limited who supplied the illustrations showing the spark plug conditions, and to Duckhams Oils who provided lubrication data. Certain other illustrations are the copyright of Peugeot Talbot Motor Company Limited, and are used with their permission. Thanks are also due to Sykes-Pickavant who supplied some of the workshop tools, and all the staff at Sparkford who assisted in the production of this Manual.

© Haynes Publishing Group 1989

A book in the **Haynes Owners Workshop Manual Series**

Printed by J. H. Haynes & Co. Ltd, Sparkford, Nr Yeovil, Somerset BA22 7JJ, England

ISBN 1 85010 517 0

British Library Cataloguing in Publication Data
Coomber, Ian, *1943-*
  Peugeot 309 owners manual.- 2nd ed.
  1. Cars. Maintenance & repair
  I. Title II. Series
  629.28'722
  ISBN 1-85010-517-0

Whilst every care is taken to ensure that the information in this manual is correct, no liability can be accepted by the authors or publishers for loss, damage or injury caused by any errors in, or omissions from, the information given.

Contents

Peugeot 309 1.3 GL

Peugeot 309 SRi

About this manual

Its aim

The aim of this manual is to help you get the best value from your vehicle. It can do so in several ways. It can help you decide what work must be done (even should you choose to get it done by a garage), provide information on routine maintenance and servicing, and give a logical course of action and diagnosis when random faults occur. However, it is hoped that you will use the manual by tackling the work yourself. On simpler jobs it may even be quicker than booking the car into a garage and going there twice, to leave and collect it. Perhaps most important, a lot of money can be saved by avoiding the costs a garage must charge to cover its labour and overheads.

The manual has drawings and descriptions to show the function of the various components so that their layout can be understood. Then the tasks are described and photographed in a step-by-step sequence so that even a novice can do the work.

Its arrangement

The manual is divided into twelve Chapters, each covering a logical sub-division of the vehicle. The Chapters are each divided into Sections, numbered with single figures, eg 5; and the Sections into paragraphs (or sub-sections), with decimal numbers following on from the Section they are in, eg 5.1, 5.2, 5.3 etc.

It is freely illustrated, especially in those parts where there is a detailed sequence of operations to be carried out. There are two forms of illustration: figures and photographs. The figures are numbered in sequence with decimal numbers, according to their position in the Chapter – eg Fig. 6.4 is the fourth drawing/illustration in Chapter 6. Photographs carry the same number (either individually or in related groups) as the Section or sub-section to which they relate.

There is an alphabetical index at the back of the manual as well as a contents list at the front. Each Chapter is also preceded by its own individual contents list.

References to the 'left' or 'right' of the vehicle are in the sense of a person in the driver's seat facing forwards.

Unless otherwise stated, nuts and bolts are removed by turning anti-clockwise, and tightened by turning clockwise.

Vehicle manufacturers continually make changes to specifications and recommendations, and these, when notified, are incorporated into our manuals at the earliest opportunity.

Whilst every care is taken to ensure that the information in this manual is correct, no liability can be accepted by the authors or publishers for loss, damage or injury caused by any errors in, or omissions from, the information given.

Project vehicles

The vehicles used in the preparation of this manual, and appearing in many photographic sequences, were a Peugot 309 1.3 GL and an SR Injection.

Introduction to the Peugeot 309

The Peugeot 309 model range was introduced in the UK in February of 1986, It has a three- or five-door hatchback body type of steel unit construction.

The engine and transmission are transversely mounted; drive being to the front roadwheels. The suspension is independent at the front and rear. The front suspension has MacPherson struts whilst the rear suspension has trailing arms and transverse torsion bars. All models have an anti-roll bar at the front.

Three engine sizes were originally available, the 1.1 and 1.3 litre engines being of overhead valve (OHV) design and the 1.6 litre being of overhead camshaft (OHC) design. In September 1988, a GTI version was introduced, powered by a 1.9 litre engine. Details of this model are included in the Supplement at the back of this manual.

The car is generally well built and economical. The wide range of models and options available should meet the needs of most purchasers looking for a practical car in this section of the market.

General dimensions, weights and capacities

Dimensions
Overall length .... 4051 mm (159.5 in)
Overall width .... 1628 mm (64.1 in)
Overall height .... 1380 mm (54.3 in)
Wheelbase .... 2469 mm (97.2 in)

Weights
Kerb weight:
    1.1 and 1.3 models .... 850 kg (1874 lb)
    1.6 carburettor models:
        Manual gearbox .... 870 kg (1918 lb)
        Automatic transmission .... 910 kg (2007 lb)
    1.6 fuel injection models .... 890 kg (1962 lb)
    1.9 GTI .... 930 kg (2051 lb)
Maximum towing weight (with braked trailer):
    All models .... 800 kg (1764 lb)
Maximum roof rack load:
    All models .... 75 kg (165 lb)

Capacities
Engine oil (including filter):
    1.1 and 1.3 engines .... 3.3 litre (5.8 pints)
    1.6 and 1.9 engines .... 5.0 litre (8.8 pints)
Manual gearbox .... 2.0 litre (3.5 pints)
Automatic transmission:
    From dry .... 6.2 litre (10.9 pints)
    Routine fluid renewal .... 2.4 litre (4.2 pints)
Power steering .... 0.65 litre (1.1 pints)
Cooling system:
    1.1 and 1.3 engines .... 6.6 litre (11.6 pints)
    1.6 carburettor engines .... 7.5 litre (13.2 pints)
    1.6 fuel injection engines .... 8.0 litre (14.1 pints)
    1.9 fuel injection engine .... 8.5 litre (15.0 pints)
Washer reservoir – front .... 1.8 litre (3.2 pints)
Washer reservoir – rear .... 1.1 litre (1.9 pints)
Fuel tank .... 55 litre (12.1 gallons)

Jacking and towing

The jack supplied with the car by the manufacturers is designed for use only when changing a roadwheel. The jack locates under the body sill on the side concerned at the jack point to the rear of the front wheel arch or to the front of the rear wheel arch as applicable. Before jacking up the car to change the roadwheel, loosen the roadwheel retaining bolts first. Ensure that the jack is securely located and standing on firm level ground. The car should be in gear and the handbrake fully applied.

If you are going to carry out work under the car it is preferable to position the car over an inspection pit. If this is not available use a workshop trolley jack or substantial screw or bottle type hydraulic jack. *Always supplement a jack with axle stands.* The sill jacking points or their adjacent re-inforced areas should be used as jacking points for raising the car. A beam may be placed under the front subframe and the front end jacked up under that. The side-members of the front subframe should be used as axle stand support points. The rear side-members may be used in a similar way.

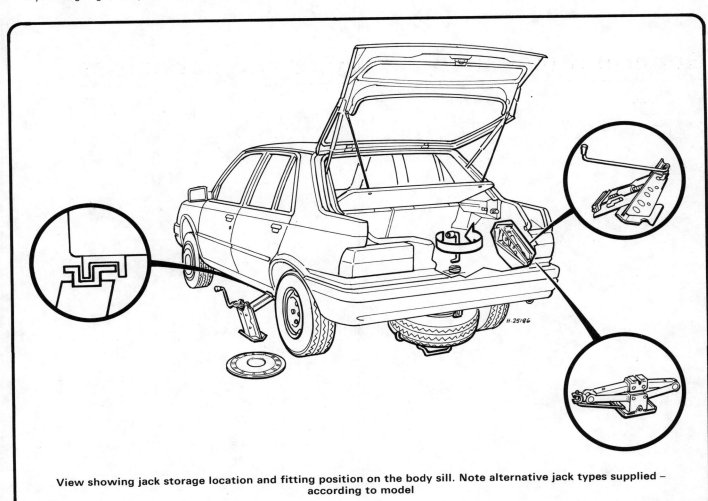

View showing jack storage location and fitting position on the body sill. Note alternative jack types supplied – according to model

Jack location points

Towing and being towed

Front and rear anchorage points are provided for securing the car during transportation on a car transporter, boat, train and so on (photo). These points can also be used for towing the car or for towing another in an emergency. For permanent towing requirements a tow-bar is necessary, properly attached to the vehicle.

Ensure that the ignition key is in the steering unlocked position (A or M as required).

On some models the blanking plate in the front bumper will need removal for access to the towing eye.

Front towing eye

Buying spare parts and vehicle identification numbers

Buying spare parts

Spare parts are available from many sources. Peugeot have many dealers throughout the UK, and other dealers, accessory stores and motor factors will also stock some spare parts suitable for Peugeot cars.

Our advice regarding spare part sources is as follows:

Officially appointed vehicle main dealers – This is the best source for parts which are peculiar to your vehicle and are otherwise not generally available (eg, complete cylinder heads, internal transmission components, badges, interior trim, etc). It is also the only place you should buy parts if your vehicle is still under warranty. To be sure of obtaining the correct parts it will always be necessary to give the storeman your vehicle's engine and chassis number, and if possible, to take the 'old' part along for a positive identification. Remember that many parts are available on a factory exchange scheme – any parts returned should always be clean. It obviously makes good sense to go straight to the specialist on your vehicle for this type of part, for they are best equipped to supply you.

Other dealers and auto accessory stores – These are often very good places to buy materials and components needed for the maintenance of your vehicle (eg, oil filters, spark plugs, bulbs, drivebelts, oils and greases, touch-up paint, filler paste, etc). They also sell general accessories, usually have the convenient opening hours, charge lower prices and can often be found not far from home.

Motor factors – Good factors will stock all the more important components which wear out relatively quickly (eg, clutch components, pistons, valves, exhaust systems, brake cylinders/pipes/hoses/seals/shoes and pads, etc). Motor factors will often provide new or reconditioned components on a part exchange basis – this can save a considerable amount of money.

Vehicle identification numbers

Modifications are a continuing and unpublicised process in vehicle manufacture. Spare parts manuals and lists are compiled on a numerical basis, the individual vehicle numbers being essential to identify correctly the component required.

Body serial number: This is located on the right-hand side wing valance within the engine compartment.

Vehicle information plate: This is located on the bulkhead on the right-hand side in the engine compartment.

Engine number (1.1 and 1.3 OHV engines): The number is stamped on a plate attached to the cylinder block on the spark plug side, just beneath the cylinder head at the flywheel end.

Engine number (1.6 and 1.9 OHC engines): The number is located at the timing case end of the cylinder block, just beneath the cylinder head on the spark plug side.

Vehicle identification plate locations

Manufacturer's plate (EEC regulations):

a	Manufacturer
b	Type approval number
c	Vehicle identification number:
	Manufacturer's identification
	Vehicle type code
	Model year G 1986
	H 1987
	Serial number

d	Gross vehicle weight (GVW)
e	Gross train weight (GTW)
f	Maximum load on front axle
g	Maximum load on rear axle
h	Paint and trim code
j	Factory build code

Serial number

General repair procedures

Whenever servicing, repair or overhaul work is carried out on the car or its components, it is necessary to observe the following procedures and instructions. This will assist in carrying out the operation efficiently and to a professional standard of workmanship.

Joint mating faces and gaskets

Where a gasket is used between the mating faces of two components, ensure that it is renewed on reassembly, and fit it dry unless otherwise stated in the repair procedure. Make sure that the mating faces are clean and dry with all traces of old gasket removed. When cleaning a joint face, use a tool which is not likely to score or damage the face, and remove any burrs or nicks with an oilstone or fine file.

Make sure that tapped holes are cleaned with a pipe cleaner, and keep them free of jointing compound if this is being used unless specifically instructed otherwise.

Ensure that all orifices, channels or pipes are clear and blow through them, preferably using compressed air.

Oil seals

Whenever an oil seal is removed from its working location, either individually or as part of an assembly, it should be renewed.

The very fine sealing lip of the seal is easily damaged and will not seal if the surface it contacts is not completely clean and free from scratches, nicks or grooves. If the original sealing surface of the component cannot be restored, the component should be renewed.

Protect the lips of the seal from any surface which may damage them in the course of fitting. Use tape or a conical sleeve where possible. Lubricate the seal lips with oil before fitting and, on dual lipped seals, fill the space between the lips with grease.

Unless otherwise stated, oil seals must be fitted with their sealing lips toward the lubricant to be sealed.

Use a tubular drift or block of wood of the appropriate size to install the seal and, if the seal housing is shouldered, drive the seal down to the shoulder. If the seal housing is unshouldered, the seal should be fitted with its face flush with the housing top face.

Screw threads and fastenings

Always ensure that a blind tapped hole is completely free from oil, grease, water or other fluid before installing the bolt or stud. Failure to do this could cause the housing to crack due to the hydraulic action of the bolt or stud as it is screwed in.

When tightening a castellated nut to accept a split pin, tighten the nut to the specified torque, where applicable, and then tighten further to the next split pin hole. Never slacken the nut to align a split pin hole unless stated in the repair procedure.

When checking or retightening a nut or bolt to a specified torque setting, slacken the nut or bolt by a quarter of a turn, and then retighten to the specified setting.

Locknuts, locktabs and washers

Any fastening which will rotate against a component or housing in the course of tightening should always have a washer between it and the relevant component or housing.

Spring or split washers should always be renewed when they are used to lock a critical component such as a big-end bearing retaining nut or bolt.

Locktabs which are folded over to retain a nut or bolt should always be renewed.

Self-locking nuts can be reused in non-critical areas, providing resistance can be felt when the locking portion passes over the bolt or stud thread.

Split pins must always be replaced with new ones of the correct size for the hole.

Special tools

Some repair procedures in this manual entail the use of special tools such as a press, two or three-legged pullers, spring compressors etc. Wherever possible, suitable readily available alternatives to the manufacturer's special tools are described, and are shown in use. In some instances, where no alternative is possible, it has been necessary to resort to the use of a manufacturer's tool and this has been done for reasons of safety as well as the efficient completion of the repair operation. Unless you are highly skilled and have a thorough understanding of the procedure described, never attempt to bypass the use of any special tool when the procedure described specifies its use. Not only is there a very great risk of personal injury, but expensive damage could be caused to the components involved.

Tools and working facilities

Introduction

A selection of good tools is a fundamental requirement for anyone contemplating the maintenance and repair of a motor vehicle. For the owner who does not possess any, their purchase will prove a considerable expense, offsetting some of the savings made by doing-it-yourself. However, provided that the tools purchased meet the relevant national safety standards and are of good quality, they will last for many years and prove an extremely worthwhile investment.

To help the average owner to decide which tools are needed to carry out the various tasks detailed in this manual, we have compiled three lists of tools under the following headings: *Maintenance and minor repair*, *Repair and overhaul*, and *Special*. The newcomer to practical mechanics should start off with the *Maintenance and minor repair* tool kit and confine himself to the simpler jobs around the vehicle. Then, as his confidence and experience grow, he can undertake more difficult tasks, buying extra tools as, and when, they are needed. In this way, a *Maintenance and minor repair* tool kit can be built-up into a *Repair and overhaul* tool kit over a considerable period of time without any major cash outlays. The experienced do-it-yourselfer will have a tool kit good enough for most repair and overhaul procedures and will add tools from the *Special* category when he feels the expense is justified by the amount of use to which these tools will be put.

It is obviously not possible to cover the subject of tools fully here. For those who wish to learn more about tools and their use there is a book entitled *How to Choose and Use Car Tools* available from the publishers of this manual.

Maintenance and minor repair tool kit

The tools given in this list should be considered as a minimum requirement if routine maintenance, servicing and minor repair operations are to be undertaken. We recommend the purchase of combination spanners (ring one end, open-ended the other); although more expensive than open-ended ones, they do give the advantages of both types of spanner.

Combination spanners - 10, 11, 12, 13, 14 & 17 mm
Adjustable spanner - 9 inch
Engine sump drain plug key
Spark plug spanner (with rubber insert)
Spark plug gap adjustment tool
Set of feeler gauges
Brake adjuster spanner
Brake bleed nipple spanner
Screwdriver - 4 in long x $1/4$ in dia (flat blade)
Screwdriver - 4 in long x $1/4$ in dia (cross blade)
Combination pliers - 6 inch
Hacksaw (junior)
Tyre pump
Tyre pressure gauge
Oil can
Fine emery cloth (1 sheet)
Wire brush (small)
Funnel (medium size)

Repair and overhaul tool kit

These tools are virtually essential for anyone undertaking any major repairs to a motor vehicle, and are additional to those given in the *Maintenance and minor repair* list. Included in this list is a comprehensive set of sockets. Although these are expensive they will be found invaluable as they are so versatile - particularly if various drives are included in the set. We recommend the ½ in square-drive type, as this can be used with most proprietary torque wrenches. If you cannot afford a socket set, even bought piecemeal, then inexpensive tubular box spanners are a useful alternative.

The tools in this list will occasionally need to be supplemented by tools from the *Special* list.

Sockets (or box spanners) to cover range in previous list
Reversible ratchet drive (for use with sockets)
Extension piece, 10 inch (for use with sockets)
Universal joint (for use with sockets)
Torque wrench (for use with sockets)
'Mole' wrench - 8 inch
Ball pein hammer
Soft-faced hammer, plastic or rubber
Screwdriver - 6 in long x $5/16$ in dia (flat blade)
Screwdriver - 2 in long x $5/16$ in square (flat blade)
Screwdriver - $1 1/2$ in long x $1/4$ in dia (cross blade)
Screwdriver - 3 in long x $1/8$ in dia (electricians)
Pliers - electricians side cutters
Pliers - needle nosed
Pliers - circlip (internal and external)
Cold chisel - $1/2$ inch
Scriber
Scraper
Centre punch
Pin punch
Hacksaw
Valve grinding tool
Steel rule/straight-edge
Allen keys (inc. splined/Torx type if necessary)
Selection of files
Wire brush (large)
Axle-stands
Jack (strong trolley or hydraulic type)

Special tools

The tools in this list are those which are not used regularly, are expensive to buy, or which need to be used in accordance with their manufacturers' instructions. Unless relatively difficult mechanical jobs are undertaken frequently, it will not be economic to buy many of these tools. Where this is the case, you could consider clubbing together with friends (or joining a motorists' club) to make a joint purchase, or borrowing the tools against a deposit from a local garage or tool hire specialist.

The following list contains only those tools and instruments freely available to the public, and not those special tools produced by the vehicle manufacturer specifically for its dealer network. You will find occasional references to these manufacturers' special tools in the text of this manual. Generally, an alternative method of doing the job without the vehicle manufacturers' special tool is given. However, sometimes, there is no alternative to using them. Where this is the case and the relevant tool cannot be bought or borrowed, you will have to entrust the work to a franchised garage.

    Valve spring compressor (where applicable)
    Piston ring compressor
    Balljoint separator
    Universal hub/bearing puller
    Impact screwdriver
    Micrometer and/or vernier gauge
    Dial gauge
    Stroboscopic timing light
    Dwell angle meter/tachometer
    Universal electrical multi-meter
    Cylinder compression gauge
    Lifting tackle
    Trolley jack
    Light with extension lead

Buying tools

For practically all tools, a tool factor is the best source since he will have a very comprehensive range compared with the average garage or accessory shop. Having said that, accessory shops often offer excellent quality tools at discount prices, so it pays to shop around.

There are plenty of good tools around at reasonable prices, but always aim to purchase items which meet the relevant national safety standards. If in doubt, ask the proprietor or manager of the shop for advice before making a purchase.

Care and maintenance of tools

Having purchased a reasonable tool kit, it is necessary to keep the tools in a clean serviceable condition. After use, always wipe off any dirt, grease and metal particles using a clean, dry cloth, before putting the tools away. Never leave them lying around after they have been used. A simple tool rack on the garage or workshop wall, for items such as screwdrivers and pliers, is a good idea. Store all normal wrenches and sockets in a metal box. Any measuring instruments, gauges, meters, etc, must be carefully stored where they cannot be damaged or become rusty.

Take a little care when tools are used. Hammer heads inevitably become marked and screwdrivers lose the keen edge on their blades from time to time. A little timely attention with emery cloth or a file will soon restore items like this to a good serviceable finish.

Working facilities

Not to be forgotten when discussing tools, is the workshop itself. If anything more than routine maintenance is to be carried out, some form of suitable working area becomes essential.

It is appreciated that many an owner mechanic is forced by circumstances to remove an engine or similar item, without the benefit of a garage or workshop. Having done this, any repairs should always be done under the cover of a roof.

Wherever possible, any dismantling should be done on a clean, flat workbench or table at a suitable working height.

Any workbench needs a vice: one with a jaw opening of 4 in (100 mm) is suitable for most jobs. As mentioned previously, some clean dry storage space is also required for tools, as well as for lubricants, cleaning fluids, touch-up paints and so on, which become necessary.

Another item which may be required, and which has a much more general usage, is an electric drill with a chuck capacity of at least 5/16 in (8 mm). This, together with a good range of twist drills, is virtually essential for fitting accessories such as mirrors and reversing lights.

Last, but not least, always keep a supply of old newspapers and clean, lint-free rags available, and try to keep any working area as clean as possible.

Spanner jaw gap comparison table

Jaw gap (in)	Spanner size
0.250	1/4 in AF
0.276	7 mm
0.313	5/16 in AF
0.315	8 mm
0.344	11/32 in AF; 1/8 in Whitworth
0.354	9 mm
0.375	3/8 in AF
0.394	10 mm
0.433	11 mm
0.438	7/16 in AF
0.445	3/16 in Whitworth; 1/4 in BSF
0.472	12 mm
0.500	1/2 in AF
0.512	13 mm
0.525	1/4 in Whitworth; 5/16 in BSF
0.551	14 mm
0.563	9/16 in AF
0.591	15 mm
0.600	5/16 in Whitworth; 3/8 in BSF
0.625	5/8 in AF
0.630	16 mm
0.669	17 mm
0.686	11/16 in AF
0.709	18 mm
0.710	3/8 in Whitworth; 7/16 in BSF
0.748	19 mm
0.750	3/4 in AF
0.813	13/16 in AF
0.820	7/16 in Whitworth; 1/2 in BSF
0.866	22 mm
0.875	7/8 in AF
0.920	1/2 in Whitworth; 9/16 in BSF
0.938	15/16 in AF
0.945	24 mm
1.000	1 in AF
1.010	9/16 in Whitworth; 5/8 in BSF
1.024	26 mm
1.063	11/16 in AF; 27 mm
1.100	5/8 in Whitworth; 11/16 in BSF
1.125	11/8 in AF
1.181	30 mm
1.200	11/16 in Whitworth; 3/4 in BSF
1.250	11/4 in AF
1.260	32 mm
1.300	3/4 in Whitworth; 7/8 in BSF
1.313	15/16 in AF
1.390	13/16 in Whitworth; 15/16 in BSF
1.417	36 mm
1.438	17/16 in AF
1.480	7/8 in Whitworth; 1 in BSF
1.500	11/2 in AF
1.575	40 mm; 15/16 in Whitworth
1.614	41 mm
1.625	15/8 in AF
1.670	1 in Whitworth; 11/8 in BSF
1.688	111/16 in AF
1.811	46 mm
1.813	113/16 in AF
1.860	11/8 in Whitworth; 11/4 in BSF
1.875	17/8 in AF
1.969	50 mm
2.000	2 in AF
2.050	11/4 in Whitworth; 13/8 in BSF
2.165	55 mm
2.362	60 mm

Conversion factors

Length (distance)
Inches (in)	X	25.4	= Millimetres (mm)	X 0.0394	= Inches (in)
Feet (ft)	X	0.305	= Metres (m)	X 3.281	= Feet (ft)
Miles	X	1.609	= Kilometres (km)	X 0.621	= Miles

Volume (capacity)
Cubic inches (cu in; in³)	X	16.387	= Cubic centimetres (cc; cm³)	X 0.061	= Cubic inches (cu in; in³)
Imperial pints (Imp pt)	X	0.568	= Litres (l)	X 1.76	= Imperial pints (Imp pt)
Imperial quarts (Imp qt)	X	1.137	= Litres (l)	X 0.88	= Imperial quarts (Imp qt)
Imperial quarts (Imp qt)	X	1.201	= US quarts (US qt)	X 0.833	= Imperial quarts (Imp qt)
US quarts (US qt)	X	0.946	= Litres (l)	X 1.057	= US quarts (US qt)
Imperial gallons (Imp gal)	X	4.546	= Litres (l)	X 0.22	= Imperial gallons (Imp gal)
Imperial gallons (Imp gal)	X	1.201	= US gallons (US gal)	X 0.833	= Imperial gallons (Imp gal)
US gallons (US gal)	X	3.785	= Litres (l)	X 0.264	= US gallons (US gal)

Mass (weight)
Ounces (oz)	X	28.35	= Grams (g)	X 0.035	= Ounces (oz)
Pounds (lb)	X	0.454	= Kilograms (kg)	X 2.205	= Pounds (lb)

Force
Ounces-force (ozf; oz)	X	0.278	= Newtons (N)	X 3.6	= Ounces-force (ozf; oz)
Pounds-force (lbf; lb)	X	4.448	= Newtons (N)	X 0.225	= Pounds-force (lbf; lb)
Newtons (N)	X	0.1	= Kilograms-force (kgf; kg)	X 9.81	= Newtons (N)

Pressure
Pounds-force per square inch (psi; lbf/in²; lb/in²)	X	0.070	= Kilograms-force per square centimetre (kgf/cm²; kg/cm²)	X 14.223	= Pounds-force per square inch (psi; lbf/in²; lb/in²)
Pounds-force per square inch (psi; lbf/in²; lb/in²)	X	0.068	= Atmospheres (atm)	X 14.696	= Pounds-force per square inch (psi; lbf/in²; lb/in²)
Pounds-force per square inch (psi; lbf/in²; lb/in²)	X	0.069	= Bars	X 14.5	= Pounds-force per square inch (psi; lbf/in²; lb/in²)
Pounds-force per square inch (psi; lbf/in²; lb/in²)	X	6.895	= Kilopascals (kPa)	X 0.145	= Pounds-force per square inch (psi; lbf/in²; lb/in²)
Kilopascals (kPa)	X	0.01	= Kilograms-force per square centimetre (kgf/cm²; kg/cm²)	X 98.1	= Kilopascals (kPa)
Millibar (mbar)	X	100	= Pascals (Pa)	X 0.01	= Millibar (mbar)
Millibar (mbar)	X	0.0145	= Pounds-force per square inch (psi; lbf/in²; lb/in²)	X 68.947	= Millibar (mbar)
Millibar (mbar)	X	0.75	= Millimetres of mercury (mmHg)	X 1.333	= Millibar (mbar)
Millibar (mbar)	X	0.401	= Inches of water (inH₂O)	X 2.491	= Millibar (mbar)
Millimetres of mercury (mmHg)	X	0.535	= Inches of water (inH₂O)	X 1.868	= Millimetres of mercury (mmHg)
Inches of water (inH₂O)	X	0.036	= Pounds-force per square inch (psi; lbf/in²; lb/in²)	X 27.68	= Inches of water (inH₂O)

Torque (moment of force)
Pounds-force inches (lbf in; lb in)	X	1.152	= Kilograms-force centimetre (kgf cm; kg cm)	X 0.868	= Pounds-force inches (lbf in; lb in)
Pounds-force inches (lbf in; lb in)	X	0.113	= Newton metres (Nm)	X 8.85	= Pounds-force inches (lbf in; lb in)
Pounds-force inches (lbf in; lb in)	X	0.083	= Pounds-force feet (lbf ft; lb ft)	X 12	= Pounds-force inches (lbf in; lb in)
Pounds-force feet (lbf ft; lb ft)	X	0.138	= Kilograms-force metres (kgf m; kg m)	X 7.233	= Pounds-force feet (lbf ft; lb ft)
Pounds-force feet (lbf ft; lb ft)	X	1.356	= Newton metres (Nm)	X 0.738	= Pounds-force feet (lbf ft; lb ft)
Newton metres (Nm)	X	0.102	= Kilograms-force metres (kgf m; kg m)	X 9.804	= Newton metres (Nm)

Power
Horsepower (hp)	X	745.7	= Watts (W)	X 0.0013	= Horsepower (hp)

Velocity (speed)
Miles per hour (miles/hr; mph)	X	1.609	= Kilometres per hour (km/hr; kph)	X 0.621	= Miles per hour (miles/hr; mph)

Fuel consumption*
Miles per gallon, Imperial (mpg)	X	0.354	= Kilometres per litre (km/l)	X 2.825	= Miles per gallon, Imperial (mpg)
Miles per gallon, US (mpg)	X	0.425	= Kilometres per litre (km/l)	X 2.352	= Miles per gallon, US (mpg)

Temperature
Degrees Fahrenheit = (°C x 1.8) + 32

Degrees Celsius (Degrees Centigrade; °C) = (°F - 32) x 0.56

*It is common practice to convert from miles per gallon (mpg) to litres/100 kilometres (l/100km), where mpg (Imperial) x l/100 km = 282 and mpg (US) x l/100 km = 235

Safety first!

Professional motor mechanics are trained in safe working procedures. However enthusiastic you may be about getting on with the job in hand, do take the time to ensure that your safety is not put at risk. A moment's lack of attention can result in an accident, as can failure to observe certain elementary precautions.

There will always be new ways of having accidents, and the following points do not pretend to be a comprehensive list of all dangers; they are intended rather to make you aware of the risks and to encourage a safety-conscious approach to all work you carry out on your vehicle.

Essential DOs and DON'Ts

DON'T rely on a single jack when working underneath the vehicle. Always use reliable additional means of support, such as axle stands, securely placed under a part of the vehicle that you know will not give way.

DON'T attempt to loosen or tighten high-torque nuts (e.g. wheel hub nuts) while the vehicle is on a jack; it may be pulled off.

DON'T start the engine without first ascertaining that the transmission is in neutral (or 'Park' where applicable) and the parking brake applied.

DON'T suddenly remove the filler cap from a hot cooling system – cover it with a cloth and release the pressure gradually first, or you may get scalded by escaping coolant.

DON'T attempt to drain oil until you are sure it has cooled sufficiently to avoid scalding you.

DON'T grasp any part of the engine, exhaust or catalytic converter without first ascertaining that it is sufficiently cool to avoid burning you.

DON'T allow brake fluid or antifreeze to contact vehicle paintwork.

DON'T syphon toxic liquids such as fuel, brake fluid or antifreeze by mouth, or allow them to remain on your skin.

DON'T inhale dust – it may be injurious to health (see *Asbestos* below).

DON'T allow any spilt oil or grease to remain on the floor – wipe it up straight away, before someone slips on it.

DON'T use ill-fitting spanners or other tools which may slip and cause injury.

DON'T attempt to lift a heavy component which may be beyond your capability – get assistance.

DON'T rush to finish a job, or take unverified short cuts.

DON'T allow children or animals in or around an unattended vehicle.

DO wear eye protection when using power tools such as drill, sander, bench grinder etc, and when working under the vehicle.

DO use a barrier cream on your hands prior to undertaking dirty jobs – it will protect your skin from infection as well as making the dirt easier to remove afterwards; but make sure your hands aren't left slippery. Note that long-term contact with used engine oil can be a health hazard.

DO keep loose clothing (cuffs, tie etc) and long hair well out of the way of moving mechanical parts.

DO remove rings, wristwatch etc, before working on the vehicle – especially the electrical system.

DO ensure that any lifting tackle used has a safe working load rating adequate for the job.

DO keep your work area tidy – it is only too easy to fall over articles left lying around.

DO get someone to check periodically that all is well, when working alone on the vehicle.

DO carry out work in a logical sequence and check that everything is correctly assembled and tightened afterwards.

DO remember that your vehicle's safety affects that of yourself and others. If in doubt on any point, get specialist advice.

IF, in spite of following these precautions, you are unfortunate enough to injure yourself, seek medical attention as soon as possible.

Asbestos

Certain friction, insulating, sealing, and other products – such as brake linings, brake bands, clutch linings, torque converters, gaskets, etc – contain asbestos. *Extreme care must be taken to avoid inhalation of dust from such products since it is hazardous to health.* If in doubt, assume that they *do* contain asbestos.

Fire

Remember at all times that petrol (gasoline) is highly flammable. Never smoke, or have any kind of naked flame around, when working on the vehicle. But the risk does not end there – a spark caused by an electrical short-circuit, by two metal surfaces contacting each other, by careless use of tools, or even by static electricity built up in your body under certain conditions, can ignite petrol vapour, which in a confined space is highly explosive.

Always disconnect the battery earth (ground) terminal before working on any part of the fuel or electrical system, and never risk spilling fuel on to a hot engine or exhaust.

It is recommended that a fire extinguisher of a type suitable for fuel and electrical fires is kept handy in the garage or workplace at all times. Never try to extinguish a fuel or electrical fire with water.

Note: *Any reference to a 'torch' appearing in this manual should always be taken to mean a hand-held battery-operated electric lamp or flashlight. It does NOT mean a welding/gas torch or blowlamp.*

Fumes

Certain fumes are highly toxic and can quickly cause unconsciousness and even death if inhaled to any extent. Petrol (gasoline) vapour comes into this category, as do the vapours from certain solvents such as trichloroethylene. Any draining or pouring of such volatile fluids should be done in a well ventilated area.

When using cleaning fluids and solvents, read the instructions carefully. Never use materials from unmarked containers – they may give off poisonous vapours.

Never run the engine of a motor vehicle in an enclosed space such as a garage. Exhaust fumes contain carbon monoxide which is extremely poisonous; if you need to run the engine, always do so in the open air or at least have the rear of the vehicle outside the workplace.

If you are fortunate enough to have the use of an inspection pit, never drain or pour petrol, and never run the engine, while the vehicle is standing over it; the fumes, being heavier than air, will concentrate in the pit with possibly lethal results.

The battery

Never cause a spark, or allow a naked light, near the vehicle's battery. It will normally be giving off a certain amount of hydrogen gas, which is highly explosive.

Always disconnect the battery earth (ground) terminal before working on the fuel or electrical systems.

If possible, loosen the filler plugs or cover when charging the battery from an external source. Do not charge at an excessive rate or the battery may burst.

Take care when topping up and when carrying the battery. The acid electrolyte, even when diluted, is very corrosive and should not be allowed to contact the eyes or skin.

If you ever need to prepare electrolyte yourself, always add the acid slowly to the water, and never the other way round. Protect against splashes by wearing rubber gloves and goggles.

When jump starting a car using a booster battery, for negative earth (ground) vehicles, connect the jump leads in the following sequence: First connect one jump lead between the positive (+) terminals of the two batteries. Then connect the other jump lead first to the negative (–) terminal of the booster battery, and then to a good earthing (ground) point on the vehicle to be started, at least 18 in (45 cm) from the battery if possible. Ensure that hands and jump leads are clear of any moving parts, and that the two vehicles do not touch. Disconnect the leads in the reverse order.

Mains electricity and electrical equipment

When using an electric power tool, inspection light etc, always ensure that the appliance is correctly connected to its plug and that, where necessary, it is properly earthed (grounded). Do not use such appliances in damp conditions and, again, beware of creating a spark or applying excessive heat in the vicinity of fuel or fuel vapour. Also ensure that the appliances meet the relevant national safety standards.

Ignition HT voltage

A severe electric shock can result from touching certain parts of the ignition system, such as the HT leads, when the engine is running or being cranked, particularly if components are damp or the insulation is defective. Where an electronic ignition system is fitted, the HT voltage is much higher and could prove fatal.

Routine maintenance

For information applicable to later models, see Supplement at end of manual

Maintenance is essential for ensuring safety and is desirable for the purpose of getting the best in terms of performance and economy from the car. Over the years the need for periodic lubrication – oiling and greasing – has been drastically reduced, if not totally eliminated. This has unfortunately tended to lead some owners to think that because no such action is required the components either no longer exist or will last for ever. This is a serious delusion. If anything, there are now more places, particularly in the steering and suspension, where joints and pivots are fitted. Although you do not grease them any more you still have to look at them – and look at them just as often as you may previously have had to grease them. The largest initial element of maintenance is visual examination. This may lead to repairs or renewal.

Every 250 miles (400 km) or weekly – whichever comes first

Engine (Chapter 1)
Check the engine oil level using the dipstick. The oil level must be maintained between the high and low markings at all times. Top up when necessary but do not overfill

Cooling system (Chapter 2)
Check the coolant level. Top up if necessary
Check for signs of leakage, and hose security

Fuel system (Chapter 3)
Check for signs of leakage, and hose security

Transmission (Chapters 6 and 13)
Check for oil/fluid leaks

Braking system (Chapter 8)
Check the level of brake fluid in the fluid reservoir. The level must be kept between the high and low markings on the reservoir wall. Top up if necessary

Suspension (Chapter 9)
Check the tyre pressures, and examine them for wear and damage

Electrical system (Chapter 12)
Check and if necessary top up the fluid level in the windscreen and tailgate washer reservoirs

After the first 1000 to 1500 miles (1600 to 2400 km)

Cars with new or overhauled components

Engine (Chapter 1)
Renew the oil and filter

Manual gearbox (Chapter 6)
Renew the oil – see also page 21

Every 6000 miles (9500 km) or six months – whichever comes first

Engine (Chapter 1)
Renew the oil
Renew the filter (every second oil change)

Braking system (Chapter 8)
Check for leaks, and hose/pipe security
Check the pads for wear. Renew if necessary.

Electrical system (Chapter 12)
Check the battery electrolyte level. Top up if necessary (not usually required on low maintenance type)

Every 12 000 miles (19 000 km) or 12 months – whichever comes first

In addition to the 6000 miles service.

Engine (Chapter 1)
Clean the filler cap filter mesh (if applicable)

Fuel system (Chapter 3)
Adjust and lubricate the throttle and choke cables (if applicable)

Ignition system (Chapter 4)
Renew the spark plugs
Lubricate the distributor
Check for cable security

Clutch (Chapter 5)
Adjust the pedal/cable

Braking system (Chapter 8)
Check the shoes for wear. Renew if necessary
Adjust the handbrake

Steering (Chapter 10)
Check the power steering fluid level (if applicable)
Adjust the power steering pump drivebelt (if applicable)

Bodywork (Chapter 11)
Check the bodywork for condition. Repair as necessary

Electrical system (Chapter 12)
Adjust the alternator/coolant pump drivebelt tension

Under bonnet view – 1.3 litre engine

1 Radiator filler cap
2 Alternator
3 Distributor
4 Engine oil dipstick
5 Right-hand engine mounting
6 Brake hydraulic system master cylinder
7 Engine oil filler cap
8 Carburettor (air filter removed)
9 Cooling system thermostat housing
10 Ignition coil
11 Front suspension strut top mounting (left-hand side)
12 Washer system reservoir
13 Engine/transmission mounting (shown with battery removed)
14 Fuel filter (in-line)
15 Cooling system bleed screw
16 Clutch adjuster
17 Starter motor
18 Fuel pump

Under bonnet view – 1.6 litre SR Injection engine

1 Alternator
2 Injectors
3 Engine mounting (right-hand)
4 Fuel filter
5 Brake hydraulic system master cylinder
6 Air filter
7 Engine oil dipstick
8 Cooling system expansion tank and filler cap
9 Ignition coil
10 Ignition distributor
11 Front suspension strut top mounting (left-hand side)
12 Washer system reservoir
13 Battery
14 Radiator cap
15 Throttle housing
16 Engine oil filler
17 Inlet manifold

View of front underside of
car with engine undershield
removed – 1.3 litre engine

1 Alternator/coolant pump
   drivebelt
2 Starter motor
3 Gearbox
4 Differential housing
5 Suspension arm
6 Anti-roll bar
7 Track rod
8 Exhaust pipe
9 Exhaust manifold
10 Driveshaft
11 Torque reaction link
12 Brake caliper
13 Sump drain plug
14 Engine coolant drain plug
   (OHV engines only)

View of rear underside of car – 1.3 litre model

1 Spare wheel
2 Towing eye
3 Shock absorber
4 Suspension arm
5 Suspension cross tube
6 Handbrake cable
7 Heat shield
8 Fuel tank
9 Torsion bar (right-hand)
10 Torsion bar (left-hand)
11 Brake backplate
12 Exhaust rear silencer

Every 24 000 miles (38 000 km) or 2 years – whichever comes first

In addition to the 12 000 miles service

Cooling system (Chapter 2)
Renew the coolant

Fuel system (Chapter 3)
Renew the air cleaner element
Clean the fuel pump filter (if applicable)
Renew the in-line filter-carburettor models (if applicable)

Ignition system (Chapter 4)
Adjust the ignition timing

Manual gearbox (Chapter 6)
Renew the oil – see also page 21

Driveshafts (Chapter 7)
Check for damage and wear

Braking system (Chapter 8)
Renew the fluid

Suspension and steering (Chapters 9 and 10)
Check the wheel bearings for wear and damage
Check the steering and suspension balljoints for wear and damage
Check the shock absorbers for operation and leaks

Automatic transmission (Chapter 13)
Renew the fluid

Every 36 000 miles (57 000 km)

Engine (Chapter 1)
Renew the camshaft (timing) drivebelt (if applicable)

Every 60 000 miles (95 000 km) or 5 years – whichever comes first

Fuel system (Chapter 3)
Renew the fuel filter – fuel injection models

Recommended lubricants and fluids

Component or system	Lubricant type/specification	Duckhams recommendation
1 Engine	Multigrade engine oil, viscosity SAE 10W/40	Duckhams QXR, Hypergrade, or 10W/40 Motor Oil
2 Manual gearbox*: Up to October 1987	Multigrade engine oil, viscosity SAE 10W/40	Duckhams QXR, Hypergrade, or 10W/40 Motor Oil
October 1987 on	Gear oil, viscosity SAE 75W/80	Duckhams Hypoid PT 75W/80
3 Braking system	Hydraulic fluid to SAE J1703C	Duckhams Universal Brake and Clutch Fluid
4 Cooling system	Ethylene glycol based antifreeze coolant mixture	Duckhams Universal Antifreeze and Summer Coolant
5 Power steering	Dexron II type ATF	Duckhams D-Matic
6 Automatic transmission	Dexron II type ATF	Duckhams D-matic

* On cars manufactured after October 1987, the manual gearbox is 'sealed for life', and renewing the oil is no longer required. It is essential to use only the specified type of oil when topping-up.

Fault diagnosis

Introduction

The vehicle owner who does his or her own maintenance according to the recommended schedules should not have to use this section of the manual very often. Modern component reliability is such that, provided those items subject to wear or deterioration are inspected or renewed at the specified intervals, sudden failure is comparatively rare. Faults do not usually just happen as a result of sudden failure, but develop over a period of time. Major mechanical failures in particular are usually preceded by characteristic symptoms over hundreds or even thousands of miles. Those components which do occasionally fail without warning are often small and easily carried in the vehicle.

With any fault finding, the first step is to decide where to begin investigations. Sometimes this is obvious, but on other occasions a little detective work will be necessary. The owner who makes half a dozen haphazard adjustments or replacements may be successful in curing a fault (or its symptoms), but he will be none the wiser if the fault recurs and he may well have spent more time and money than was necessary. A calm and logical approach will be found to be more satisfactory in the long run. Always take into account any warning signs or abnormalities that may have been noticed in the period preceding the fault – power loss, high or low gauge readings, unusual noises or smells, etc – and remember that failure of components such as fuses or spark plugs may only be pointers to some underlying fault.

The pages which follow here are intended to help in cases of failure to start or breakdown on the road. There is also a Fault Diagnosis Section at the end of each Chapter which should be consulted if the preliminary checks prove unfruitful. Whatever the fault, certain basic principles apply. These are as follows:

Verify the fault. This is simply a matter of being sure that you know what the symptoms are before starting work. This is particularly important if you are investigating a fault for someone else who may not have described it very accurately.

Don't overlook the obvious. For example, if the vehicle won't start, is there petrol in the tank? (Don't take anyone else's word on this particular point, and don't trust the fuel gauge either!) If an electrical fault is indicated, look for loose or broken wires before digging out the test gear.

Cure the disease, not the symptom. Substituting a flat battery with a fully charged one will get you off the hard shoulder, but if the underlying cause is not attended to, the new battery will go the same way. Similarly, changing oil-fouled spark plugs for a new set will get you moving again, but remember that the reason for the fouling (if it wasn't simply an incorrect grade of plug) will have to be established and corrected.

Don't take anything for granted. Particularly, don't forget that a 'new' component may itself be defective (especially if it's been

Carrying a few spares can save you a long walk!

A simple test lamp is useful for tracing electrical faults

Do not use on fuel injection system circuits

Jump start lead connections for negative earth vehicles –
connect leads in order shown

Crank engine and check for spark. Note use of insulated
tool

rattling round in the boot for months), and don't leave components out of a fault diagnosis sequence just because they are new or recently fitted. When you do finally diagnose a difficult fault, you'll probably realise that all the evidence was there from the start.

Electrical faults

Electrical faults can be more puzzling than straightforward mechanical failures, but they are no less susceptible to logical analysis if the basic principles of operation are understood. Vehicle electrical wiring exists in extremely unfavourable conditions – heat, vibration and chemical attack – and the first things to look for are loose or corroded connections and broken or chafed wires, especially where the wires pass through holes in the bodywork or are subject to vibration.

All metal-bodied vehicles in current production have one pole of the battery 'earthed', ie connected to the vehicle bodywork, and in nearly all modern vehicles it is the negative (–) terminal. The various electrical components – motors, bulb holders etc – are also connected to earth, either by means of a lead or directly by their mountings. Electric current flows through the component and then back to the battery via the bodywork. If the component mounting is loose or corroded, or if a good path back to the battery is not available, the circuit will be incomplete and malfunction will result. The engine and/or gearbox are also earthed by means of flexible metal straps to the body or subframe; if these straps are loose or missing, starter motor, generator and ignition trouble may result.

Assuming the earth return to be satisfactory, electrical faults will be due either to component malfunction or to defects in the current supply. Individual components are dealt with in Chapter 12. If supply wires are broken or cracked internally this results in an open-circuit, and the easiest way to check for this is to bypass the suspect wire temporarily with a length of wire having a crocodile clip or suitable connector at each end. Alternatively, a 12V test lamp can be used to verify the presence of supply voltage at various points along the wire and the break can be thus isolated.

If a bare portion of a live wire touches the bodywork or other earthed metal part, the electricity will take the low-resistance path thus formed back to the battery: this is known as a short-circuit. Hopefully a short-circuit will blow a fuse, but otherwise it may cause burning of the insulation (and possibly further short-circuits) or even a fire. This is why it is inadvisable to bypass persistently blowing fuses with silver foil or wire.

Spares and tool kit

Most vehicles are supplied only with sufficient tools for wheel changing; the *Maintenance and minor repair* tool kit detailed in *Tools and working facilities*, with the addition of a hammer, is probably sufficient for those repairs that most motorists would consider attempting at the roadside. In addition a few items which can be fitted without too much trouble in the event of a breakdown should be carried. Experience and available space will modify the list below, but the following may save having to call on professional assistance:

Spark plugs, clean and correctly gapped
HT lead and plug cap – long enough to reach the plug furthest from the distributor
Distributor rotor
Drivebelt(s) – emergency type may suffice
Spare fuses
Set of principal light bulbs
Tin of radiator sealer and hose bandage
Exhaust bandage

Roll of insulating tape
Length of soft iron wire
Length of electrical flex
Torch or inspection lamp (can double as test lamp)
Battery jump leads
Tow-rope
Ignition waterproofing aerosol
Litre of engine oil
Sealed can of hydraulic fluid
Emergency windscreen
Worm drive clips
Tube of filler paste

If spare fuel is carried, a can designed for the purpose should be used to minimise risks of leakage and collision damage. A first aid kit and a warning triangle, whilst not at present compulsory in the UK, are obviously sensible items to carry in addition to the above.

When touring abroad it may be advisable to carry additional spares which, even if you cannot fit them yourself, could save having to wait while parts are obtained. The items below may be worth considering:

Clutch and throttle cables
Cylinder head gasket
Alternator brushes
Fuel pump repair kit
Tyre valve core

One of the motoring organisations will be able to advise on availability of fuel etc in foreign countries.

Engine will not start

Engine fails to turn when starter operated
Flat battery (recharge, use jump leads, or push start)
Battery terminals loose or corroded
Battery earth to body defective
Engine earth strap loose or broken
Starter motor (or solenoid) wiring loose or broken
Ignition/starter switch faulty
Major mechanical failure (seizure)
Starter or solenoid internal fault (see Chapter 12)

Starter motor turns engine slowly
Partially discharged battery (recharge, use jump leads, or push start)
Battery terminals loose or corroded
Battery earth to body defective
Engine earth strap loose
Starter motor (or solenoid) wiring loose
Starter motor internal fault (see Chapter 12)

Starter motor spins without turning engine
Flat battery
Starter motor pinion sticking on sleeve
Flywheel gear teeth damaged or worn
Starter motor mounting bolts loose

Engine turns normally but fails to start
Damp or dirty HT leads and distributor cap (crank engine and check for spark)
No fuel in tank (check for delivery at carburettor)
Excessive choke (hot engine) or insufficient choke (cold engine)
Fouled or incorrectly gapped spark plugs (remove, clean and regap)
Other ignition system fault (see Chapter 4)
Other fuel system fault (see Chapter 3)
Poor compression
Major mechanical failure (eg camshaft drive)

Engine fires but will not run
Insufficient choke (cold engine)
Air leaks at carburettor or inlet manifold
Fuel starvation (see Chapter 3)
Ballast resistor defective, or other ignition fault (see Chapter 4)

Engine cuts out and will not restart

Engine cuts out suddenly – ignition fault
Loose or disconnected LT wires
Wet HT leads or distributor cap (after traversing water splash)
Coil failure (check for spark)
Other ignition fault (see Chapter 4)

Engine misfires before cutting out – fuel fault
Fuel tank empty
Fuel pump defective or filter blocked (check for delivery)
Fuel tank filler vent blocked (suction will be evident on releasing cap)
Carburettor needle valve sticking
Carburettor jets blocked (fuel contaminated)
Other fuel system fault (see Chapter 3)

Engine cuts out – other causes
Serious overheating
Major mechanical failure (eg camshaft drive)

Engine overheats

Ignition (no-charge) warning light illuminated
Slack or broken drivebelt – retension or renew (Chapter 12)

Ignition warning light not illuminated
Coolant loss due to internal or external leakage (see Chapter 2)
Thermostat defective
Low oil level
Brakes binding
Radiator clogged externally or internally
Electric cooling fan not operating correctly
Engine waterways clogged
Ignition timing incorrect or automatic advance malfunctioning
Mixture too weak

Note: *Do not add cold water to an overheated engine or damage may result*

Low engine oil pressure

Gauge reads low or warning light illuminated with engine running
Oil level low or incorrect grade
Defective gauge or sender unit
Wire to sender unit earthed
Engine overheating
Oil filter clogged or bypass valve defective
Oil pressure relief valve defective
Oil pick-up strainer clogged
Oil pump worn or mountings loose
Worn main or big-end bearings
Note: *Low oil pressure in a high-mileage engine at tickover is not necessarily a cause for concern. Sudden pressure loss at speed is far more significant. In any event, check the gauge or warning light sender before condemning the engine.*

Engine noises

Pre-ignition (pinking) on acceleration
Incorrect grade of fuel
Ignition timing incorrect
Distributor faulty or worn
Worn or maladjusted carburettor
Excessive carbon build-up in engine

Whistling or wheezing noises
Leaking vacuum hose
Leaking carburettor or manifold gasket
Blowing head gasket

Tapping or rattling
Incorrect valve clearances
Worn valve gear
Worn timing chain or belt
Broken piston ring (ticking noise)

Knocking or thumping
Unintentional mechanical contact (eg fan blades)
Worn drivebelt
Peripheral component fault (generator, water pump etc)
Worn big-end bearings (regular heavy knocking, perhaps less under load)
Worn main bearings (rumbling and knocking, perhaps worsening under load)
Piston slap (most noticeable when cold)

Chapter 1 Engine

For modifications, and information applicable to later models, see Supplement at end of manual

Contents

Specifications

Part A: OHV engines
General
Type .... Four-cylinder, in-line, overhead valve (OHV), water-cooled, transverse mounting

Engine type references:
    1.1 litre engine .... EIA
    1.3 litre engine .... GIA
Bore X stroke:
    EIA engine .... 74 x 65 mm
    GIA engine .... 76.7 x 70 mm
Capacity:
    EIA engine .... 1118 cc
    GIA engine .... 1294 cc
Compression ratio:
    EIA engine .... 9.6 : 1
    GIA engine .... 9.5 : 1
Firing order .... 1 – 3 – 4 – 2 (No 1 at flywheel end)

Cylinder block

	1118 cc	**1294 cc**
Cylinder bore diameter:		
Class A	73.9920 to 73.9995 mm	76.6870 to 76.6945 mm
Class B	73.9995 to 74.0070 mm	76.6945 to 76.7020 mm
Class C	74.0070 to 74.0145 mm	76.7020 to 76.7095 mm
Class D	74.0145 to 74.0220 mm	76.7095 to 76.7170 mm
Bore oversizes	+ 0.1 mm, + 0.4 mm	+ 0.1 mm, + 0.4 mm
Width of centre bearing bore	26.58 to 26.62 mm	26.58 to 26.62 mm
Camshaft bore diameter (bearings fitted):		
No 1 (flywheel end)	35.484 to 35.520 mm	35.484 to 35.520 mm
No 2	40.984 to 41.020 mm	40.984 to 41.020 mm
No 3	41.484 to 41.520 mm	41.484 to 41.520 mm

Crankshaft and connecting rods
Number of main bearings 5
Main bearing journal diameter .... 51.966 to 51.976 mm
Undersizes for regrinding .... 0.1, 0.2 and 0.5 mm
Main bearing running clearance .... 0.04 to 0.078 mm
Big-end journal diameter .... 40.949 to 40.957 mm
Undersizes for regrinding .... 0.1, 0.2 and 0.5 mm
Big-end running clearance .... 0.03 to 0.064 mm
Crankshaft stroke:
    1118 cc .... 65 mm
    1294 cc .... 70 mm
Crankshaft endfloat .... 0.09 to 0.27 mm
Thrustwasher thickness .... 2.31 to 2.36 mm
Connecting rod endfloat .... 0.010 to 0.027 mm

Pistons
Material .... Aluminium alloy
Number of rings .... 2 compression, 1 oil control
Maximum weight difference between any two pistons .... 3 g

	1118 cc	**1294 cc**
Piston diameter:		
Class A	73.9625 to 73.9700 mm	75.6575 to 76.6650 mm
Class B	73.9700 to 73.9775 mm	76.6650 to 76.6725 mm
Class C	73.9775 to 73.9850 mm	76.6725 to 76.6800 mm
Class D	73.9850 to 73.9925 mm	76.6800 to 76.6875 mm
Piston oversizes	+ 0.1 mm, + 0.4 mm	+ 0.1 mm, + 0.4 mm
Piston-to-bore clearance (nominal)	0.22 to 0.037 mm	0.22 to 0.037 mm
Piston ring end gap:		
Compression rings	0.025 to 0.45 mm	0.025 to 0.45 mm
Oil control ring	0.020 to 0.40 mm	0.020 to 0.40 mm

Gudgeon pin
Material .... Steel
Outside diameter .... 21.991 to 21.995 mm
Inside diameter .... 13 mm
Length:
    1118 cc .... 64 mm
    1294 cc .... 66.7 mm
Fit .... Clearance in piston, interference in connecting rod

Camshaft and valve gear

Camshaft journal diameter:	
No 1 (flywheel end)	35.439 to 35.459 mm
No 2	40.939 to 40.959 mm
No 3	41.439 to 41.459 mm
Camshaft endfloat	0.10 to 0.20 mm
Valve timing:	
Inlet opens	16° 30' BTDC
Inlet closes	37° 06' ABDC
Exhaust opens	52° BBDC
Exhaust closes	16° 20' ATDC
Inlet cam lift	5.41 mm
Exhaust cam lift	5.71 mm
Cam followers (tappets):	
Outside diameter	22.974 to 23.000 mm
Clearance in bores	Zero to 0.047 mm
Length	39.5 to 40.5 mm
Pushrods:	
Length (to bottom of rocker arm ball seat)	201 mm

Cylinder head

	1118 cc	1294 cc
Maximum amount to be skimmed from gasket face	1.0 mm	0.6 mm
Gasket thickness for use with machined head	2.2 mm	1.8 mm
Standard gasket thickness	1.2 mm	1.2 mm
Valve guides:		
Material	Cast iron	Cast iron
Inside diameter	8.022 to 8.040 mm	8.022 to 8.040 mm
Valve seats/face angle	44° to 44° 30'/45°	44° to 44° 30'/45°
Valve lift:		
Inlet	8.12 mm	8.12 mm
Exhaust	8.58 mm	8.58 mm

Valves

Valve clearances – cold:	
Inlet	0.25 mm (0.010 in)
Exhaust	0.25 mm (0.010 in)
Valve sequence (from flywheel end)	I,E,I,E,E,I,E,I
Inlet valves:	
Stem diameter	7.970 to 7.985 mm
Stem-to-guide clearance	0.037 to 0.070 mm
Exhaust valves:	
Stem diameter	7.950 to 7.965 mm
Stem-to-guide clearance	0.057 to 0.090 mm
Valve springs free length	48.4 mm

Lubrication system

Oil pressure (minimum) at pressure switch take-off:	
At idle speed:	
Oil temperature of 40° to 80°C (104° to 176°F)	2.6 bar (37.7 lbf/in²)
Oil temperature of 120°C (248°F)	1.2 bar (17.4 lbf in²)
At 3000 rpm:	
At temperature of 40° to 120°C (104° to 248°F)	3.6 to 5.6 bar (52.2 to 81.2 lbf/in²)
Oil pump	Externally mounted gear type
Endfloat – oil pump driveshaft	0.05 to 0.50 mm
Pump driveshaft bush diameter	12.030 to 12.055 mm
Oil type/specification	Multigrade engine oil, viscosity SAE 10W/40 (Duckhams QXR, Hypergrade, or 10W/40 Motor Oil)

Torque wrench settings

	Nm	lbf ft
Rocker cover	5	4
Spark plugs	30	22
Main bearing cap bolts	65	48
Big-end cap bolts	38	28
Flywheel to crankshaft	55	41
Crankshaft pulley	150	111
Inlet manifold	15	11
Exhaust manifold	20	15
Timing cover to block:		
7 mm bolts	13	10
8 mm bolts	30	22
Timing cover	20	15
Sump to block	13	10
Sump baseplate	10	7
Oil pump to block	13	10
Oil pressure relief valve plug	40	30
Oil pump strainer to block	13	10
Camshaft sprocket	15	11
Camshaft thrust plate bolt	15	11

Torque wrench settings (continued)

	Nm	lbf ft
Crankshaft oil seal housing	13	10
Oil strainer gauze to housing	15	11
Sump drain plug	35	26
Cylinder block coolant drain plug	4	3
Engine to right mounting support nuts	50	37
Flexible mounting nuts	20	15
Gearbox (left-hand) mounting support nuts	35	26
Suspension lower balljoint bolts	35	26
Bearing to housing	17	13
Engine lower mounting bolt (on engine side)	45	33
Engine lower mounting bolt (crossmember side)	55	41
Driveshaft nuts	265	196
Cylinder head bolts:		
Stage 1	50	37
Stage 2	70	52
Stage 3 (after running engine – see Section 47) – loosen bolts in turn and retighten to	70	52

Part B: OHC engine

General

Type	Four-cylinder, in-line, overhead camshaft (OHC), water cooled, transverse mounting
Engine type references:	
1.6 litre engine, carburettor	XU5-1C
1.6 litre engine, fuel injection	XU5-JA
Bore	83 mm
Stroke	73 mm
Capacity	1580 cc
Compression ratio	9.39 : 1
Firing order	1–3–4–2 (No 1 at flywheel end)

Camshaft

Drive	Toothed belt
Action	Directly onto bucket tappets
Endfloat (not adjustable)	0.07 to 0.16 mm
Lift:	
Early models	10.4 mm
Later models	9.7 mm

Connecting rods

Type	Forged steel
Big-end bore	48.655 to 48.671 mm
Small-end bore	21.959 to 21.971 mm

Crankshaft and main bearings

Number of main bearings	5
Main bearing bore in crankcase	63.708 to 63.727 mm
Main journal diameter:	
New	59.981 to 60.000 mm
After regrinding	59.681 to 59.700 mm
Crankpin diameter:	
New	44.971 to 44.990 mm
After regrinding	44.671 to 44.690 mm
Journal or crankpin out-of-round	0.007 mm max
Endfloat	0.07 to 0.27 mm
Thrust washer thicknesses available	2.30, 2.35, 2.40, 2.45 and 2.50 mm

Cylinder liners

Type	Wet, removable, matched to piston
Protrusion from block (without seal)	0.08 to 0.15 mm
Protrusion difference between liners	0.05 mm max
Coding mark	One, two or three slashes

Pistons

Type	Aluminium alloy with three compression rings and one scraper; matched to liner
Fitting orientation	DT mark and arrow point towards timing case end of engine
Coding marks:	
For gudgeon pin	Figure 1 (blue), 2 (white) or 3 (red)
For liner	One, two or three slashes

Gudgeon pin

Nominal diameter	22 mm
Coding mark	Coloured paint (see piston specs)
Fit	Clearance in piston, interference in connecting rod

Cylinder head

Material	Aluminium alloy
Warp limit	0.05 mm
Number of camshaft bearings	5
Cylinder head gasket thickness (service exchange)	1.4 mm
Cylinder head gasket thickness (new engine)	1.2 mm
Maximum amount to be skimmed from gasket face	0.20 mm

Valves

Head diameter:	
Inlet	40 mm
Exhaust	32.95 mm
Stem diameter:	
Inlet	7.965 to 7.980 mm
Exhaust	7.945 to 7.960 mm
Length:	
Inlet	109.29 mm
Exhaust	108.72 mm
Valve clearances (cold):	
Inlet	0.15 to 0.25 mm (0.006 to 0.010 in)
Exhaust	0.35 to 0.45 mm (0.014 to 0.018 in)
Adjustment method	Shims between tappet and valve stem

Valve timing

Inlet opens	10° 16' BTDC
Inlet closes	28° 26' ABDC
Exhaust opens	41° 20' BBDC
Exhaust closes	4° 37° ATDC

Lubrication system

Type	Wet sump, pressure feed and splash
Filter type	Full flow, disposable cartridge
Oil pressure (at oil temperature of 80°C/176°F):	
Minimum at 900 rpm	1.4 bar (20.3 lbf/in²)
Minimum at 4000 rpm	3.5 bar (50.8 lbf/in²)
Oil pressure warning light operation:	
Bulb extinguished above pressure of	0.8 bar (11.6 lbf/in²)
Bulb lights if pressure falls below	0.6 bar (8.7 lbf/in²)
Oil type/specification	Multigrade engine oil, viscosity SAE 10W/40 (Duckhams QXR, Hypergrade, or 10W/40 Motor Oil)

Torque wrench settings

	Nm	lbf ft
Cam cover	10	7
Cylinder head bolts:		
Stage 1 (All bolts, in sequence)	60	44
Stage 2: Slacken bolt 1, then	20 + 120°	15 + 120°
Repeat Stage 2 on remaining bolts in sequence		
Camshaft bearing caps	15	11
Camshaft sprocket bolt (M10)	40	30
Camshaft sprocket bolt (M12)	80	59
Crankshaft pulley bolt	110	81
Camshaft thrust plate	10	7
Main bearing cap nuts and bolts	50	37
Main bearing side bolts	25	18
Big-end cap bolts	50	37
Oil pump-to-block bolts	20	15
Oil seal carrier	15	11
Sump bolts	20	15
Suction drain pipe (oil)	5	4
Flywheel to crankshaft*	50	37
Engine mounting bracket bolts (timing case end)	20	15
Engine mounting nut (centre) – left-hand mounting	35	26
Coolant pump bolts	20	15
Timing cover bolts	15	11
Timing belt tensioner	15	11
Oil pressure switch	25	18
Clutch housing bolts	45	33
Starter motor bolts	35	26

*Apply locking solution to bolt threads

PART A: OHV ENGINES

1 General description

The Peugeot 309 models fitted with the overhead valve type engine are the XE and GE models (1.1 litre engine), and the XE, XL, GE, GL, Style and GR Profile models (1.3 litre engine). Whichever engine type is fitted, the basic design is the same, being a water-cooled, four-cylinder, four-stroke petrol engine. The different engine capacities are obtained by using different cylinder bore diameters and lengths of piston stroke.

The engine is located in a transverse position and is inclined rearwards at an angle of 38°. This lowers the centre of gravity and also improves accessibility to the ancillary components mounted on the front of the engine.

Fig. 1.1 Side and end section views of the OHV engine (Sec 1)

The combined crankcase and cylinder block is of cast iron construction and houses the pistons, connecting rods, crankshaft and camshaft. The cast aluminium alloy pistons are retained on the connecting rods by gudgeon pins which are an interference fit in the connecting rod small-end bore. The connecting rods are attached to the crankshaft by renewable shell type big-end bearings.

The forged steel crankshaft is carried in five main bearings, also of the renewable shell type. Crankshaft endfloat is controlled by semi-circular thrust washers on the upper half of the centre main bearing.

The camshaft runs in three bearings recessed into bores in the cylinder block. Camshaft drive is by a double row timing chain from a sprocket on the crankshaft.

The cylinder head is an aluminium alloy die-casting of crossflow configuration. Inclined inlet and exhaust valves operate in renewable valve guides pressed into the cylinder head. Valve actuation is by rocker arms, pushrods and cam followers activated by the camshaft lobes.

2 Routine maintenance

The following maintenance procedures must be carried out at the intervals given in Routine Maintenance at the beginning of the manual.
1 The oil level in the engine should be checked with the car standing on level ground, with the engine switched off and preferably when the engine is cold.
2 The manufacturers specify a normal oil consumption figure of 0.5 litre per 1000 km (700 miles per pint), but this will depend on the condition of the engine and the conditions under which it is driven, therefore check the engine oil level at the intervals specified.
3 Withdraw the dipstick, wipe it clean, re-insert it and then withdraw it for the second time. The oil level should be between the high and low marks. If it is too low, top up through the filler cap (photo), but take care not to overfill. Refit the filler cap.
4 To drain the engine oil it is preferable for the engine to be hot. First raise the front of the car on ramps or with a jack. Unscrew the socket-headed plug in the sump, remove the filler cap and allow the oil to drain into a suitable container (photo).
5 When the oil has drained, wipe clean the drain plug then refit and tighten it.
6 If the oil filter is due for renewal, now is the time to change it. The removal and refitting details are described in Section 4.
7 Lower the car to the ground then fill the engine with the specified quantity and grade of oil.
8 Start the engine. There will be a short delay before the oil warning lamp goes out. This is normal and is caused by the new filter having to fill with oil.
9 Switch off the engine, wait ten minutes and check the oil level and top up if necessary.
10 Periodically, partioularly on an engine which has covered a high mileage, remove the engine oil filler cap and, if fitted, check the filter mesh incorporated in the cap (photo). The filter is a breather for the crankcase ventilation system and should be cleaned or renewed if it is blocked with sludge.

3 Lubrication system – description

An external spur type oil pump is bolted to the rear face of the cylinder block and is driven by a skew gear off the camshaft. Oil is pumped through a full-flow filter to the crankshaft main oil gallery and then through drillings in the cylinder block to the camshaft, timing gears and valve train. The cylinder bores, gudgeon pins and valve stems are splash lubricated by oil thrown off the moving parts.

4 Oil filter – removal and refitting

1 The oil filter is of disposable cartridge type. Unscrew it with an oil filter wrench, but first wrap it in cloth as some oil will run out. If a proper wrench is not available a large worm drive hose clip can be fitted to the filter and the screw used as a gripping point. If all else fails, a screwdriver can be driven right through the cartridge and this used as a lever to unscrew it.
2 It is very important to purchase and fit the correct type of filter as some engines have a bypass valve incorporated in the filter mounting base of the crankcase whilst others have the valve incorporated in the filter cartridge.
3 No problem will arise if genuine Peugeot filters are used as they all incorporate a bypass valve. This will have no bearing upon the fact that a valve may already be built into the crankcase.
4 Clean the filter mounting ring on the crankcase and apply engine oil to the rubber seal on the cartridge. Do not use grease as it may make the filter difficult to unscrew (photo).
5 Check that the threaded sleeve is tight on the crankcase, offer up the new filter and screw it on using hand pressure only.
6 Top up the engine oil, run the engine and check for any signs of oil leakage from the filter seal.

5 Major operations possible with engine in car

The following operations are possible with the engine in position in the car.

Removal and refitting of the cylinder head, valves and rocker gear.
Removal and refitting of the oil pump
Removal and refitting of the sump
Removal and refitting of the big-end bearings (after removal of the sump)
Removal and refitting of the piston/connecting rod assemblies (after removal of the cylinder head and sump)
Removal and refitting of the timing gear components
Removal and refitting of the engine mountings
Removal and refitting of the flywheel (after removal of the gearbox).

2.3 Topping-up the engine oil (OHV engine)

2.4 Engine oil drain plug (OHV engine)

2.10 Oil filler cap showing filter mesh (OHC engine shown)

Fig. 1.2 Engine lubrication system circuit – OHV engine (Sec 3)

4.4 Lubricate filter seal with oil before fitting

Removal and refitting of the major ancillary components – inlet and exhaust manifolds, starter motor, water pump, distributor, alternator and oil filter.

6 Major operations requiring engine removal

The following operations can only be carried out with the engine removed from the car.
Removal and refitting of the main bearings
Removal and refitting of the crankshaft
Removal and refitting of the camshaft

7 Engine removal methods

1   The engine and transmission assembly are removed from beneath the vehicle. Once removed from the vehicle, the two units can be separated. If required the gearbox can be separated and removed with the engine *in situ*, but again its withdrawal is from underneath (see Chapter 6 for details).
2   If the gearbox is removed first, the engine can then be removed from above, but in view of the additional operations required, this is not a method that is normally recommended for removal and subsequent refitting.

8 Engine/transmission – removal

1 Open and support the bonnet in the full open position. It is advisable though not necessary, to unbolt and remove the bonnet (see Chapter 12) to prevent damaging it and to improve access (photo).
2 Disconnect and remove the battery as described in Chapter 12.
3 Remove the air cleaner unit and ductings (Chapter 3).
4 Remove the engine undersheild and side shields, then drain the cooling system as described in Chapter 2.
5 Undo the sump drain plug and drain the engine oil into a suitable container for disposal.
6 Undo the two drain plugs and drain the oil from the gearbox and differential unit into a suitable container for disposal (see Chapter 6).
7 Disconnect and remove the radiator top hose.
8 Disconnect the heater hose at the thermostat and at the three-way connector on the front side of the engine (photo).
9 Disconnect the vacuum servo hose at the inlet manifold and release it from the guide clip on the rocker cover.
10 Disconnect the fuel supply and return hose from the location bracket on the left-hand mounting and move the hose out of the way.
11 Disconnect the ignition HT leads from the coil and the spark plugs. Detach the LT lead connector from the distributor body. Remove the distributor cap and leads (photos).
12 Disconnect the accelerator and choke cables at the carburettor (see Chapter 3).
13 Disconnect the following items from the transmission:

  (a) Reverse stop cable (unscrew)
  (b) Clutch cable (see Chapter 5)
  (c) Speedometer cable (see Chapter 12)
  (d) Earth cable (note connection point)
  (e) Reversing light switch wire

14 Disconnect the oil pressure and level switch leads, also the temperature switch leads, noting their connections. Detach the wiring harness from the clip on the gearbox, the diagnostic socket bracket and the clip on the coolant hose between the inlet manifold and the three-way connector.
15 Whilst the vehicle is still free-standing, loosen (but do not remove at this stage) the front wheel hub nuts.
16 If they are available, fit Peugeot special cables No 0903 to the front suspension struts as described in Chapter 9 (Section 4).
17 Raise and support the vehicle at the front end and rear end using safety (axle) stands for support. There should be a minimum front skirt-to-ground clearance of about 27 inches (686 mm) to allow engine and transmission removal clearance. The following operations are carried out underneath the vehicle, so ensure that it is securely supported.
18 Refit the drain plugs to the engine and transmission.
19 Unbolt and detach the exhaust downpipe from the manifold flange.
20 Unclip the heat shield from the gear control relay lever then detach the gear control rods from the gearbox at their balljoints by prising them free using needle-nosed pliers or an open-ended spanner.

Fig. 1.3 Engine undershield and side shield removal – pull on clips to withdraw them (Sec 8)

21 Pivot the gearbox relay lever through 90° (either direction) to ensure that it is out of the way when removing the engine.
22 Detach the radiator bottom hose at the engine end, and the heater return hose at the radiator end.
23 Detach the wiring connectors from the starter motor and the alternator, also the coolant level indicator sensor on the radiator.
24 Undo the clamp bolt from the steering stub axle lower balljoint on each side and withdraw the bolts. Note that the bolts are fitted from the front. With the bolts removed, prise free the joints by levering down on the suspension arm. Take care not to damage the gaiters.
25 Remove the balljoint protector shields. If strut retainer cables were not fitted (as suggested in paragraph 16), it will be necessary to unbolt and remove the suspension arm inner pivot bolt in order to allow the full separation of the balljoint. Turn the hub onto full lock when separating the balljoint in this manner.
26 Undo the left-hand front hub nut, then detach and remove the left-hand drive shaft (see Chapter 7).
27 Unbolt and remove the torque reaction link from its location between the engine and the subframe on the right-hand side (photo).
28 Remove the right-hand driveshaft as described in Chapter 7.
29 Fit the lift sling to the engine and transmission. Lift sling attachment eyes are located at the right-hand side mounting and on the rear of the transmission on the left-hand side above the selector shaft. Attach the lift hoist to the sling and take up any slack but do not raise the engine/transmission.
30 Undo the left and right-hand mounting nuts.

8.1 Unbolt and remove the bonnet

8.8 Detach the hoses indicated from the three-way connector

8.11A Disconnect the LT lead connector, and distributor cap and HT leads ...

8.11B ... from the distributor and coil

8.27 Torque reaction link and right-hand driveshaft

8.31 Lowering the engine and transmission from the car

31 Check that all attachments are clear of the engine and transmission, then carefully lower the engine and transmission unit (photo). As the two assemblies are separated from their mountings, collect the special flat washer from the left-hand mounting and the standard flat washer from the right-hand mounting.

32 When fully lowered, withdraw the engine and transmission from the front end of the vehicle. Lowering onto a suitable trolley will ease removal.

9 Engine – separation from the transmission

1 If the engine has been removed complete with the transmission assembly, it is necessary to separate the two units before dismantling work on the engine can begin.

2 To do this, first undo and remove the bolts securing the starter motor flange to the bellhousing and the bolt securing the lower support bracket to the cylinder block. Lift away the starter motor.

3 Undo and remove the bolts securing the ignition coil mounting plate to the bellhousing and lift off this assembly.

4 Unbolt and remove the clutch housing cover plate with the TDC wire and sensor (where fitted). Loosen the small bolt and pivot the plate free.

5 Support the gearbox, remove any retaining bolts remaining. The gearbox can now be withdrawn from the engine but as they are separated, do not allow the weight of the transmission to hang on the input shaft. Recover any loose dowels (photo).

9.5 Engine and transmission separation

10 Engine – dismantling (general)

1 Ideally, the engine is mounted on a proper stand for overhaul but it is anticipated that most owners will have a strong bench on which to place it. If a sufficiently large strong bench is not available then the work can be done at ground level. It is essential, however, that some form of substantial wooden surface is available. Timber should be at least 3/4 inch thick, otherwise the weight of the engine will cause projections to punch holes straight through it.

2 It will save a great deal of time later if the engine is thoroughly cleaned down on the exterior before any dismantling begins. This can be done by using paraffin and a stiff brush or more easily, probably, by the use of a water soluble solvent which can be brushed on and then the dirt swilled off with a water jet. This will dispose of all the heavy grease and grit once and for all so that later cleaning of individual components will be a relatively clean process and the paraffin bath will not become contaminated with abrasive metal.

3 As the engine is stripped down, clean each part as it comes off. Try to avoid immersing parts with oilways in paraffin as pockets of liquid could remain and cause oil dilution in the critical first few revolutions after reassembly. Clean oilways with wire or, preferably, an air jet.

4 Where possible, avoid damaging gaskets on removal, especially if new ones have not been obtained. They can be used as patterns if new ones have to be specially cut.

5 It is helpful to obtain a few blocks of wood to support the engine while it is in the process of dismantling. Start dismantling at the top of the engine and then turn the block over and deal with the sump and crankshaft etc, afterwards.

6 Nuts and bolts should be refitted in their locations where possible to avoid confusion later. As an alternative keep each group of nuts and bolts together in a jar or tin.

7 Many items which are removed must be refitted in the same position, if they are not being renewed. These include valves, rocker arms, cam followers, pistons, pushrods, bearings and connecting rods. Some of these are marked on assembly to avoid any possibility of mixing them up during overhaul. Others are not, and it is a great help if adequate preparation is made in advance to classify these parts. Suitably labelled tins or jars and, for small items, egg trays, tobacco tins and so on, can be used. The time spent in this operation will be amply repaid later.

8 Other items which will be useful are a notebook and pencil, masking tape (for labelling components) and a good supply of plastic bags. Do make notes of the positions of washers, shims etc – you may think you will remember as you are dismantling but it can be a different story when the time comes for reassembly!

11 Engine ancillary components – removal

1 Before engine dismantling begins it is necessary to remove the externally mounted ancillary components. The extent and sequence of their removal is dependent on the amount to which the engine is being

11.1 General view of the 1.3 litre engine prior to dismantling

dismantled. If the engine is being fully dismantled, the following items must be removed (photo).

(a) *Thermostat housing complete – refer to Chapter 2 for details*
(b) *Inlet manifold with carburettor – refer to Chapter 3 for details*
(c) *Exhaust manifold – refer to Chapter 3 for details*
(d) *Fuel pump – refer to Chapter 3 for details*
(e) *Distributor – refer to Chapter 4 for details*
(f) *Alternator and mounting bracket – refer to Chapter 12 for details*
(g) *Clutch unit – refer to Chapter 5 for details*
(h) *Engine oil filter – refer to Section 4 for details*

2   With the major ancillary components removed, the engine sub-assemblies can now be dismantled as required, as described in the following Sections.

12 Cylinder head – removal (engine in car)

1   Disconnect the battery earth terminal and then drain the cooling system as described in Chapter 2.
2   Remove the air cleaner assembly as described in Chapter 3.
3   Undo and remove the nuts securing the exhaust front pipe to the manifold flange and recover the heat shield and gasket. If it is necessary to jack up the car for this operation, make sure that it is well supported on axle stands.
4   Slacken the retaining clip and remove the brake servo vacuum hose from the inlet manifold.
5   Undo and remove the two nuts and one bolt securing the air cleaner hot air box to the rocker cover. Lift off the air box.
6   Slacken the retaining clips and withdraw the radiator top hose and heater hose from their outlets on the thermostat housing.
7   Slacken the hose clips and detach the coolant hoses from the inlet manifold and carburettor as necessary.
8   Mark the positions of the HT leads and then pull them off the spark plugs. Note that No 1 cylinder is nearest to the flywheel.
9   Detach the fuel inlet pipe and distributor vacuum advance pipe from the carburettor.
10 Refer to Chapter 3, and disconnect the accelerator cable and choke cable from the carburettor.
11 Detach the electrical lead from the temperature gauge transmitter at the rear of the cylinder head.
12 Undo and remove the remaining securing nuts and lift off the rocker cover complete with breather hose. Recover the rocker cover

gasket. The engine must be cold before proceeding any further to avoid distortion of the cylinder head.
13 Slacken all the cylinder head bolts one turn at a time in the order shown in Fig. 1.4 and then undo and remove them completely.
14 Lift off the rocker shaft assembly, holding it at both ends to prevent it springing apart. After removal secure the assembly with wire to keep it together.
15 Lift out each pushrod in turn, using a twisting motion to release them from the cam followers. Punch eight holes in a stiff piece of cardboard, number them one to eight and place the pushrods in order of removal through the cardboard.
16 The cylinder head, complete with manifolds and carburettor, can now be removed by lifting it upwards. If the head is stuck, try to rock it to break the seal or strike it sharply with a hide or plastic mallet. Under no circumstances should the head be struck directly with a metal hammer, nor should any attempt be made to prise it apart from the cylinder block using a screwdriver or cold chisel. Cranking the engine on the starter motor may be effective in breaking the seal of a stubborn gasket.
17 Having removed the cylinder head, lift out the cam followers. Withdraw them one at a time, keeping each follower in its correct order of removal so that it can be fitted in its original bore.
18 If further work is to be carried out on the cylinder head, remove the thermostat housing and manifolds before proceeding.
19 It should be noted that the cylinder head gasket must be renewed when refitting and it is essential that the correct type is fitted according to model (see Figure 1.5).

Fig. 1.4 Numerical sequence for loosening the cylinder head bolts – OHV engine (Sec 12)

H.20119

Fig. 1.5 Cylinder head gasket identification – OHV engines (Sec 12)

E series (1.1 litre) engine – 2 notches
G Series (1.3 litre) engine – 3 notches

13 Cylinder head – removal (engine out of car)

Remove the engine ancillary components as described in Section 11, and then proceed as directed in paragraphs 12 to 17 inclusive of the previous Section.

14 Valves – removal

With the cylinder head removed from the engine, the valves can be removed as follows.

1 First remove the spark plugs.
2 Using a conventional valve spring compressor, compress each valve spring in turn until the two halves of the collets can be removed. Release the compressor and remove the spring and spring cup, valve oil seal, spring seat and the valve itself.
3 As before, identify all the parts so that they may be refitted into the same positions from which they were taken.
4 If when the valve spring compressor is screwed down, the valve spring cup refuses to free and expose the split collets, do not screw the compressor further down in an effort to force the cup free. Gently tap the top of the tool directly over the spring cup with a light hammer. This will usually free the cup. Whilst tapping the tool, hold the compressor firmly with your other hand to prevent the tool jumping off the cup when it is released.

15 Sump – removal

1 The sump consists of two parts: a lower pressed steel baseplate, containing the drain plug, and a light alloy main body incorporating anti-surge baffles. A separate compartment on the front face of the main body houses the water pump and water inlet elbow.
2 If the sump is to be removed with the engine in the car it is first necessary to remove the engine undertray, then drain the engine oil and the cooling system. Also to be removed are the alternator dirt shield, alternator and water pump hoses. Full information covering these operations will be found in the relevant Sections and Chapters of this manual.
3 If the engine is out of the car and on the bench, turn it over on its side so that the sump bolts are accessible.
4 Undo and remove the fourteen baseplate retaining bolts and lift off the plate.
5 Undo and remove the three retaining bolts and withdraw the oil pick-up and strainer assembly (photo).
6 Undo and remove the bolts inside and along the outer edge of the main body and lift off this assembly. If it is stuck, tap it free using a hide or plastic mallet. Recover the cork and paper gaskets from the baseplate, main body and strainer mating faces.

16 Flywheel – removal

1 If this component is to be removed with the engine in the car, it will first be necessary to remove the bellhousing and gearbox assembly, and then the clutch, as described in Chapter 6 and Chapter 5 respectively.
2 If the engine is on the bench, turn it the right way up and stand it on wooden blocks positioned beneath the crankcase.
3 Lock the flywheel to prevent it turning by engaging a strip of angle iron with the ring gear teeth and resting it against a bar inserted through the rear engine-to-bellhousing retaining bolt hole.
4 Undo and remove the flywheel retaining bolts in a progressive, diagonal sequence, recover the seating plate, and lift off the flywheel. Be careful not to drop it, it is heavy.

17 Timing cover, gears and chain – removal

1 Remove the sump as described in Section 15.
2 Place a block of wood between the crankshaft and the side of the crankcase to prevent rotation of the crankshaft.
3 Using a socket and extension bar, undo and remove the crankshaft pulley retaining bolt and then lever off the pulley using two screwdrivers. The retaining bolt is very tight.
4 Undo and remove the timing cover retaining bolts, ease the cover off its locating dowels and remove it from the front face of the engine.
5 Undo and remove the three bolts securing the camshaft sprocket to the camshaft.

Fig. 1.6 Using a spring compressor to release the valve collets (Sec 14)

15.5 Oil pick-up and strainer shown with sump baseplate removed

6 Lift off the camshaft sprocket complete with chain and then using two screwdrivers, lever off the crankshaft sprocket. Recover the Woodruff key from the end of the crankshaft.

18 Camshaft and oil pump driveshaft – removal

It is theoretically possible to remove the camshaft with the engine in the car. However, the preliminary work is so extensive – removal of cylinder head, sump, starter motor, oil pump and fuel pump, followed by the lowering of the front of the engine – that the procedure is not recommended. With the engine on the bench and the camshaft sprocket removed as described in Section 17, proceed as follows.
1 Undo and remove the two bolts that secure the distributor mounting plate to the side of the cylinder block and lift off the plate.
2 Withdraw the distributor driving dog from the splined end of the oil pump driveshaft.
3 Prior to removing the shaft, if a dial gauge is available, the driveshaft endfloat should be checked and noted (also the camshaft).

4   Using a pair of pliers, extract the small circlip from the end of the shaft, lift out the driven gear and washer, and then slide out the driveshaft from the oil pump side of the cylinder block.
5   Rotate the camshaft until the cut-outs on the front flange are aligned with the thrust plate retaining bolts. Relieve the locktabs (if applicable), then undo and remove the thrust plate retaining bolts.
6   Lift off the thrust plate and then carefully withdraw the camshaft from the front of the engine. Take care to avoid scratching the soft bearing surfaces with the camshaft lobes.

19 Piston and connecting rod assemblies – removal

1   This operation may be carried out with the engine in the car after removal of the cylinder head, described in Section 12, and the sump, described in Section 15.
2   Before removing the piston and connecting rod assemblies, clean off all traces of carbon from the top of the cylinder bores. If a wear ridge can be felt, reduce this as much as possible, using a sutiable scraper, to avoid damaging the pistons and rings during removal.
3   Rotate the crankshaft in the normal direction of rotation until No 1 piston is at the bottom of its stroke.
4   Undo and remove the big-end bearing nuts on No 1 connecting rod and take off the cap and lower bearing shell. If the cap is tight, tap it gently from side to side using a hammer.
5   Push the piston and connecting rod assembly up through the bore and withdraw it from the top of the cylinder block. Take care not to score the crankshaft journal with the big-end bolts.
6   Refit the bearing cap and lower shell to the connecting rod and secure with the nuts finger tight. Make sure that the upper and lower bearing shells are not interchanged if they are to be re-used. Identification numbers may be stamped on the connecting rod and big-end cap to indicate the cylinder to which they are fitted. If numbers are not visible, suitably mark the cap and rod using a centre punch (photo).
7   Repeat the above procedure for the remaining three piston and connecting rod assemblies, turning the crankshaft as necessary to gain access to the big-end nuts.

20 Crankshaft and main bearings – removal

1   In order to be able to remove the crankshaft it will be necessary to have completed the following tasks:

(a) Removal of engine
(b) Separation of engine from transmission
(c) Removal of cylinder head
(d) Removal of sump and flywheel
(e) Removal of timing cover, gears and chain
(f) Removal of big-end bearings

2   It is not essential to have extracted the pistons and connecting rods, but it makes for a less cluttered engine block during crankshaft removal.
3   Before removing the crankshaft, it is advisable to check the crankshaft endfloat as described in Section 38. If the crankshaft endfloat is in excess of the maximum amount specified, it is indicative of excessive wear of the crankshaft and bearings. Remove the crankshaft as follows.
4   Begin by removing the five retaining bolts and lifting off the oil seal housing at the rear of the crankshaft and cylinder block.
5   Check that the main bearing caps have identification numbers marked on them; No 1 should be at the flywheel end and No 5 at the timing gear end. If identification is not visible, use a centre punch to mark the caps. Also note the direction of fitting of the caps.
6   Slacken the main bearing cap retaining bolts by one turn only to begin with. Once all have been loosened, proceed to unscrew and remove them.
7   The bearing caps can now be lifted away, together with the shells inside them. Finally the crankshaft can be removed, followed by the upper shells seated in the crankcase.

19.6 Connecting rod and cap identification marks

21 Gudgeon pins – removal

The pistons are retained on the connecting rods by gudgeon pins, which are an interference fit in the connecting rod small-end bore. If new pistons are to be fitted, it is strongly recommended that you take the assemblies to your Peugeot dealer or motor engineering specialist to have this done, otherwise damage to the piston or distortion of the connecting rod may result.

22 Piston rings – removal

1   To remove the piston rings, slide them carefully over the top of the piston, taking care not to scratch the aluminium alloy; never slide them off the bottom of the piston skirt. It is very easy to break the cast iron piston rings if they are pulled off roughly, so this operation should be done with extreme care. It is helpful to make use of an old 0.5 mm (0.020 in) feeler gauge.
2   Lift one end of the piston ring to be removed out of its groove and insert under it the end of the feeler gauge.
3   Slide the feeler gauge slowly round the piston and, as the ring comes out of its groove, apply slight upward pressure so it rests on the land above. It can then be eased off the piston with the feeler gauge stopping it from slipping into an empty groove if it is any but the top piston ring that is being removed.
4   Repeat the procedure on the remaining piston rings. Keep the rings with their pistons if they are to be re-used (photo).

23 Engine components – examination for wear

When the engine has been stripped down and all parts properly cleaned, decisions have to be made as to what needs renewal. The following Sections tell the examiner what to look for. In any border-line case it is always best to decide in favour of a new part. Even if a part may still be serviceable, its life will have to be reduced by wear and the degree of trouble needed to renew it in the future must be taken into consideration. However, these things are relative and it depends on whether a quick 'survival' job is being done or whether the car as a whole is being regarded as having many thousands of miles of useful and economical life remaining.

22.4 Piston, connecting rod and piston rings dismantled for inspection

24 Crankshaft, main and big-end bearings – examination and renovation

1   With careful servicing and regular oil and filter changes, bearings will last for a very long time. But they can still fail for unforeseen reasons. With big-end bearings, an indication is a regular rhythmic loud knocking from the crankcase. The frequency depends on engine speed and is particularly noticeable when the engine is under load. This symptom is accompanied by a fall in oil pressure although this is not normally noticeable unless an oil pressure gauge is fitted. Main bearing failure is usually indicated by serious vibration, particularly at higher engine revolutions, accompanied by a more significant drop in oil pressure and a 'rumbling' noise.

2   Big-end bearings can be removed with the engine still in the car. If the failure is sudden and the engine has a low mileage since new or overhaul, this is probably worth doing. Bearing shells in good condition have bearing surfaces with a smooth, even matt silver/grey colour all over. Worn bearings will show patches of a different colour when the bearing metal has worn away and exposed the underlay. Damaged bearings will be pitted or scored. It is always well worthwhile fitting new shells as their cost is relatively low. If the crankshaft is in good condition, it is merely a question of obtaining another set of standard size shells (but see below). A reground crankshaft will need new bearing shells as a matter of course (photo).

3   Look at the main bearing journals and the crankpins. If there are any deep scratches or score marks, the shaft will need regrinding. Such conditions will nearly always be accompanied by similar deterioration in the matching bearing shells.

4   Each bearing journal must also be perfectly round and can be checked with a micrometer (photo) or caliper gauge around the periphery at several points. If there is more the 0.02 mm (0.001 in) of ovality, regrinding is necessary.

5   A main Peugeot agent or motor engineering specialist will be able to decide to what extent regrinding is necessary and also supply the special oversize shell bearings to match whatever may need grinding off.

6   Before taking the crankshaft for regrinding, check also the cylinder bore and pistons as it may be advantageous to have the whole engine done at the same time.

7   If the crankshaft is not being reground, but the bearings are to be renewed, take the old shells along to your supplier and check that you are getting the correct size bearings.

8   Check the spigot bush in the end of the crankshaft for wear, and if necessary renew it. To remove the bush, fill it with grease and then drive in a close-fitting rod. The bush will come out by the hydraulic pressure generated.

Fig. 1.7 Crankshaft and flywheel assembly (Sec 24)

1 Pulley retaining bolt	5 Crankshaft	8 Starter ring gear	11 Flywheel bolt
2 Pulley	6 Gasket	9 Flywheel	12 Spigot bush
3 Shell bearing	7 Oil seal cover	10 Locking plate	13 Crankshaft rear flange seal
4 Thrust washers			

24.2 Bearing shell identification mark (on rear face of shell)

24.4 Measure crankshaft journals for wear using a micrometer

25 Cylinder bores – examination and renovation

1   A new cylinder is perfectly round and the walls parallel throughout its length. The action of the piston tends to wear the walls at right-angles to the gudgeon pin due to side thrust. This wear takes place principally on that section of the cylinder swept by the piston rings.

2   It is possible to get an indication of bore wear by removing the cylinder head with the engine still in the car. With the piston down in the bore, first signs of wear can be seen and felt just below the top of the bore where the top piston ring reaches and there will be a noticeable lip. If there is no lip it is fairly reasonable to expect that bore wear is not severe and any lack of compression or excessive oil consumption is due to worn or broken piston rings or pistons.

3   If it is possible to obtain a bore measuring micrometer, measure the bore in the thrust plane below the lip and again at the bottom of the cylinder in the same plane. If the difference is more than 0.15 mm (0.006 in), a rebore is necessary. Similarly, a difference of 0.08 mm (0.003 in) or more between two measurements of the bore diameter taken at right angles to each other is a sign of ovality, calling for a rebore.

4   Any bore which is significantly scratched or scored will need reboring. This symptom usually indicates that the piston or rings are damaged also. In the event of only one cylinder being in need of reboring it will still be necessary for all four to be bored and fitted with new oversize pistons and rings. Your Peugeot agent or local motor engineering specialist will be able to rebore and obtain the necessary matched pistons. If the crankshaft is undergoing regrinding also, it is a good idea to let the same firm renovate and reassemble the crankshaft and pistons to the block. A reputable firm normally gives a guarantee for such work.

5   If the cylinders are in a satisfactory condition and a rebore is not necessary but new pistons and/or rings are to be fitted, the cylinder bores must be deglazed. This entails removing the high surface polish or glaze on the cylinder walls which will otherwise prevent the new rings from properly bedding in, with resultant high oil consumption.

6   Deglazing can be carried out using a fine grade emery cloth wrapped around a suitable former. Use liberal amounts of paraffin to keep the emery unclogged and use a criss-cross action so that the resulting finish is of a cross-hatch pattern. On completion thoroughly wash the block and remove all traces of emery grit.

26 Piston and piston rings – examination and renovation

1   Worn pistons and rings can usually be diagnosed when the symptoms of excessive oil consumption and low compression occur

and are sometimes, though not always, associated with worn cylinder bores. Compression testers that fit into the spark plug hole are available and these can indicate where low compression is occurring. Wear usually accelerates the more it is left so when the symptoms occur, early action can possibly save the expense of a rebore.

2   Another sympton of piston wear is piston slap – a knocking noise from the crankcase not to be confused with big-end bearing failure. It can be heard clearly at low engine speed when there is no load (idling for example) especially when the engine is cold and is much less audible when the engine speed increases. Piston wear usually occurs in the skirt or lower end of the piston and is indicated by vertical streaks

Fig. 1.8 Measuring cylinder bore wear with bore gauge
(Sec 25)

Fig. 1.9 Desired cross-hatch pattern in a cylinder bore after deglazing (Sec 25)

in the worn area which is always on the thrust side. It can also be seen where the skirt thickness is different.

3   Piston ring wear can be checked by first removing the rings from the pistons as described in Section 22. Then place the rings in the cylinder bores from the top, pushing them down about 38 mm (1.5 in) with the head of a piston (from which the rings have been removed) so that they rest square in the cylinder. Now measure the gap at the ends of the rings with a feeler gauge and compare the dimension obtained with the figures given in Specifications. It the gaps are excessive the rings must be renewed (photo).

4   The grooves in which the rings locate in the pistons can also become enlarged in use. These clearances can be measured with the rings in position on the piston after cleaning away any carbon deposits. Excessive clearances may be overcome by fitting thicker piston rings, but the grooves will need to be machined out to suit. This is a specialist's job and must therefore be entrusted to a Peugeot dealer or automotive machine shop.

5   If any of the pistons are excessively worn or damaged they must be renewed as a set. Removal of the pistons from the connecting rods whether for repair or renewal is a task which must be entrusted to your

Peugeot dealer or motor engineering specialist (see Section 21).

6   If the engine has been using an excessive amount of oil, but no significant wear or defects can be found in the cylinder bores and/or the pistons and rings, consult your Peugeot dealer or motor engineering specialist concerning the possibility of fitting a ring expander to the oil control rings, or fitting an alternative type of oil control ring.

27 Connecting rods – examination and renovation

1   The connecting rods are not subject to wear but can, in the case of engine seizure, become bent or twisted. If any distortion is visible or suspected, have the rods checked for alignment by your Peugeot dealer or motor engineering specialist. A small amount of twist or distortion of the rods can usually be straightened, but again this must be entrusted to a specialist. If the rods are excessively twisted, distorted or are damaged in any way they must be renewed as a set.

2   Removal of the pistons and gudgeon pins from the connecting rods is a specialist task (see Section 21).

3   Check that the oil squirt hole is clear (photo).

28 Camshaft and camshaft bearings – examination and renovation

1   The camshaft lobes and bearing journals should be carefully examined for any indications of flat spots, deep scoring, pitting or breakdown of the surface hardening. If any of these conditions exist the camshaft must be renewed, together with a complete set of cam followers.

2   If only very slight scoring marks on the lobes are noticed, these can be removed by a very gentle rubbing down with fine emery cloth or an oil stone. The greatest care should be taken to keep the cam profiles smooth.

3   Removal of the camshaft bearings in the cylinder block can be carried out using the following method.

4   First drive out the camshaft bearing sealing plug from the flywheel end bearing, using a long tubular drift (Fig. 1.10).

5   Removal of the front, rear and centre camshaft bushes is best accomplished by the use of a length of threaded rod and nuts with suitable tubular distance pieces (Fig. 1.11).

6   Note the precise positioning of each bearing bush before removal and ensure that the bearing seats are not damaged during the removal operation.

7   Fit the new bearing bushes using the same method as for removal, starting with the centre one. It is essential that the bearing oil hole is in exact alignment with the one drilled in the bearing seat and marks

26.3 Checking a piston ring gap using a feeler gauge

27.3 Connecting rod oil squirt hole

Fig. 1.10 Removing the camshaft sealing plug (Sec 28)

Fig. 1.11 Camshaft bush removal using a threaded rod, nuts and distance pieces (Sec 28)

should be made on the edge of the bearing bush and seat before pulling into position.
8   Fit a new camshaft front bearing sealing cap.

29 Cam followers and pushrods – examination and renovation

1   The cam followers (tappets) should be checked in their respective bores in the crankcase and no excessive side play should be apparent. The faces of the followers which bear against the camshaft lobes should also have a clear smooth shiny surface. If they show signs of pitting or serious wear they should be renewed.
2   The pushrods should be checked for straightness by rolling them along a flat surface. Also check for wear of the ball end which locates in the cam follower, and the cup end that accepts the rocker adjusting ball. Renew as necessary.

30 Cylinder head, valves and piston crowns – decarbonising

1   When the cylinder head is removed, either in the course of an overhaul or for inspection of bores or valve condition when the engine is in the car, it is normal to remove all carbon deposits from the piston crowns, cylinder head and valves.
2   This is best done using a scraper, but when working on the cylinder head and piston crowns, take care not to damage the relatively soft alloy in any way.
3   When the engine is in the car, certain precautions must be taken when decarbonising the piston crowns in order to prevent dislodged pieces of carbon falling into the interior of the engine which could cause damage to the cylinder bores, piston and rings, or if allowed into the water passages, damage to the water pump. Turn the engine so that the piston being worked on is at the top of its stroke and then mask off the adjacent cylinder bores and all surrounding orifices with paper and adhesive tape. Press grease into the gap all round the piston to keep the carbon particles out and then scrape all carbon away. When completed, carefully clear out the grease around the rim of the piston with a matchstick or something similar – bringing any carbon particles with it. Repeat the process on the other piston crown. It is not recommended that a ring of carbon is left round the edge of the piston on the theory that it will aid oil consumption. This was valid in the earlier days of long stroke, low revving engines but modern engines, fuels and lubricants cause less carbon deposits anyway, and any left behind tends merely to cause hot spots.
4   The valves are best cleaned using a rotary wire brush.

31 Cylinder head, valves and rocker gear – examination and renovation

1   Examine the cylinder head for signs of cracks around the valve seats or spark plug holes and for water erosion around the passages

and outlets in the cylinder head face. Also check for distortion of the cylinder head face using a straight-edge. If any cracks are apparent the head must be renewed. Minor erosion or distortion of the cylinder head face can be rectified by having the face skimmed by a motor engineering specialist or machine shop. If this work is carried out, refer to the Specifications for the maximum amount of metal that can be removed from the head face and note also that a thicker gasket must be used on reassembly.
2   The valve seats should be examined for signs of pitting or ridging. Slight pitting can be ground away using carborundum paste and an *old* valve (photo). New valves are specially plated and **must not** be used to grind in the seats. If the valve faces are burnt or cracked, new valves must be obtained. If the valve seats require re-cutting ensure that the seat width and seat angle are maintained (Fig. 1.12).
3   The rocker gear should be dismantled and thoroughly cleaned of the sludge deposits which normally tend to accumulate on it. The gear is dismantled by simply sliding the pedestals, springs and rockers off the shafts (photo). The shafts may be removed from the centre pedestal after drifting out the retaining roll pin.
4   The rocker arms should be a slide fit over the shaft with very little play. If play is excessive, or if ridges are apparent in the shaft, renew these components. Also check the domed ends of the rocker adjusting screws for wear and renew any that are deformed. The pad of the rocker that bears against the valve stem should also be examined. It is normal to detect a slight wear ridge using the edge of your fingernail. If the ridge is visibly apparent then it has penetrated the surface hardening of the pad and the rocker arm should be renewed. A very slight ridge can be dressed with an oilstone.
5   Refit the valve into its guide in the head and note if there is any sideways movement which denotes wear between the stem and guide. Here again the degree of wear can vary. If excessive, the performance of the engine can be noticeably affected and oil consumption increased. Wear is normally in the guide rather than on the valve stem

31.2 Valve seat refacing using an old valve and carborundum paste

Fig. 1.12 Valve seat angles (Sec 31)

30°

44 +0°30 +0

31.3 Check the rocker gear for excessive wear

but check a new valve in the guide if possible first. Valve guide renewal is a tricky operation and should be left to a Peugeot dealer.
6 Check that the end face of the valve stem is not 'hammered' or ridged by the action of the rocker arm. If it is, dress it square and smooth with an oilstone.

32 Oil pump – examination and renovation

1 Separate the two halves of the oil pump body and examine the gears and internal walls of the housing for scoring, pitting or wear ridges. Check for excessive endfloat of the gears using a straight-edge and feeler gauges as shown (photos). Peugeot do not stipulate any allowable wear tolerances for the endfloat of the gears and it will therefore be necessary to compare the amount of wear present against

a new pump to assess if excessive wear is present. If in doubt, renew the pump unit.
2 Remove the domed nut and sealing washer and then, using an Allen key, unscrew the pressure relief valve plunger. Take out the plunger, spring and ball. Thoroughly clean away any sludge deposits from the relief valve and then check the ball and housing for pitting or ridging (photos).
3 If the oil pump or pressure relief valve are worn or in any way suspect, renew the pump or worn parts as necessary. It is always a good idea to renew the pump if the engine is being overhauled or reconditioned, particularly if it has covered a high mileage.

32.1A Separate the two halves of the oil pump ...

32.1B ... and remove the gears to check for excessive wear

32.1C Checking the gears for excessive endfloat

32.2A Unscrew the pressure relief valve plunger ...

32.2B ... to withdraw the ball and spring

33 Oil pump driveshaft bushes – examination and renovation

1   The two bushes in the cylinder block in which the oil pump/dipstick driveshaft runs should be examined for wear by refitting the shaft and checking for excessive side play (unless checked when dismantling).

2   If wear has taken place the bushes should be renewed. To remove them, draw each one out using a threaded rod, nuts, and distance piece as shown in Fig. 1.14.

3   New bushes can be fitted using the following procedure.

4   Fit the shorter bush to the distributor side, pulling it in tight to the machined surface of the cylinder block. It is vital that the oil hole in the bush aligns with the crankshaft bearing oil passage.

5   Fit the bush to the oil pump side, again using the threaded rod and nut method and avoid damage to the bush just fitted. There is no need to align the oil hole on this bush as it opens into a circular oil chamber in the cylinder block.

6   Test the driveshaft in the bushes for ease of rotation. A hard spot will indicate mis-alignment or distortion.

Fig. 1.13 Sectional view of the oil pump and driveshaft assembly (Sec 33)

1 Fixing bolt	4 Driven gear	7 Driveshaft	10 Drivegear
2 Idler gear	5 Body	8 Camshaft	11 Driveshaft bushes
3 Cover	6 Crankcase	9 Circlip	

Fig. 1.14 Extracting the oil pump driveshaft bushes (Sec 33)

1 Rod	4 Nut	A Shaft bush	M Side towards distributor
2 Plate	5 Nut	B Old gudgeon pin	N Side towards oil pump
3 Sleeve			

Fig. 1.15 Drifting off the flywheel ring gear (Sec 34)

34 Flywheel – examination and renovation

1   The clutch friction disc mating surface of the flywheel should be examined for scoring. If this is apparent then it should either be exchanged for a new unit or if the scoring is very light it may be skimmed.
2   The starter ring gear should be examined and if the teeth are worn or chipped it must be renewed.
3   To remove the ring, support the flywheel and drive off the ring gear using a bronze or steel bar (Fig. 1.15).
4   Take care not to damage the flywheel locating dowels during this operation or they will have to be renewed.
5   To fit a new ring gear requires heating the ring to 220°C (428°F). This can be done by polishing four equal spaced sections of the gear, placing it on a suitable heat resistant surface (such as fire bricks) and heating it evenly with a blow lamp or torch until the polished areas turn a light yellow tinge. Do not overheat, or the hard wearing properties will be lost. The gear has a chamfered inner edge which should go against the shoulder when put on the flywheel. When hot enough, place the gear in position quickly, tapping it home if necessary, and let it cool naturally without quenching in any way.

35 Timing gears, chain and cover – examination and renovation

1   Carefully examine the teeth of the timing gears and the links of the chain for wear. Place the chain over the gears and ensure that it is a snug fit without slackness. Renew any of the components where necessary.
2   The camshaft timing chain sprocket has an anti-rattle band located in its central groove. Check this for deterioration and renew it if necessary (photo).
3   The crankshaft front oil seal in the timing cover should be renewed as a matter of course. The old seal may be drifted out using a hammer and a suitable tube, or levered out with a screwdriver or stout bar. Tap a new seal into position using a hammer and a block of wood. The lips of the seal must face toward the engine when installed (photo).

36 Engine – reassembly (general)

1   It is during the process of engine reassembly that the job is either made a success or a failure. From the word go there are certain basic rules which it is folly to ignore, namely:

(a) *Absolute cleanliness. The working area, the components of the engine and the hands of those working on the engine must be completely free of grime and grit. One small piece of carborundum dust or swarf can ruin a big-end in no time, and nullify all the time and effort you have spent.*

(b) *Always, no matter what the circumstances may be, use new gaskets, locking tabs, seals, nyloc (self-locking) nuts and any other parts mentioned in the Sections in this Chapter. It is pointless to dismantle an engine, spend considerable money and time on it and then waste all this for the sake of something as small as a failed oil seal. Delay the rebuilding if necessary.*

(c) *Don't rush it. The most skilled and experienced mechanic can easily make a mistake if he is rushed.*

(d) *Check that all nuts and bolts are clean and in good condition and ideally renew all spring washers, lockwashers and tab washers as a matter of course. A supply of clean engine oil and clean cloths (to wipe excess oil off your hands) and a torque spanner are the only things which should be required in addition to all the tools used in dismantling the engine.*

(e) *The torque wrench is an essential requirement when reassembling the engine (and transmission) components. This is because the various housings are manufactured from aluminium alloy and whilst this gives the advantage of less weight, it also means that the various fastenings must be accurately tightened as specified to avoid distortion and/or damage to the components.*

35.2 Camshaft sprocket showing the anti-rattle band

35.3 Renew the timing cover oil seal

37 Engine – preparation for reassembly

1   Assuming that the engine has been completely stripped for reconditioning and that the block is now bare, before any reassembly takes place it must be thoroughly cleaned both inside and out.

2   Clean out the oilways using a bottle brush, wire or other suitable implement, and blow through with compressed air. Squirt some clean engine oil through to check that the oilways are clear.

3   If the core plugs are defective and show signs of weeping, they must be renewed at this stage. To remove, carefully drive a punch through the centre of the plug and use the punch to lever the plug out. Clean the aperture thoroughly and prior to fitting the new plug, smear the orifice with sealant. Use a small-headed hammer and carefully drive the new core plug into position with the convex side outwards. Check that it is correctly seated on completion.

4   As the components are assembled, lubricate them with clean engine oil and use a suitable sealant where applicable.

5   Make sure that all blind tapped holes are clean, with any oil mopped out of them. This is because it is possible for a casting to fracture when a bolt is screwed in owing to hydraulic pressure.

6   Before fitting the retaining bolts, their threads must be cleaned and lightly oiled, unless otherwise stated or where a locking compound or sealant is specified.

38 Crankshaft and main bearings – refitting

1   Ensure that the crankcase is thoroughly clean and all oilways are clear. A thin twist drill is useful for clearing the oilways, or if possible, they may be blown out with compressed air. Treat the crankshaft in the same fashion, then inject engine oil into the oilways (photo).

2   Wipe the bearing shell seats in the crankcase clean, then fit the upper halves of the new main bearing shells into their seats (photo). All upper half shells have oil grooves in them but the cap shells differ in

Fig. 1.16 Position of grooved and plain main bearing shells (Sec 38)

A   Lower (cap) shells
B   Upper (cylinder block) shells
C   Timing cover end
D   Flywheel end

that numbers 2 and 4 have oil grooves, whilst numbers 1, 3 and 5 are plain shells.

3   Note that there is a tab on the back of each bearing shell which engages with a groove in the seating.

4   Wipe the seats in the main bearing caps clean and fit the remaining shells to their seats (photo).

5   Fit the semi-circular thrust washers to each side of the centre main bearing in the crankcase. Retain the thrust washers with a smear of grease and position them with the oil grooves facing outwards (photo).

6   Liberally lubricate the main bearing shells in the crankcase and then carefully lower the crankshaft into position (photos).

38.1 Check that the crankcase and oilways are clean prior to reassembly

38.2 Locate the main bearing upper shells in the crankcase ...

38.4 ... and the lower shells in the caps

38.5 Fit the thrust washers with the oil grooves facing out

38.6A Lubricate the bearings ...

38.6B ... then lower the crankshaft into position ...

38.7 ... and fit the main bearing caps

38.8 Tighten the cap retaining bolts to the specified torque

38.10 Check the crankshaft endfloat using a feeler gauge

7   Lubricate the bearing shells in the caps and then refit the caps and retaining bolts to their correct locations in the crankcase (photos).

8   With all the caps in place, tighten the retaining bolts progressively to the specified torque wrench setting (photo). Check the crankshaft for ease of rotation. If new bearing shells have been fitted, it may be fairly stiff to turn, but there should be no high spots.

9   Should the crankshaft be very stiff to turn or possess high spots, a most careful inspection should be made – preferably by a skilled mechanic – to trace the cause of the trouble. It is very seldom that trouble of this nature will be experienced when fitting the crankshaft.

10 Using a screwdriver, ease the crankshaft fully forward and measure the endfloat, with feeler gauges, between the side of the crankshaft centre journal and the thrust washers. Ensure that the clearance is within the limits given in the Specifications. Oversize thrust washers are available (photo).

11 Position a new oil seal housing gasket, lightly smeared with jointing compound, on the rear face of the crankcase.

12 Lubricate the lips of the oil seal and then carefully ease it over the crankshaft flange using a twisting action (photo).

13 Refit the oil seal housing retaining bolts finger tight, rotate the crankshaft one full turn to centralise the seal and then progressively tighten the bolts to the specified torque wrench setting.

39 Gudgeon pins – refitting

As interference fit gudgeon pins are used (see Section 21), this operation must be carried out by your Peugeot dealer or motor engineering specialists.

40 Piston rings – refitting

1   Check that the piston ring grooves and oilways are thoroughly clean and unblocked. Piston rings must always be fitted over the head of the piston and never from the bottom.

2   The easiest method to use when fitting rings is to wrap a 0.38 mm (0.015 in) feeler gauge round the top of the piston and place the rings one at a time, starting with the bottom oil control ring, over the feeler gauge (photo).

3   The feeler gauge, complete with ring, can then be slid down the piston over the other piston ring grooves until the correct groove is reached. The piston ring is then slid gently off the feeler gauge into the groove.

4   An alternative method is to fit the rings by holding them slightly open with the thumbs and both of the index fingers. This method requires a steady hand and great care, as it is easy to open the ring too much and break it.

5   The top compression ring and oil control ring may be fitted either way up; however the second ring must be fitted with the word TOP uppermost (photo). (Fig. 1.17).

6   When all the rings are in position on the pistons, move them around to bring each ring gap approximately 120° away from the adjacent ring (Fig. 1.18).

38.12 Fit the crankshaft rear oil seal

40.2 Method used to refit the piston rings

40.5 Orientation and size mark on the top piston ring

Fig. 1.17 Piston ring identification (Sec 40)

Fig. 1.18 Space the ring gaps when fitted as indicated
(Sec 40)

Fig. 1.19 Connecting rod orientation when fitting (Sec 41)

A   Oil groove towards camshaft side
B   Identification marks

7   If special oil control rings are being fitted, follow the maker's
instructions closely.

41 Piston and connecting rod assemblies – refitting

1   Clean the cylinder bores with a non-fluffy rag and then liberally
lubricate them with engine oil.
2   Apply clean engine oil to the piston rings of No 1 piston and insert
this piston connecting rod assembly into No 1 cylinder bore (photo).
3   It is essential that the piston and rod assemblies are correctly
orientated when fitted, with lubrication groove on the big-end face
and the connecting rod and cap identity marks facing towards the
camshaft side of the engine (Figs. 1.19 and 1.20) (photo).
4   Make sure that the piston ring gaps are still correctly staggered and
then compress the rings using a piston ring compressing tool. A large
diameter worm drive hose clip will serve as a ring compressor if a
proper tool is not available.
5   Now tap the top of the piston down through the ring compressor
and into the cylinder using a block of wood or hammer handle (photo).
Guide the big-end of the connecting rod near to its position on the
crankshaft, taking care not to scratch the crankpin with the big-end
bolts.

Fig. 1.20 Piston orientation when fitting. Slot C must face
the timing cover end (Sec 41)

41.2 Inserting a piston and connecting rod into its bore

41.3 The lubrication groove on the connecting rod big-end side face fits facing the camshaft side

4.15 Tap the piston and rod down the bore whilst supporting the ring compressor

41.9 Fit the connecting rod big-end bearing cap ...

41.10 ... and tighten the cap retaining bolts to the specified torque

6   Wipe the shell seat in the big-end of the connecting rod clean, and the underside of the new shell bearing. Fit the shell into position in the connecting rod with its locating tongue engaged with the appropriate groove in the big-end.

7   Generously lubricate the crankpin journals with engine oil and turn the crankshaft so that it is in its most advantageous position for the rod to be drawn onto it.

8   Wipe the bearing shell seat in the bearing cap clean, and then the underside of the new shell. Fit the shell into the cap, engaging the shell tongue with the groove in the cap.

9   Draw the big-end of the connecting rod onto the crankpin, then fit the cap into position (photo). Make sure it is the correct way around, then fit new nuts.

10 Tighten the nuts progressively to the specified torque wrench

setting (photo) and then check that the crankshaft is still free to rotate without tight spots. (A certain additional amount of resistance is to be expected from the friction between piston rings and cylinder bore).

11 Repeat this procedure for the remaining piston/connecting rod assemblies.

42 Camshaft, timing gears, chain and cover – refitting

1   Liberally lubricate the camshaft bearings and insert the camshaft, taking care not to damage the bearings as the cam lobes pass through them (photos).

2   Engage the camshaft thrust plate with the groove behind the

42.1A Lubricate the camshaft bearings ...

42.1B ... and fit the camshaft

42.2A Locate the camshaft thrust plate ...

42.2B ... fit and tighten the retaining bolt to the specified torque

42.3 Check the camshaft endfloat

42.5 Fit the crankshaft sprocket

camshaft flange (photo), and refit the retaining bolts, tightened to the specified torque wrench setting (photo). Knock up the lockwasher tabs (if fitted).

3   Pull the camshaft fully forward and check the endfloat using feeler gauges inserted between the thrust plate and flange (photo). If the endfloat is outside the specified tolerance, various sizes of thrust plate are available.

4   Rotate the crankshaft until Nos 1 and 4 pistons are at TDC.

5   Refit the Woodruff key to the slot in the crankshaft and slide on the crankshaft sprocket (photo).

6   Temporarily position the camshaft sprocket on the camshaft and align the bolt holes.

7   Rotate the camshaft and sprocket until the dot on the edge of the sprocket is aligned between the two lines on the crankshaft sprocket.

8   Remove the camshaft sprocket without rotating the camshaft and lift the timing chain over both sprockets. Refit the camshaft sprocket and check that the timing marks are still in alignment, using a straight-edge if necessary (photo). (Fig. 1.21).

9   Refit the three camshaft sprocket retaining bolts and tighten to the specified torque wrench setting (photo). Knock up the tabs of the lockwashers (if used).

10 Lightly smear a new timing cover gasket with jointing compound and position it on the cylinder block. Refit the timing cover and retaining bolts and then tighten the bolts to the specified torque (photos). Note that the engine mounting support is returned by the upper bolts, and this can be fitted at this stage.

43 Oil pump driveshaft – refitting

1   Temporarily refit the crankshaft pulley and then rotate the crankshaft until the notch on the pulley is aligned with the specified BTDC mark on the timing scale of the timing cover. No 1 cylinder must be on its compression stroke, ie the cam lobes for No 1 cylinder will point downwards.

Fig. 1.21 Alignment of timing marks and sprockets (Sec 42)

2   Smear the oil pump driveshaft with engine oil and insert it into its bushes from the oil pump side of the cylinder block (photo).

3   With the shaft in position, slide on the washer and driven gear from the distributor side of the cylinder block, ensuring that the flanged side of the gear faces outward (photo).

4   Secure the gear and shaft with the circlip and then check that the endlfoat of the shaft is as specified (photo).

5   With the crankshaft positioned as described above (paragraph 1), slide the distributor driving dog onto the end of the shaft, so that when installed the dog slot positioned as shown (photo); three teeth anti-clockwise from vertical.

6   Refit the distributor mounting plate so that its boss is towards the timing cover and secure with the retaining bolts (photo).

42.8 Fit the camshaft sprocket and chain, aligning the timing marks on the sprockets

42.9 Tighten the camshaft sprocket retaining bolts

42.10A Position a new gasket on the endface of the crankcase ...

42.10B ... then fit the timing cover

43.2 Insert the oil pump driveshaft

43.3 Fit the driven gear onto the driveshaft ...

43.4 ... and secure it with the circlip

43.5 Fit the distributor driving dog with the slot positioned as shown

43.6 Refit the distributor mounting plate

44 Flywheel and crankshaft pulley – refitting

1   Place the flywheel in position on the crankshaft flange and turn it as necessary until all the offset bolt holes are aligned.
2   Apply a drop of thread locking compound to the retaining bolts and then refit the bolts and seating plate (photo).
3   Lock the flywheel using a piece of angle iron and bar engaged in the ring gear, or a block of wood between the crankshaft and crankcase.
4   Tighten the flywheel retaining bolts in a diagonal sequence to the specified torque wrench setting (photo).

5   Lubricate the lips of the timing cover oil seal and slide on the crankshaft pulley.
6   Refit the retaining bolt and tighten to the specified torque wrench setting (photos).

45 Sump – refitting

1   Ensure that the mating surfaces of the sump and crankcase are clean, smear both sides of the new gasket with jointing compound and position it on the crankcase.
2   Place the sump main body over the gasket and secure with the

44.2 Fit the flywheel and retaining bolts. Apply locking compound to the bolt threads

44.4 Tighten the retaining bolts to the specified torque

44.6 Fit the crankshaft pulley and retaining bolt

45.2 Refit the sump main body

45.3A Locate the oil pick-up gasket

45.3B Assemble the pick-up and strainer unit ...

45.3C ... then fit it into position ...

45.3D ... and tighten the securing bolts

45.4 Refit the sump baseplate

internal and external retaining bolts (photo), using thread locking compound.

3   Smear the oil pick-up/strainer assembly gasket with jointing compound, position it on the sump and refit the pick-up/strainer assembly (photos).

4   Finally refit the baseplate, again using a new gasket with jointing compound, and secure with the retaining bolts, correctly tightened (photo).

46 Valves – refitting

1   Place new oil seals over the valve guides (photo).

2   Liberally lubricate the valve stems and then insert them into the valve guides from which they were removed (photo).

3   Refit the lower spring seat, valve spring and spring cup over the valve stem and then position the spring compressor over the assembly (photos).

4   Compress the spring sufficiently to allow the cotters to be slipped into place in the groove machined in the top of the valve stem (photo). Now release the spring compressor.

5   Repeat this operation until all eight valves have been assembled into the cylinder head.

6   With all the valves installed, gently tap the top of the valve stems once or twice, using a soft-faced mallet, to seat the cotters and centralise the components.

47 Cylinder head – refitting

1   Before refitting the cylinder head, insert the cam followers, liberally lubricated, into their original bores in the cylinder block (photo).

46.1 Fit the new oil seals onto the valve guides

46.2 Insert the valves ...

46.3A ... fit the lower spring seat ...

46.3B ... spring and upper cup ...

46.4 ... then locate the compressor and fit the collets

47.1 Fit the cam followers into their original positions

47.2 Alignment dowels must be securely fitted

47.4A Position cylinder head gasket with ALTO marking uppermost

47.4B New cylinder head gasket fitted into position

47.5 Refitting the cylinder head

47.6 Locate the pushrods into their original positions

2 Make sure that the two alignment dowels are in position on the cylinder block face and then wipe the block and cylinder head faces with a petrol-moistened rag. Allow time to air dry (photo).

3 Make sure that the head gasket being fitted is of the correct type. If any machining operations have been carried out on the cylinder head face, a gasket of the correct thickness must be used (see Specifications).

4 Locate the new cylinder head gasket in position on the block, ensuring that the word ALTO is visible on the upper surface (photos). The gasket should normally be fitted dry, but if there has been evidence of water leaks from the previous head gasket, or if there is slight eroding of the aluminium face around the water passages, then a thin film of a suitable sealant (eg Hylomar) should be applied to both sides of the gasket. This is a non-setting jointing compound, particularly resistant to oil, water and heat, and will also provide protection against further erosion of the head. Refer to Fig. 1.5 and check that the gasket type is correct.

5 Lower the cylinder head gently into position on the cylinder block and engage the locating dowels (photo).

6 Fit the pushrods in their correct locations, carefully engaging their lower ends in the cam followers (photo).

7 If the rocker shaft has been dismantled for removal of worn components, it should be reassembled with the parts fitted in the sequence shown in Fig. 1.22. Note that the shafts are assembled with their plugged ends facing outward.

8 Make sure that the rocker pillar alignment dowels are in position and lower the rocker gear into place over the dowels (photo). Make sure that the adjusting screw ball on each rocker arm engages with its respective pushrod.

9 Refit the cylinder head retaining bolts, having first cleaned their threads with a wire brush. Oil the threads also.

10 Using a torque wrench, tighten the cylinder head bolts progressively and evenly, in the sequence shown in Fig. 1.23, to the torque wrench setting given in the Specifications (photo), but note that the

Fig. 1.23 Tightening sequence for cylinder head retaining bolts (Sec 47)

Fig. 1.22 Correct reassembly of the rocker gear (Sec 47)

air cleaner, as described in Chapter 3, and the rocker cover as described in Section 12 of this Chapter. The crankshaft can be rotated for adjustment of the clearances by engaging a socket on the crankshaft pulley bolt.

3   It is important that the clearances are adjusted only when the appropriate piston is at TDC on the compression stroke. The following table shows the order in which the valves should be adjusted (which also avoids turning the crankshaft more than necessary):

Valves rocking on cylinder No	Adjust valves on cylinder No
4	1
2	3
1	4
3	2

tightening procedure for all OHV engine models must be as follows whenever the cylinder head is being refitted:

(a) *Tighten to the Stage 1 torque*
(b) *Tighten to the Stage 2 torque*
(c) *After the engine has been restarted, run it up to its normal operating temperature (but do not exceed 3000 rpm), then switch it off and allow it to cool for a minimum period of 6 hours*
(d) *Final tightening: Loosen each head bolt in turn and retighten it to the Stage 3 torque in the specified order of sequence. Readjust the valve clearances*

48 Valve clearances – checking and adjusting

1   The importance of correct rocker arm/valve stem clearance cannot be over-stressed as it vitally affects the performance of the engine. If the clearances are set too wide, the efficiency of the engine is reduced as the valves open later and close earlier than intended. If, however, the clearances are too tight, there is a danger that as the valve stems expand with heat there will be insufficient clearance to allow the valves to close properly. This will cause loss of compression and possible burning of the valve head and seat.

2   Valve clearances must only be adjusted with the engine cold. With the engine in the car, access to the rockers is gained after removing the

4   Turn the crankshaft in the normal direction of rotation and observe the movement of the exhaust valves. (Counting from the flywheel end, exhaust valves are Nos 2, 4, 5 and 7). When one is moving upward to its closed position, continue turning slowly until the inlet valve on the same cylinder just starts to open. This is the 'valves rocking' position. The piston in the appropriate cylinder shown in the table is now at TDC on the compression stroke and its valve clearances can be checked and if necessary adjusted.

5   Insert a feeler blade of the specified thickness into the gap between the valve stem and the rocker arm. The blade should be a firm sliding fit.

6   If adjustment is necessary, slacken the hexagon locknut on the rocker arm, then screw the adjusting screw in or out as necessary until the feeler blade is a firm sliding fit (photo). Hold the adjusting screw to prevent it turning further and tighten the locknut, then recheck the clearance. Repeat the operation if necessary.

7   Check the adjacent valve of that cylinder in the same way and then repeat the procedure until all eight valves have been adjusted.

8   If the engine is in the car, refit the rocker cover on completion, using a new gasket if the old one was damaged during removal, and then the air cleaner assembly (photo).

47.8 Refit the rocker gear assembly

47.10 Tighten the cylinder head bolts to the specified torque

48.6 Adjusting the valve-to-rocker arm clearance

48.8 Refitting the rocker cover (note new gasket)

49.3 Refit the alternator mounting bracket and plate

49.6A Reassemble the oil pump ...

49.6B ... locate the new gasket and fit the pump unit ...

49.6C ... and secure the retaining bolts

49 Engine ancillary components – refitting

1   Begin by refitting the clutch assembly to the flywheel. Full details of the fitting procedure and centralisation of the clutch friction disc are given in Chapter 5.

2   Place a new gasket, lightly coated with jointing compound, in position on the water pump housing and then refit the pump and retaining bolts. With the pump in position refit the pulley, and the pump-to-timing cover water hose. (Refer to Chapter 2 for full details).

3   Fit the alternator mounting bracket and plate (photo).

4   The alternator and drivebelt can be fitted and adjusted at this stage or later after the engine is fitted. Refer to Chapter 12 for details.

5   Position new gaskets on both sides of the fuel pump insulator block. Hold the block in place on the engine and refit the fuel pump, ensuring that the operating arm goes over the camshaft eccentric, not under it. Secure the pump with the two bolts.

6   Liberally lubricate the oil pump gears and the inside of the housing. Place a new gasket between the two halves of the pump body and join them together. Using another new gasket refit the pump to the cylinder block and secure with the retaining bolts (photos).

7   Smear clean engine oil onto the rubber seal of a new oil filter and screw the filter onto its housing on the oil pump (photo). Tighten the filter by hand only. Do not use any tools.

8   Refit the distributor to the engine, using the procedure described in Chapter 4 to ensure that the ignition timing is correct.

9   Refit the oil pressure switch using a new washer (photo).

10 Fit the three-way coolant connector to the side of the sump using a new gasket smeared with sealant (photo).

49.7 Fit the new oil filter to the pump

49.9 Oil pressure switch location

49.10 Coolant three-way connector

49.13A Right-hand engine support bracket ...

49.13B ... and support plate

49.14 Driveshaft bearing/torque reaction link bush housing

11 Refit the inlet manifold (together with carburettor if applicable) and reconnect the coolant hoses. Use a new manifold gasket.
12 Stick a new gasket onto the thermostat housing, engage the housing with the hose from the inlet manifold and refit the bolts. Secure the hose clip in position. Fit the down hose between the inlet manifold and the three-way connector.
13 If not already fitted, locate the right-hand engine mounting bracket and its support plate as shown (photos).
14 Refit the driveshaft bearing/torque reaction link bush housing (photo).
15 Refit the exhaust manifold using a new gasket. Ensure that both mating faces are clean before fitting.
16 Refit the fault diagnosis socket retaining bracket.
17 The engine is now reassembled and ready for reconnection to the gearbox and refitting to the car.

50 Engine – reconnecting to gearbox

1 If the engine and transmission were removed from the car as a unit, the two assemblies must now be reconnected before being refitted to the car.
2 The reconnecting procedure is a straightforward reverse of the

removal sequence. If difficulty is experienced engaging the manual gearbox input shaft splines, engage a gear by moving the shift rod and then rotate the crankshaft slightly. This should align the clutch friction disc and input shaft splines and allow the shaft to enter the disc. On no account allow the weight of the gearbox to hang unsupported on the input shaft.

51 Engine – refitting

1 Refitting the engine is a reversal of the removal procedure. A little trouble taken in getting the engine properly slung (so it takes up a suspended angle similar to its final position) will pay off when it comes to locating the engine mountings. Note the following special points when refitting the engine and transmission unit to the car.

(a) *Ensure that all loose leads, cables, hoses, etc, are tucked out of the way. If not, it is easy to trap one and cause additional work after the engine is refitted in the car*
(b) *An assistant will be required to help guide the power unit into position*
(c) *Fit the special washer to the centre stud in the left-hand engine mounting. This washer prevents the engine from placing the mounting under excessive tension. Tighten the mounting nuts to the specified torque settings*
(d) *Use a final drive oil seal protector when inserting the right-hand driveshaft. Remove the protector when the driveshaft is fitted. See Chapter 7 for full details*
(e) *Adjust the clutch cable with reference to Chapter 5*
(f) *Adjust the throttle cable with reference to Chapter 3*
(g) *Tighten the exhaust flange bolts as described in Chapter 3*
(h) *Ensure that the heater hose is located in the strap attached to the bracket on alternator upper retaining bolt. This is necessary to keep the hose clear of the alternator drive pulley (Fig. 1.24).*
(i) *Refill and bleed the cooling system as described in Chapter 2*
(j) *Top up the engine and gearbox oil levels (see Chapters 1 and 6)*

52 Engine – initial start-up after major repair or overhaul

1 Make sure that the battery is fully charged and that all lubricants, coolant and fuel are replenished.
2 If the fuel system has been dismantled, it will require several

SPACER

BRACKET

CLEARANCE

Fig. 1.24 Heater hose arrangement to clear alternator and drivebelt (Sec 51)

revolutions of the engine on the starter motor to pump petrol to the carburettor. It will help to remove the spark plugs, which will enable the engine to turn over much easier, and enable oil to be pumped around the engine before starting it.

3   Refit the spark plugs and as soon as the engine fires and runs, keep it going at a fast tickover only (no faster) and bring it up to normal working temperature.

4   As the engine warms up, there will be odd smells and some smoke from parts getting hot and burning off oil deposits. Look for water or oil leaks which will be obvious if serious. Check also the clamp connection of the exhaust pipe to the manifold as these do not always find their exact gastight position until the warmth and vibration have acted on them, and it is almost certain that they will need tightening further. This should be done, of course, with the engine stationary.

5   When the engine running temperature has been reached, adjust the idling speed as described in Chapter 3.

6   Stop the engine and wait a few minutes to see if any lubricant or coolant leaks.

7   Road test the car to check that the timing is correct and that the engine is giving the necessary smoothness and power. Do not race the engine. If new bearings and or pistons and rings have been fitted, it should be treated as a new engine and run in at reduced revolutions for 500 miles (800 km).

8   Re-tighten the cylinder head bolts, with the engine cold, after the first 1000 miles have been covered. It is best to slacken each bolt $1/4$ turn to break the 'stiction' before tightening. Follow the tightening sequence shown in Fig. 1.23 and check the valve clearances on completion.

9   Also after the first 1000 miles, it is a good idea to change the engine

oil and filter if many new engine parts have been fitted. This is because the small metal particles produced by new components bedding in to each other will be circulating in the oil, or trapped in the filter.

PART B: OHC ENGINE

53 General description

The single overhead camshaft (OHC) engine covered in this Part of Chapter 1 is of 1.6 litre capacity. A 1.9 litre variant is described in Chapter 13.

The engine is a four-cylinder (in-line), four-stroke water-cooled type with a single overhead camshaft.

The engine is mounted transversely and inclined at an angle of 30° from vertical.

Wet cylinder liners are used and the crankshaft runs in five main bearings.

Camshaft drive is by toothed belt. The belt is tensioned by a spring-loaded wheel and also drives the coolant pump. The camshaft operates directly on bucket tappets; valve clearance adjustment is by shims inserted between the tappet and the valve stem. The distributor is driven directly from the tail of the camshaft.

The oil pump is located in the sump and is chain driven from the crankshaft.

Fig. 1.25 Side and end section views of the OHC engine (Sec 53)

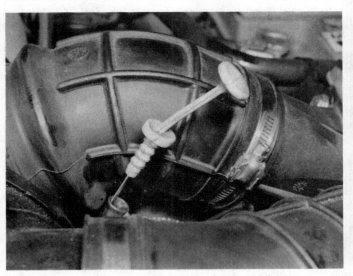

54.1A Engine oil dipstick location – OHC engine (SRi)

54.1B Engine oil drain plug removal – OHC engine

Fig. 1.26 Engine lubrication circuit – OHC engine (Sec 55)

54 Routine maintenance

The main procedures for the OHC engine variants are in general the same as those described for the smaller engine OHV variants in Section 2 of this Chapter. The dipstick and drain plug locations applicable to the OHC engine are shown in the accompanying photos.

55 Lubrication system – description

The oil pump is located in the sump and is chain driven from the crankshaft. A forced feed lubrication system is employed. Oil from the pump passes to the oil filter then to the oil gallery, crankshaft and camshaft. The valve stems are lubricated by oil returning from the camshaft to the sump. The oil pump chain and sprockets are lubricated by oil in the sump. Fig. 1.26 shows the lubrication system circuit round the engine.

56 Oil filter – removal and refitting

1   The oil filter is located on the inlet manifold side of the engine in the lower side face of the crankcase. The filter must be renewed at the specified intervals (see Routine Maintenance at the front of the manual).
2   Removal and renewal of the oil filter is the same as that described for the smaller engine variants, therefore refer to Section 4. For access, remove the engine undertray and renew the filter from underneath (photo).

57 Major operations possible with the engine in the car

The following operations are possible with the engine in the car.

Valve clearances checking and adjustment
Camshaft drivebelt renewal
Camshaft removal and refitting
Cylinder head removal and refitting
Sump and oil pump removal and refitting
Big-end renewal (after removal of sump)
Piston and connecting rod assembles removal and refitting (after removal of sump and cylinder head)
Removal and refitting of engine mountings
Removal and refitting of major ancillary items such as inlet/exhaust manifolds, starter motor, water pump etc
Clutch and flywheel removal and refitting (after removal of transmission)

58 Major operations requiring engine removal

The following operations can only be carried out with the engine removed from the car.

Main bearings renewal
Crankshaft removal and refitting

59 Camshaft (timing) drivebelt – removal and refitting (engine in car)

1   Although the manufacturers do not recommend that the timing belt be renewed at any specific period, it is advisable to renew the timing belt every 36 000 miles, or whenever the engine is dismantled for overhaul and it is known that the drivebelt has covered a high mileage. If the drivebelt comes into contact with oil or grease at any time it must be renewed irrespective of its age.
2   Disconnect the battery earth lead.
3   Remove the alternator drivebelt.
4   Remove the inner shield from the right-hand wheel arch and wedge the radiator bottom hose under the sump.
5   Remove the shield from the camshaft sprocket.
6   Turn the crankshaft until the dowel hole in the pulley is at about 12

o'clock and the hole in the camshaft sprocket is at about 7 o'clock. In this position a 10 mm dowel should pass through each hole and into the timing recess behind. Verify this and then remove the dowels (photo). Note that there are three holes in the crankshaft pulley spaced at 120° intervals but only one hole is 10 mm in diameter, the other two are larger.
7   Remove the clutch bottom shield. Have an assistant jam the starter ring gear while the crankshaft pulley bolt is undone. This bolt is very tight. **Do not** jam the pulley by means of the timing dowel: damage will result. Remove the bolt and washer.
8   Check that the 10 mm dowels will still enter the timing holes: adjust the crankshaft position if necessary by means of the starter ring gear. Remove the crankshaft pulley, retrieving the Woodruff key if it is loose.
9   Remove the plastic covers from the front of the camshaft drivebelt. Note the location of the various bolts.
10 Slacken the two nuts on the front of the drivebelt tensioner and the single nut at the rear. Use a spanner on the 6 mm square end of the tensioner cam spindle to turn the cam to the horizontal position and so compress the tensioner spring. Tighten the cam locknut (photo).
11 Remove the camshaft drivebelt, taking care not to kink it or contaminate it with oil if it is to be re-used.
12 Commence refitting by positioning the belt on the crankshaft sprocket, then refitting the pulley and verifying the correct position of the crankshaft by means of the dowel. (Observe the arrows on the belt showing the direction of rotation, and the timing lines which align with marks on the crankshaft and camshaft sprockets) (photo).
13 Fit the belt to the camshaft sprocket, round the tensioner and to the coolant pump socket.
14 Release the tensioner cam locknut and turn the cam downwards to release the spring. Tighten the locknut and the tensioner front nuts (photo).
15 Remove the timing dowels and turn the crankshaft through two full turns in the normal direction of rotation. Turn the crankshaft further to bring No 1 piston to TDC on the firing stroke.
16 Slacken the tensioner front nuts and the cam locknut, then retighten them.
17 Turn the crankshaft further and make sure that the timing dowels can still be inserted. If not, remove the drivebelt and start again.
18 At this point, the remaining procedure depends on whether a new timing belt has been fitted. If the old timing belt is refitted, remove the crankshaft pulley and proceed from paragraph 23, but ignore the alternator drivebelt removal reference.
19 If a new belt has been fitted, it must be run in and retensioned as follows.
20 Tighten the crankshaft pulley bolt to the specified torque, then refit and tension the alternator drivebelt. Temporarily refit the camshaft sprocket cover.
21 Run the engine up to operating temperature, indicated by the cooling fan operating, then stop it and allow it to cool for at least two hours.
22 Rotate the crankshaft to the TDC position, No 1 cylinder firing, then slacken and retighten the tensioner nuts once more.
23 Remove the alternator drivebelt and the crankshaft pulley. Refit and secure the plastic covers, then refit the pulley and tighten its bolt to the specified torque. Refit and tension the alternator drivebelt.
24 Check the ignition timing and adjust if necessary.

56.2 Engine oil filter location – OHC engine

59.6 Timing dowels in position – shown with engine removed for clarity

59.10 Turning the tension cam spindle

59.12 Line on belt aligns with mark on sprocket

59.14 Drivebelt tensioner front nuts

60.4 Lift out the camshaft lubrication manifold

60 Camshaft – removal and refitting (engine in car)

1   Remove the camshaft drivebelt as described in Section 59.
2   Remove the camshaft cover. For ease of access, remove the distributor cap and HT leads, air cleaner and brake servo vacuum hose.
3   Remove the distributor, as described in Chapter 4.
4   Remove the camshaft lubrication manifold (photo).
5   Lock the camshaft sprocket (eg with a timing dowel – see previous Section), and remove the sprocket retaining bolt. Remove the sprocket and the cover plate behind it. Remove the thrust plate (photos).
6   Progressively slacken the camshaft bearing cap securing nuts. Make identifying marks if necessary, then remove the caps. Be prepared for the camshaft to spring upwards. Remove the camshaft (photo).

7   Commence refitting by making sure that the crankshaft is in the correct (dowelled) position – if not, move it to this position to avoid possible piston/valve contact.
8   Lubricate the camshaft bearing journals with clean engine oil then fit the camshaft into position. On carburettor models fitted with a mechanical fuel pump, push the pump operating rod in as the camshaft is fitted. Lubricate and fit the camshaft bearing caps to their original positions as noted during removal. When fitting the No 1 bearing cap, smear the joint and lower mating faces with sealant. Tighten the cap nuts progressively to the specified torque. Refit and secure the thrust plate (photo).
9   Fit a new oil seal to the sprocket end of the camshaft.
10 Refit the sprocket rear cover plate, locate it correctly with a 10 mm dowel and tighten its fastenings (photo). Fit the camshaft sprocket, dowel it and tighten its securing bolt to the specified torque.

60.5A Camshaft sprocket locked with a 10 mm rod (or drill as in this case)

60.5B Undo the retaining screw ...

60.5C ... and remove the camshaft thrust plate

60.6 Removing the camshaft (cylinder head removed in this instance)

60.8 Tighten the camshaft bearing cap nuts to the specified torque

60.10 Locate the cover plate with a 10 mm rod

11 Check and if necessary adjust the valve clearances as described in Section 62.
12 Refit the lubrication manifold and distributor.
13 Refit the camshaft cover, HT leads and distributor cap, air cleaner, and brake servo vacuum hose.
14 Refit the camshaft drivebelt (Section 59).

61 Cylinder head – removal and refitting (engine in car)

1 Disconnect the battery earth lead.
2 Drain the engine coolant as described in Chapter 2.
3 Remove the timing belt as described in Section 59.
4 Remove the air cleaner unit as described in Chapter 3.
5 Remove the distributor cap and leads then the distributor referring to Chapter 4 for details.
6 Working underneath the vehicle, remove the engine undertray then unbolt and detach the engine torque reaction link from the lower engine mounting (photo).
7 Unscrew and remove the right-hand engine mounting rubber retaining nut (photo).
8 Position a jack under the sump with a protector or suitable piece of wood located on the jack saddle to avoid damaging the sump. Raise the engine about 3 inches (70 to 80 mm) so that the two bolts securing the right-hand mounting bracket to the cylinder head can be removed, then lower the engine to its original position.
9 Disconnect the coolant and vacuum hoses from the cylinder head noting their fitting locations. Mark them to avoid confusion.
10 Referring to the appropriate Sections in Chapter 3 disconnect and remove the following (as applicable).

   (a) Carburettor and inlet manifold
   (b) Fuel injectors, fuel feed tube rail and inlet manifold

11 Unbolt and detach the exhaust downpipe from the exhaust manifold. If required the exhaust manifold can be removed together with, or separate from the cylinder head.
12 Disconnect all electrical leads from the cylinder head and note their connections.

Fig. 1.27 Cylinder head bolt tightening sequence (Sec 61)

13 Disconnect the oil filter spout and the engine oil dipstick guide tube location bolt from the cylinder head (bulkhead side).
14 Unbolt and remove the diagnostic socket/retainer.
15 Remove the camshaft cover from access to the cylinder head bolts. Loosen the head bolts in a progressive sequence in the reverse order of that shown for tightening (Fig. 1.27). Remove the bolts.
16 Before removing the cylinder head the following must be noted. The cylinder head is positioned during assembly by means of two dowels. When removing the cylinder head it is most important not to lift it directly from the cylinder block; it must be twisted slightly. This action prevents the cylinder liners from sticking to the cylinder head face and being lifted with it, thus breaking their bottom seals. Before the cylinder head can be twisted, the dowel at the flywheel end must be tapped down flush with the top of the cylinder block, using a drift. Tap the cylinder head at the flywheel end to twist it free.
17 Fit cylinder liner clamps, or large washers secured with nuts and bolts, to keep the liners in position (photo). *If the liners are disturbed, the engine will have to be removed for new seals to be fitted.*
18 Before refitting the cylinder head, ensure that the joint faces are clean, also the bolt hole threads. If possible, clean the threads with a suitable 11 x 50 mm thread tap. Commence refitting by fitting the dowels to the cylinder block. Keep the flywheel and dowel raised by inserting a 5 mm punch or large nail through the hole in the front of the

61.6 Torque reaction link and lower engine mounting

61.7 Right-hand engine mounting – undo nut arrowed

61.17 Cylinder liners clamped with washers and bolts

61.18A Dowel is retained with a nail or rod on its underside

61.18B Oil filter gauze location in cylinder head oilway

Fig. 1.28 Driving cylinder head dowel down flush with block (Sec 61)

61.20 Fit and progressively tighten the cylinder head bolts to the Stage 1 torque setting. Note spacer location (arrowed)

61.23 Home-made disc used for measuring the Stage 3 cylinder head bolt tightening angle. Disc is fixed and pointer rotates.

62.6 Measuring a valve clearance

block (photo). Remove the liner clamps. Ensure that the new plastic filter is in its location port (photo).

19 Fit the new gasket, dry, with the tab at the flywheel end. Lower the cylinder head into position, making sure that it mates with the dowels. Remove the punch or nail.

20 Fit the cylinder head bolts, their threads clean and lightly oiled. Remember to fit the spacer to the bolt above the coolant pump (bolt number 8) (photo).

21 Progressively tighten the bolts in the order shown in Fig. 1.27 to the Stage 1 specified torque.

22 Raise the engine slightly and refit the two bolts which secure the right-hand mounting bracket to the cylinder head. Tighten these bolts and slacken the one which holds the same bracket to the engine block. Lower the engine and tighten the right-hand mounting nut and the lower mounting rubber nut and bolt.

23 Slacken cylinder head bolt No 1, then immediately retighten it to the Stage 2 specified torque. Tighten further by the angle specified. Repeat for all the bolts, following the tightening sequence (photo).

24 Check the valve clearances and adjust if necessary (Section 62). After the engine is restarted follow the check procedures in Section 94.

25 Refit the remaining components in the reverse order of removal.

26 Refill and bleed the cooling system (Chapter 2).

27 Start the engine and warm it up until the cooling fan cuts in, then switch off and allow it to cool for at least two hours.

28 Retighten the cylinder head bolts as described in paragraphs 22 and 23 then recheck the valve clearances. If Torx type cylinder head bolts are fitted, note the different final tightening angle, and also that no subsequent re-tightening is required (see Chapter 13).

29 If a new camshaft drivebelt has been fitted, retension it as described in Section 39, Paragraph 19 on.

30 Tighten the engine mounting bracket bolt.

62 Valve clearances – checking and adjustment

Valve clearances – checking

1 The valve clearances must be checked with the engine cold; therefore do not run the engine for a minimum period of two hours prior to making the checks.

2 Detach the distributor cap and the spark plug leads.

3 Remove the camshaft cover; trying not to damage the gasket.

4 Prepare to rotate the crankshaft, either by jacking up one front wheel and turning the wheel with 4th or 5th gear engaged, or with a spanner on the crankshaft pulley bolt. The crankshaft will be easier to rotate if the spark plugs are first removed.

5 Have ready a pencil and paper to record the measured clearances.

6 Turn the crankshaft until the cam lobe nearest the pulley end of the engine is pointing vertically upwards. Use feeler gauges to measure the clearance between the base of the cam and the tappet (photo). Record the clearance.

7 Repeat the measurement for the other seven valves, turning the crankshaft as necessary so that the cam lobe in question is always vertically upwards.

8 Calculate the difference between each measured clearance and the desired value (see Specifications). Note that the value for inlet valves is different from that for exhaust. Counting from either end of the engine, the valve sequence is:

Exhaust – Inlet – Inlet – Exhaust – Exhaust – Inlet – Inlet – Exhaust

9 If any clearance measured is outside the specified tolerance adjustment must be carried out as described below.

10 If all clearances are within tolerance, refit the camshaft cover, using a new gasket if necessary. Note the copper washer under the bolt at the timing belt end.

Valve clearances – adjustment

11 Remove the camshaft as described in Section 60.

12 Lift off a tappet and its shim. Be careful that the shim does not fall out of the tappet. Clean the shim and measure its thickness with a micrometer (photos).

13 Refer to the clearance recorded for the valve concerned. If the clearance was larger than specified, a thicker shim must be fitted; if the clearance was too small, a thinner shim must be fitted.

Sample calculation – clearance too large:
    Desired clearance (A) 0.20 mm
    Measured clearance (B) 0.28 mm
    Difference (B–A) = +0.08 mm
    Original shim thickness 2.62 mm
    Required shim thickness 2.62 + 0.08 = 2.70 mm

Sample calculation – clearance too small:
    Desired clearance (A') 0.40 mm
    Measure clearance (B') 0.23 mm
    Difference ('B–A') = 0.17 mm
    Original shim thickness 2.86 mm
    Required shim thickness 2.86 – 0.17 = 2.69 mm

Fig. 1.29 Valve clearance is measured at point J and altered by selective thickness shim (4) (Sec 62)

62.12A Lift off the tappet

62.12B Measuring the thickness of a shim using a micrometer

14 Shims are available in thicknesses from 1.650 to 4.000 mm, in steps of 0.025 mm in the middle of the range and at the ends in steps of 0.075 mm. Clean new shims before measuring or fitting them.
15 Repeat the operations on the other tappets and shims, keeping each tappet identified so that it can be refitted in the same position.
16 When reassembling, oil the shim and fit it on the valve stem, then oil the tappet and lower it smoothly into position. If the tappet is raised at any stage the shim may be dislodged.
17 When all the tappets are in position with their shims, refit the camshaft. Check the valve clearances before refitting the camshaft drivebelt in case a mistake has been made and the camshaft has to be removed again.

63 Engine – removal methods

Refer to Section 7. The engine and transmission removal and refitting methods are the same as for the OHV variants.

64 Engine/transmission – removal

1 The removal procedures for the OHC engines are much the same as those described for the OHV engine variants in Section 8. Therefore follow the procedures given but make allowances for differences between the two engine types with items such as coolant hose and wiring connections.
2 On fuel injection models ignore references made to the carburettor and its associated components and remove or disconnect (as applicable) the following; with reference to Chapter 3 where necessary.

Throttle cable from the throttle body
Air cleaner unit
Air flow sensor unit
Throttle switch leads connection
Supplementary air device and temperature sensor leads
Pressure regulator and fuel supply hoses

65 Engine – separation from transmission

1 Assuming the engine has been removed complete with the transmission unit, it is necessary to separate the two units before dismantling operations on the engine can commence.
2 Unbolt and remove the starter motor as described in Chapter 12.
3 Remove the remaining engine-to-transmission bolts and note the

position of any ancillary items which may be secured by the bolts, such as hose retaining clips.
4 Support the engine and pull the transmission away from it. Do not allow the weight of the transmission to hang on the input shaft during withdrawal of the transmission. Recover any loose location dowels.

66 Engine – dismantling (general)

Refer to Section 10 of this Chapter.

67 Engine ancillary components – removal

Refer to Section 11 of this Chapter.

68 Cylinder head – removal (engine out of car)

1 Slacken the ten cylinder head bolts, working in the reverse sequence of that used when tightening (Fig. 1.27). Remove the bolts and washers.
2 Remove the cylinder head. Refer to Section 61, paragraph 16.
3 Fit liner clamps if it is not proposed to remove the pistons and liners. See Section 61, paragraph 17.

69 Timing covers, timing belt and associated components – removal

1 Unbolt and remove the crankshaft pulley. Jam the flywheel teeth when undoing the pulley bolt to stop the crankshaft rotating.
2 Remove the camshaft drivebelt covers, noting the location of the various sizes of bolt.
3 Unbolt and remove the camshaft cover.
4 Rotate the crankshaft by means of the flywheel until a 10 mm diameter rod can be passed through the hole in the camshaft sprocket and into the timing recess. The pistons are now at mid-stroke so piston/valve contact cannot occur.
5 Release the camshaft drivebelt tensioner by slackening its nuts (two at the front and one behind the front plate) and using the square end of the cam spindle to bring the cam into a horizontal position.

6 Remove the camshaft drivebelt, taking care not to kink it and noting its direction of travel if it is to be re-used.
7 Unbolt and remove the camshaft drivebelt tensioner.
8 Remove the belt side covers and crankshaft sprocket. Recover the Woodruff key.
9 Unbolt and remove the camshaft sprocket. Restrain the sprocket from turning if necessary using the 10 mm diameter rod inserted through the timing hole in the sprocket (see photo 60.5).
10 Unbolt and remove the engine mounting bracket, the camshaft sprocket backplate and the coolant pump.

70 Flywheel – removal

Refer to Section 16 of this Chapter. Note that the flywheel is located by dowels. If the dowels are loose they must be renewed.

71 Sump and oil pump – removal

1 If the engine is in the car, remove the engine undertray and drain the engine oil.
2 Remove the suction drain pipe from the side of the sump.
3 Unbolt and remove the sump. Note the location of the three Allen-headed bolts (photo).
4 Remove the bolts which secure the oil pump, noting the special centering bolt at the rear.
5 Unbolt and remove the oil seal carrier plate.
6 Lower the oil pump into the engine so that its chain can be removed. Withdraw the pump and recover the spacer, the dowel and the chain.
7 Pull the oil pump sprocket off the crankshaft and recover the Woodruff key.

72 Connecting rods, pistons and liners – removal

1 If the engine is in the car remove the sump (Section 71) and the cylinder head (Section 61).
2 Unscrew the connecting rod cap bolts. Before removing the caps check that they are marked in numerical order, also the connecting rods, liners and pistons. Mark them if they are not (1 to 4 from the flywheel end).
3 If the cylinder liners are being removed, then the pistons, rods and liners can be lifted out of the block as individual units, but mark their relative positions.

73 Crankshaft and main bearings – removal

1 Before removing the crankshaft, its endfloat should be checked and noted to assess for wear during examination and renovation procedures later. To check the endfloat proceed as described in Section 85.
2 Remove the bolts from main bearing caps 1, 2, 4 and 5. Also remove the two nuts and the two side bolts from the centre cap. Make alignment marks on the bearing caps and remove them. Keep the bearing shells with their caps if they are to be re-used. Recover the thrust washer segments from either side of No 2 bearing cap.
3 Remove the oil seal from the flywheel end of the crankshaft.
4 Lift the crankshaft out of the crankcase. Recover the upper half main bearing shells and the other two thrust washer segments.
5 If the cylinder liners have been left clamped in position in the cylinder block, their protrusions above the cylinder block face must be checked, as described in Section 81 before reassembling the engine.

74 Cylinder head – dismantling

1 If not already done, remove the distributor, the fuel pump and the spark plugs. Also remove the manifolds and their gaskets.
2 Unbolt and remove the coolant outlet housing. Do not overlook the

recessed securing screw in the end (photo). Remove the thermostat elbow from the housing and withdraw the thermostat.
3 Lift out the camshaft lubrication manifold (photo 60.4).
4 Unbolt and remove the camshaft thrust fork plate (photos 60.5B and 60.5C).
5 Progressively slacken the camshaft bearing cap nuts. Remove the caps – be prepared for the camshaft to spring upwards. Remove the oil seal from the sprocket end, then remove the camshaft (photo 60.6).
6 Remove the tappets and shims, identifying their locations if they are to be re-used.
7 Extract the oil filter gauze from the oilway (photo 61.18B).
8 Use a universal type valve spring compressor to compress a valve spring. Remove the collets, carefully release the compressor and extract the valve and spring. Repeat for the other seven valves.
9 Using long-nosed pliers, carefully remove the valve stem oil seals from their locations in the head. Dismantling of the cylinder head is now complete.

75 Engine components – examination and renovation (general)

The inspection requirement procedures concerning the following engine components are as described for the equivalent items in Part A

71.3 Allen-head bolt locations on sump

74.2 Undoing the recessed securing screw in the coolant outlet housing

of this Chapter, but refer to the Part B Specifications for the tolerance requirements applicable to the OHC engine.

   (a) *General guidance on examination for wear – Section 23*
   (b) *Crankshaft, main and big-end bearings – Section 24*
   (c) *Pistons and rings – Section 26*
   (d) *Connecting rods – Section 27*
   (e) *Gudgeon pins – Sections 21 and 39*
   (f) *Flywheel – Section 34*

76 Camshaft and tappets – examination and renovation

1 Inspect the camshaft lobes and bearing journals for wear and damage; if evident, renewal is probably necessary. Also inspect the bearing surfaces in the cylinder head and bearing caps.
2 Clean the camshaft lubrication manifold with solvent and then blow through it with compressed air. All the holes must be clear (photo).
3 Inspect the tappets for wear and scuffing; renew them as necessary. New tappets **must** be fitted if the camshaft is renewed; it is also advisable to renew the valve springs.
4 Renew the camshaft drivebelt as a matter of course unless it is in perfect condition and is known to have covered only a nominal mileage. Renew the sprockets if they are damaged.

77 Cylinder head, valves and piston crowns – decarbonising, examination and renovation

1 With the cylinder head and associated components dismantled they can be cleaned and examined as described in Sections 30 and 31 of this Chapter, but ignore the references to the rocker arms.
2 Note that, with the OHC engine, the manufacturers state that only

0.2 mm machining of the cylinder head surface is permitted. A badly warped head must therefore be renewed.
3 Factory exchange cylinder heads may have had 0.2 mm machined off the mating face. These heads are identified by the letter 'R' stamped on a boss at the distributor end of the head. A gasket 0.2 mm thicker than normal must be used with such a head; the thicker gasket is identified by a cut-out in the tab at the clutch end.

78 Timing belt, tensioner and sprockets – examination and renovation

1 Renew the drivebelt as a matter of course unless it is in perfect condition and is known to have covered only a nominal mileage.
2 Inspect the sprockets for any signs of damage. Renew them if necessary.
3 The drivebelt tensioner must be examined for roughness of the wheel bearing and wear or distortion of the spring. Renew as necessary. The wheel, bearing and backplate must be renewed as an assembly (photo).

79 Oil pump, drive chain and sprockets – examination and renovation

1 Remove the six bolts which hold the two halves of the oil pump together. Separate the halves, being prepared for the release of the relief valve spring and plunger (photo).
2 Inspect the rotors and their housing for wear and damage. No wear limits are published for this pump; any visible wear on the moving parts suggests that renewal is necessary. With the exception of the relief valve spring and plunger, individual components are not available (photos).
3 Lubricate the pump components well before reassembly. Bolt the two halves together, being careful not to trap the spring.

76.2 The pinholes in the camshaft lubrication manifold must be clear

78.3 Camshaft drivebelt tensioner components

79.1 Separating the two halves of the oil pump

79.2A Inspect the oil pump gears for excessive wear

79.2B Oil pump relief valve spring and plunger

4   If the pump is to be renewed it is wise to renew the chain and the crankshaft sprocket also.

5   Examine the teeth of both sprockets for wear. Each tooth on a sprocket is an inverted V-shape and wear is apparent when one side of the tooth becomes more concave in shape than the other. When badly worn, the teeth become hoop-shaped and the sprockets must be renewed.

6   If the sprockets need to be renewed then the chain will have worn also and should be renewed as well. If the sprockets are satisfactory, examine the chain and look for play between the links. When the chain is held out horizontally, it should not bend appreciably. Remember, a chain is only as strong as its weakest link, and being a relatively cheap item, it is worthwhile fitting a replacement anyway.

80 Cylinder liners – examination and renovation

1   The liner bores may be examined for wear either in or out of the engine block; the cylinder head must, of course, be removed in each case.

2   First of all examine the top of the cylinder about a quarter of an inch below the top of the liner and with a finger feel if there is any ridge running round the circumference of the bore. In a worn cylinder bore a ridge will develop at the point where the top ring on the piston comes to the uppermost limit of its stroke. An excessive ridge indicates that the bore below the ridge is worn. If there is no ridge, it is reasonable to assume that the cylinder is not badly worn. Measurement of the diameter of the cylinder bore both in line with the piston gudgeon pin and at right angles to it, at the top and bottom of the cylinder, is another check to be made. A cylinder is expected to wear at the sides where the thrust of the piston presses against it. In time this causes the cylinder to assume an oval shape. Furthermore, the top of the cylinder is likely to wear more than the bottom of the cylinder. It will be necessary to use a proper bore measuring instrument in order to measure the differences in bore diameter across the cylinder, and variations between the top and bottom ends of the cylinder. As a general guide it may be assumed that any variation more than 0.25 mm (0.010 in) indicates that the liners should be renewed. Provided all variations are less than 0.25 mm (0.010 in) it is probable that the fitting of new piston rings will cure the problem of piston-to-cylinder bore clearances. Once again it is difficult to give a firm ruling on this as so much depends on the amount of time, effort and money which the individual owner is prepared, or wishes to spend, on the task. Certainly if the cylinder bores are obviously deeply grooved or scored, the liners must be renewed, regardless of any measurement differences in the cylinder diameter.

3   If new liners are to be fitted, new pistons will be required also, as they are supplied as matched sets.

4   If the existing liners are to be refitted, it is advisable to check their protrusions when fitted at this stage rather than during engine reassembly. This is because the protrusion heights are not adjustable and if the old liners cannot meet the specified protrusion they may well have to be scrapped and new ones fitted. Consult your Peugeot dealer if in doubt. Refer to Section 81 for details on checking the protrusions of each liner.

81 Cylinder liner protrusion – checking

1   The protrusion of the cylinder liners when assembled to the block must be within prescribed limits so that a gastight seal can be achieved when the head is bolted on. One liner protruding too much or not enough will, despite the cylinder head gasket, make it impossible to secure a gas or watertight joint.

2   An O-ring seal is fitted between each liner mating flange and the cylinder block. These seals compress when the cylinder head is tightened down to effect a watertight seal (Fig. 1.30).

3   Although the actual liner protrusion check method is the same, the procedure differs if the engine is assembled or dismantled.

4   If the cylinder head has been removed with the engine *in situ* the liners must be held under compression with the use of liner clamps. Remove the dowels from the cylinder block top face to allow the clamps to be fitted, if necessary.

5   If the engine is dismantled, check that the seal mating surfaces of the liners and the cylinder block are clean, then insert each liner into its respective position in the cylinder block without its seal.

6   Check each liner protrusion in turn measuring the distance between the top face of the liner and the top face of the cylinder block. Use a dial test indicator if available but, failing this, use a metal rule and feeler gauges to assess the protrusion (photo).

7   As the protrusion of each liner in turn is checked, ensure that it is squarely located in the cylinder block. The protrusion of each liner should be within the limits specified (see Specifications at the start of this Chapter). New liners can be rotated half a turn (180°), and/or fitted in a different position in the block, to bring protrusion within tolerance. Old liners which will not produce the desired results are best scrapped. Consult a Peugeot dealer for advice.

8   Finally check the difference in height between adjacent liners. Use the dial test indicators or rule and feeler gauges to measure the difference in height, if any, between adjacent liners at a point on each lying along the centre axis parallel with the crankshaft on the top face. Each difference in level must not exceed the maximum specified.

9   If the checks reveal a discrepancy on an installed engine it will be necessary to renew the liner O-rings or even one or more liners.

10 Once the checks have shown the liners to be within limits of protrusion and squareness reassembling can continue or, if appropriate, temporary retainer clamps/straps should be fitted to hold them

Fig. 1.30 Cylinder line O-ring seal location (Sec 81)

81.6 Measuring a cylinder liner projection

H.20120

Fig. 1.31 Mark top of cylinders and block numerically from the flywheel end to ensure correct relocation (Sec 81)

in position. *Don't turn the crankshaft if the liners are not restrained from movement.* Cover the exposed engine internal parts if there is likely to be a delay before completing reassembly.

11 With new liners, once correctly located, mark their sequence in the block (see Fig. 1.31) and withdraw them so that their piston/rods can be fitted.

82 Engine – reassembly (general)

Refer to Section 36 of this Chapter.

83 Engine – preparation for reassembly

Refer to Section 37 of this Chapter.

84 Pistons and liners – reassembly and refitting

1 Fit the piston rings to the pistons. Always fit the rings from the piston crown end. Use three old feeler blades equally spaced behind the ring so that it will slide down to the lower grooves without dropping into the higher ones (see photo 40.2).
2 Make sure that the rings are correctly located and the right way up. If genuine Peugeot piston rings are being used, refer to Fig. 1.32. If special proprietary rings are being fitted, follow the manufacturer's instructions.
3 Twist the piston rings so that the gap in the oil control ring expander aligns with the gudgeon pin and the gaps in the rails are offset from the gudgeon pin by between 20.0 and 50.0 mm (0.79 and 1.97 in). The gaps in the top two compression rings should be equally spaced (120°) from the gap in the oil control expander around the piston.
4 If new piston/liner assemblies have been supplied, the identification marks on the piston and liner should be:

Piston	Liner
A	One file mark on rim
B	Two file marks on rim
C	Three file marks on rim

5 All four pistons should be of the same grading.
6 Fit the liners to the piston/connecting rod assemblies so that when installed in the cylinder block, the rim mark on the liner will be towards the oil gallery side and the arrow on the piston crown facing towards the timing cover end of the engine (photo). Piston-to-rod relationship is not important.
7 Oil the piston rings liberally and fit a compressor to the piston and

compress the rings fully. When fitted, the top edge of the ring compressor should be 4 to 5 mm below the crown of the piston.
8 Lubricate the bore of the liner and insert the piston. As this is done, the compressor will be pushed off (photo).
9 Push the piston down so that the piston crown is level with or just below the top edge of the liner.
10 With the pistons and liners reassembled, fit a new O-ring seal over the bottom end of each liner in turn, ensuring that the seals are not twisted as they are fitted (photo).
11 Remove the big-end caps, wipe the recesses in rod and cap absolutely clean and fit the bearing shells. If the original shells are being used again, make sure that they are being returned to their original locations.
12 Push the liner/rod assemblies into the block, without disturbing the seals and aligning the location marks (photo).
13 Fit clamps to hold the liners in the block.

85 Crankshaft and main bearings – refitting

1 Position the cylinder block for access to the bottom end then fit the upper half main bearing shells, with grooved shells to the No 2 and No 4 main bearing.
2 Locate the 2.30 mm thick thrust washers to the No 2 bearing (from flywheel end), with its grooved face out (toward the crankshaft). Retain the washers each side of the bearing by smearing them with grease.
3 Oil the bearing shells and lower the crankshaft into position, taking care not to dislodge the thrust washer segments (photo). Inject some oil into the crankshaft oilways.
4 Check the crankshaft endfloat by pushing it in one direction then the other along its length. A dial gauge or feeler gauges should be used to measure the endfloat. If the endfloat measured is not within the specified limits change the thrust washer segments and fit alternatives of suitable thickness, but the four thrust washers used must all be of the same thickness. Thrust washers are available in a choice of four thicknesses.
5 Fit new side seals to No 1 main bearing cap. Carefully fit the cap with its bearing shell; lubricate the shell, the sides of the cap and the

Fig. 1.32 Positioning the piston ring gaps on assembly (Sec 84)

1   Scraper ring
    (b) Expander gap on axis of gudgeon pin hole
    (c) Scraper rings gaps on alternate sides of gudgeon pin axis within 20 to 50 mm (0.79 to 1.96 in)
2   Tapered face ring gap 120° from gudgeon pin axis
3   Curved face ring gap 120° from gudgeon pin axis in opposite direction

84.6 Arrow mark on piston crown must point towards the timing cover end of engine. Letter and number indicate the liner and gudgeon pin grade

84.8 Insert the piston into its liner

84.10 Fit the liner O-ring seal

84.12 Installing piston/liner assembly

85.3 Fitting the crankshaft

85.5A Fitting a side seal to No 1 main bearing cap

85.5B Protect the side seals with feeler blades

85.7 Tightening the No 3 main bearing side bolt

85.10 Crankshaft oil seal – flywheel end

locating surfaces in the block. There is a risk of displacing or distorting the side seals as the cap is fitted, so protect them with a couple of feeler blades or thin strips of tin which can be withdrawn rearwards after fitting the cap (photos).

6 Fit the shells to the other main bearing caps, lubricate them and fit the caps. Fit the thrust washer segments (grooved side outwards) to the No 2 cap. Observe the mating marks made when dismantling; the lug on each bearing cap points towards the timing sprockets. Ensure that the thrust washer segment on each side of the number two main bearing cap is of equal thickness to the corresponding upper segment washer selected when setting the crankshaft endfloat.

7 Fit the main bearing cap nuts and bolts and tighten them to the specified torque. Tighten the side bolts on No 3 cap last (photo).

8 Check the protrusion of No 1 cap side seals above the sump mating face; it should be 2 mm. Trim off any excess.

9 Recheck the crankshaft endfloat (paragraph 4), and ensure that it rotates freely.

10 Fit a new oil seal, lips inwards and lubricated, to the flywheel end of the crankshaft. Drive it into place with a piece of tube (photo).

11 If not already fitted, fit new O-ring seals to the cylinder liners, then fit the pistons and liners with reference to paragraphs 10 to 13 inclusive in Section 84.

12 Push each piston down its liner and simultaneously engage the connecting rod with the crankshaft journal. Fit the mating big-end cap with the bearing and shells well lubricated. Ensure that the cap/rod match marks are in alignment to make sure that the shell tongues are correctly located on the same side.

13 Fit and tighten the big-end nuts to the specified torque, then check that the crankshaft can still be rotated. Extra effort will be required to turn the crankshaft.

86.1A Fitting the oil pump drive sprocket

86.1B Locate the oil pump drive chain

86.2A Fitting the oil pump. Engage the chain first

86.2B Locate the oil pump spacer

86.3 Oil pump special bolt location

86 Oil pump and sump – refitting

1   Fit the Woodruff key and oil pump drive sprocket to the crankshaft nose. Fit the chain over the sprocket (photos).
2   Make sure that the locating dowel is in position, then engage the oil pump sprocket in the chain and offer the pump to the block. Engage the pump on the dowel, then lift it up far enough to slide the L-shaped spacer in underneath it (photos).
3   Fit the oil pump securing bolts, remembering that the special centering bolt is nearest the flywheel, and tighten them to the specified torque. Generously lubricate the pump and the chain (photo).
4   Refit the pulley oil seal carrier plate, using silicone jointing compound on the block mating faces. Fit a new oil seal, lubricated lips inwards, and drive it home with a piece of tube.
5   Fit the sump, using a new gasket, and tighten its securing bolts progressively to the specified torque. Remember the correct location of the three Allen-headed bolts.
6   Refit the suction drain pipe, using a new O-ring. Do not overtighten the securing nuts, refer to the Specifications for the correct torque setting.

87 Flywheel and clutch – refitting

1   Fit the flywheel to the crankshaft flange and secure with new bolts, using thread locking compound. Tighten the bolts progressively to the specified torque.
2   Fit the clutch friction plate and pressure plate, as described in Chapter 5.

88 Valves – refitting

1   Commence reassembly by fitting new valve stem oil seals, then fit the valves, springs and collets. Oil the valve stems liberally; a smear of grease will hold the collets in position while the spring is compressed. The valve springs can be fitted either way up.
2   Lubricate the tappet bores. Secure each shim to its valve stem with a dab of grease and carefully fit the tappets. If new components have been fitted so that the valve clearances are unknown, fit the thinnest possible shims to all valves.

89 Cylinder head and camshaft – refitting

1   Refer to Section 61 and proceed as described in paragraphs 18 to 21 inclusive, then paragraph 23.
2   Refer to Section 60 and proceed as described in paragraphs 8 to 11 inclusive to fit the camshaft.
3   Note that the cylinder head bolts will need to be retightened again after the engine is restarted and warmed up (see Section 94 for details). This does not apply to Torx head bolts.

90 Timing covers, timing belt and associated components – refitting

1   Fit the camshaft sprocket backplate, using a 10 mm rod through the timing hole to locate it precisely before tightening its securing bolts.
2   Fit the camshaft sprocket, washer and bolt. Use the 10 mm rod to lock the sprocket in the correct position and tighten the bolt to the specified torque. Remove the rod.

3   Fit and secure the coolant pump, using a new gasket. Tighten the bolts to the specified torque (Chapter 2).

4   Fit the covers around the coolant pump, noting the locations of the various special bolts (Fig. 1.33). Smear the large bolt threads with sealant.

5   Fit the Woodruff key and the crankshaft sprocket.

6   Fit the camshaft drivebelt tensioner, but leave the nuts slack. Compress the spring by locking the cam in the horizontal position.

7   Temporarily fit the crankshaft pulley, its washer and bolt; lightly tighten the bolt. Carefully turn the crankshaft until a 10 mm rod will pass through the timing hole in the pulley and into the timing recess. If piston/valve contact occurs, back off and try again with the camshaft in a slightly different position. **Do not** try to force the crankshaft if a piston contacts a valve.

8   Use the 10 mm rod to position the camshaft sprocket, then remove the crankshaft pulley and fit the camshaft drivebelt. Be careful not to kink the belt as it is fitted, and observe the arrows showing the correct direction of rotation. The two white strips on the belt should align with the timing marks on the sprockets.

9   Withdraw the timing rod. Tension the belt by turning the tensioner cam so that it points downwards; secure it with its locknut. Tighten the two nuts at the front of the tensioner.

10 Turn the crankshaft through two full turns in the normal direction of rotation; rotate it further to bring Nos 1 and 4 pistons to TDC with the valves on No 1 cylinder open.

11 Slacken the two nuts and the cam locknut on the drivebelt tensioner, then retighten them.

12 Temporarily refit the crankshaft pulley, rotate the crankshaft and check that the timing rods can be inserted simultaneously in the crankshaft pulley and camshaft sprocket holes. If not, remove the belt and try again. Remove the pulley.

13 Fit the engine mounting bracket and tighten its bolts.

14 Refit the drivebelt covers, but note that they will have to be removed later to retension the drivebelt if a new one has been fitted (Fig. 1.34).

15 Fit the crankshaft pulley, washer and bolt, making sure that the Woodruff key is still in position. Jam the starter ring gear teeth and tighten the bolt to the specified torque.

H.251/2

Fig. 1.33 Drivebelt cover special bolts (Sec 90)

Fig. 1.34 Fit the timing covers in the numerical sequence shown (Sec 90)

16 If not already fitted, locate the camshaft oil lubrication manifold, then refit the camshaft cover, noting the copper washer at the sprocket end bolt. Use a new gasket.

91 Engine ancillary components – refitting

1 Refit the ancillary components listed below; it may be preferable to leave delicate items such as the alternator and distributor until after the engine is refitted:

    (a) Oil filler/breather pipe
    (b) Oil pressure switch
    (c) Coolant housing and pipe
    (d) Spark plugs, distributor and HT leads (refer to Chapter 4)
    (e) Inlet and exhaust manifolds (Chapter 3)
    (f) Alternator and drivebelt (Chapter 12)
    (g) Oil filter (Section 56)

92 Engine – reconnection to gearbox

1 Check that the clutch release components are correctly fitted in the gearbox and that the pressure plate and friction disc are fitted to the flywheel.
2 Smear a little anti-seize compound on the nose and splines of the transmission input shaft, then offer the transmission to the engine. Do not allow the weight of the transmission to hang on the input shaft. If the input shaft does not wish to pass the clutch, it is possible that the clutch disc is not centred.
3 Engage the engine-to-transmission dowels and loosely fit the bolts. Also fit the starter motor, which is secured by three Allen bolts and a bracket. Tighten the bolts to the specified torque.

93 Engine – refitting

1 Refitting is a reversal of the removal procedures given in Section 64, but the following special points should be noted.

(a) Fit the special washer to the centre stud in the left-hand engine mounting stud. This prevents the mounting from being under excessive tension. Tighten the nut to the specified torque.
(b) Use a final drive oil seal protector when inserting the right-hand driveshaft. Remove the protector when the driveshaft is fitted (see Chapter 7 for full details).
(c) Adjust the clutch cable, with reference to Chapter 5, and the throttle cable, with reference to Chapter 3.
(d) Tighten the exhaust flange bolts, as described in Chapter 3.
(e) Refill and bleed the cooling system as described in Chapter 2.
(f) When refitting the heater hose, arrange it as shown in Fig. 1.35 and secure it with the retaining straps. When located the hose must be 50 mm clear of the alternator (at the front).
(g) Refer to Chapter 3 when reconnecting the fuel injection components on the SRi model.
(h) Top up the engine and gearbox oil levels with the correct grade and quantity of oils.

94 Engine – initial start-up after major repair or overhaul

1 Refer to Section 52 of this Chapter, but when retightening the cylinder head bolts (not Torx type bolts) the procedure is as follows.
2 Allow the engine to cool for at least two hours. Loosen the bolt which secures the engine right-hand mounting bracket to the block then retighten the cylinder head bolts, as described in Section 61, paragraph 23.
3 Tighten the mounting bracket bolt on completion. No subsequent retightening is necessary.
4 Recheck the valve clearances, then refit the cam cover.
5 If a new camshaft drivebelt was fitted, retension it as described in Section 59, paragraphs 22 and 23.

Fig. 1.35 Heater hose routing showing securing clip locations (arrowed) and clearance requirement from alternator (Sec 93)

PART C: ALL ENGINES

95 Fault diagnosis – engine

Symptom	Reason(s)
Engine will not turn over when starter switch is operated	Flat battery Bad battery connections Bad connections at solenoid switch and/or starter motor Starter motor jammed Defective solenoid Starter motor defective
Engine turns over normally but fails to fire and run	No sparks at plugs No fuel reaching engine Too much fuel reaching engine (flooding)
Engine starts but runs unevenly and misfires	Ignition and/or fuel system faults Incorrect valve clearance Burnt out valves Blown cylinder head gasket, dropped liners (if applicable) Worn out piston rings Worn cylinder bores
Lack of power	Ignition and/or fuel system faults Incorrect valve clearances Burnt out valves Blown cylinder head gasket Worn out piston rings Worn cylinder bores
Excessive oil consumption	Oil leaks from crankshaft oil seal, timing cover gasket and oil seal, rocker cover gasket, crankcase or gearbox joint Worn piston rings or cylinder bores resulting in oil being burnt by engine (smoky exhaust is an indication) Worn valve guides and/or defective valve stem Worn valve seals
Excessive mechanical noise from engine	Wrong valve clearances Worn crankshaft bearings Worn cylinders (piston slap) Slack or worn timing chain and sprockets (OHV engine) Worn timing belt and/or sprockets (OHC engine) Worn oil pump drive chain or sprockets (OHC engine)

Chapter 2 Cooling system

For modifications, and information applicable to later models, see Supplement at end of manual

Contents

Specifications

General

Type	Pressurised system with front-mounted radiator, electric cooling fan, water pump and thermostat
System coolant capacity:	
1.1 and 1.3 litre (OHV) engines	6.6 litre (11.6 pints)
1.6 litre models except fuel injection	7.5 litre (13.2 pints)
1.6 litre fuel injection models	8.0 litre (14.1 pints)
Pressure cap setting	1.0 bar (14.5 lbf/in²)
Thermostat opening temperature:	
1.1 and 1.3 litre (OHV engines)	89°C (192°F)
1.6 litre (OHC) engine	82°C (180°F)
Antifreeze type/specification	Ethylene glycol based antifreeze coolant mixture (Duckhams Universal Antifreeze and Summer Coolant)
Antifreeze mixture:	
Protection to – 15°C (5°F)	27% antifreeze
Protection to – 35°C (–31°F)	50% antifreeze

Torque wrench settings

	Nm	lbf ft
OHV engines		
Coolant pump	12	9
Pump pulley bolts	15	11
Coolant pump drain plug	18	13
Coolant drain plug on crankcase	18	13
OHC engines		
Coolant pump	15	11
Coolant outlet housing (to cylinder head)	15	11

1 General description

The cooling system is of the pressurised type. The system includes a front-mounted cross-flow radiator, thermoswitch controlled electric cooling fan, water pump and thermostat. The car interior heater matrix is supplied with a continuous supply of coolant since there is no water valve and the hot air supply is controlled by an air flap.

On OHV engine models, the water pump is driven in tandem with the alternator drivebelt. On OHC models the water pump is driven by the engine camshaft (timing) drivebelt.

The cooling system functions in the following way. After a cold start the thermostat valve is shut and coolant circulation is restricted to the engine and heater matrix. When the coolant reaches the normal engine operating temperature the thermostat starts to open and coolant circulation also flows through the radiator. The engine temperature is then controlled by the thermostat and the electric cooling fan located on the front of the radiator.

Fig. 2.1 Engine cooling system and heater system coolant circuits – OHV engine (Sec 1)

Fig. 2.2 Engine cooling system and heater system coolant circuits – OHC engine (Sec 1)

2 Routine maintenance

Carry out the following procedures at the intervals given in Routine Maintenance at the beginning of the manual.

1 With the engine cold, check the level of coolant in the radiator or the expansion tank (where applicable). Where an expansion tank is *not* fitted, the coolant level should be six inches below the top of the radiator filler neck. Where an expansion tank *is* fitted, a level guide is fitted inside the filler neck. Do not remove the filler cap when the engine is hot as the system will be pressurized and steam or coolant will be suddenly released under pressure and scalding could result. If it is essential to remove the cap with the engine hot, cover the cap with a cloth and slowly release the cap to its first position. Leave at this position until the pressure in the system is fully released before removing the cap, again covered with a cloth to guard against scalding (photo).

2 If necessary top up the cooling system level as required then refit the cap. Note that cold coolant must not be added to a hot engine (photo).

3 Check the cooling system hoses, thermostat housing and water pump for leakage and rectify as necessary.

4 Drain the coolant, flush the cooling system and fill with fresh coolant, as described in Section 4.

5 On OHV engine models, check the tension and condition of the alternator/coolant pump drivebelt (see Chapter 12).

3 Coolant mixture – general

1 Plain water should never be used in the cooling system. Apart from giving protection against freezing, an antifreeze mixture protects the engine internal surfaces and components against corrosion. This is very important in an engine with alloy components.

2 Always use a top quality glycol-based antifreeze which is recommended for alloy engines.

3 Ideally a 50% mixture of antifreeze and soft or demineralised water should be used to maintain maximum protection against freezing and corrosion. On no account use less than 25% antifreeze.

4 Renew the coolant at the specified intervals as the inhibitors contained in the antifreeze gradually lose their effectiveness.

5 Even when operating in climates where antifreeze is not required never use plain water, but add a corrosion inhibitor to it.

4 Cooling system – draining, flushing and refilling

1 If the engine is cold, remove the filler cap from the radiator/ expansion tank by turning the cap anti-clockwise. If the engine is hot, then turn the filler cap very slightly until pressure in the system has had time to be released. Use a rag over the cap to protect your hand from escaping steam. If, with the engine very hot, the cap is released suddenly, the drop in pressure can result in the water boiling. With the

2.1 Coolant expansion tank (where fitted)

pressure released the cap can be removed. Remove the engine undershield.

2 If antifreeze is used in the cooling system, drain into a bowl having the necessary capacity (see Specifications). If the system coolant is under two years old, it can be re-used, otherwise it must be discarded.

3 The drain plug location is dependent on model as follows:

   (a) OHV engines: *Radiator and coolant (water) pump base (photo)*
   (b) OHC engines: *Radiator, cylinder block and coolant manifold (photo)*

When draining the radiator on both engine types, undo the small diameter expansion hose from the lower connection on the rear face of the radiator on the left-hand side.

4 When the coolant has finished draining, probe the drain points with a piece of wire to dislodge any sediment or rust particles which may cause blockage.

5 Remember that, without dismantling, it is impossible to drain the system dry as some coolant will be retained in the heater matrix. If there is no antifreeze in the system, frost damage is still possible in winter even though the system is 'drained'.

6 If you intend to re-use the coolant, cover it to prevent dust or other contaminants from affecting it.

7 To flush the cooling system, cover the engine and all electrical circuits with a sheet of plastic to stop water getting on them, as you are bound to cause some splashing. Insert a hose in the radiator filler neck and flush the system with fresh water for ten to fifteen minutes.

2.2 Filler cap removal from expansion tank (take care if coolant is hot – see text)

4.3A Coolant drain plug in the water pump – OHV engine

4.3B Coolant drain plug in the radiator – OHC engine

Fig. 2.3 Cooling system bleed screw locations (arrowed) – OHV engine (Sec 4)

8 In extreme cases of sediment formation it may be necessary to use a proprietary chemical cleaner and/or to reverse flush the system. In the latter case disconnect the bottom hose from the radiator and remove the thermostat (Section 7). Direct the hose into the thermostat housing so that water is forced through the engine coolant passages and out of the bottom hose. To reverse flush the radiator it is advisable to remove it as described in Section 5 and invert it whilst flushing.

9 Flushing should be continued until the water runs clear and you are satisfied that the system is clean; then close the drain tap and refit any components which were removed.

10 Whenever the engine coolant level is to be topped up or the coolant renewed, it is essential that the engine is cold.

11 Reconnect the radiator hoses and refit the drain plugs.

12 Loosen the cooling system bleed screws (Fig. 2.3), then refill the cooling system through the radiator filler neck (photos). Ensure that the correct ratio of antifreeze is used (Section 3).

13 As the system is filled, coolant will flow from the bleed screws. When the flow of coolant from each screw is continuous, retighten the bleed screw.

14 Fill the system so that the coolant level reaches the top of the radiator filler neck, then refit the radiator cap. Wipe any spilt coolant from the paintwork.

15 On models with an expansion tank, refit the radiator filler cap then

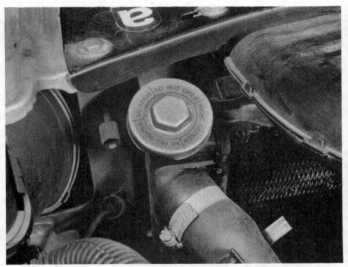

4.12A Radiator filler cap on SRi model fitted with an expansion tank. The cap should not be removed unless refilling or flushing the system

4.12B Cooling system bleeder on the inlet manifold (arrowed) – OHV engine

4.12C Cooling system bleed screw on the thermostat housing (arrowed) – OHC engine

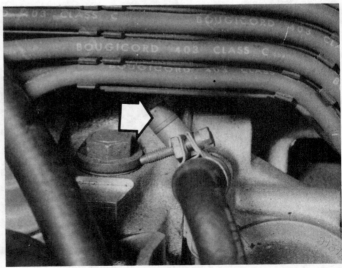

4.12D Cooling system bleed screw in heater hose at bulkhead – OHC engine

continue refilling the expansion tank to top up the level, then refit its cap.

16 Start the engine and run it up to its normal operating temperature and the cooling fan cuts in. Run the engine for a further five minutes and turn it off. Check for any signs of leaks and allow the engine to cool for about two hours, then recheck the coolant level in the radiator or expansion tank (as applicable). Top up if necessary.

17 The cooling system should be drained and flushed, then new antifreeze solution added at regular intervals (see Routine Maintenance).

5 Radiator – removal, inspection, cleaning and refitting

1 Drain the cooling system as described in Section 4.
2 Loosen the clips securing the top and bottom hoses to the radiator and carefully ease the hoses off the connecting tubes.
3 Disconnect the electrical leads to the fan thermal switch and the coolant level warning switch (photos).
4 Lift the radiator upwards to disengage its bottom location pegs from their holes in the body frame, on the left and right-hand sides. Then, when clear, pivot the radiator at the bottom towards the engine, pull it downwards and disengage the radiator from its upper fixings and lift it clear (photo).
5 Radiator repairs are best left to a specialist as without the relevant equipment it is quite easy to make matters worse, although minor repairs can be tackled with a proprietary compound. The radiator matrix, header and bottom tanks should be thoroughly examined for signs of damage, deterioration and leakage; very often a rusty sediment will have been deposited where a leak has occurred.
6 After inspection, the radiator should be flushed as described in Section 4 and the matrix and exterior cleaned of dirt and dead flies with a strong jet of water.

7 Refitting the radiator is a reversal of the removal procedure but the following additional points should be noted:

(a) *Examine and renew any clips, hoses and rubber mounting washers which have deteriorated*
(b) *Refill the cooling system as described in Section 4*

6 Cooling fan – removal and refitting

1 Disconnect the battery earth lead.
2 Remove the radiator as described in the previous Section.
3 Unbolt and remove the top front cross panel.
4 Detach the air intake duct from the locating wire at the front.
5 Disconnect the wiring from the cooling fan at the in-line connectors.
6 Lift out the cooling fan and the location frame (photo).
7 Undo the three retaining nuts to remove the fan unit from the frame (photo).
8 Refitting is a reversal of the removal procedure. If renewing the fan unit, note that the motor output is dependent on the engine type.
9 Check for satisfactory operation on completion by running the engine at a fast idle speed until the engine is warmed up when the fan should cut in, then out when the engine has cooled sufficiently.

7 Thermostat – removal, testing and refitting

1 Drain the cooling system as described in Section 4.
2 Disconnect the radiator top hose from the thermostat housing (photo). On SRi models first remove the air inlet duct from the air cleaner.

5.3A Coolant temperature switch location in radiator – OHV engine

5.3B Coolant level warning switch removal from radiator – OHV engine

5.4 Radiator removal from the car – OHV engine

6.6 Cooling fan and location frame removal

6.7 Cooling fan retaining nuts removal

7.2 Thermostat housing and radiator top hose (arrowed) – OHV engine

7.3 Thermostat housing cover removal – OHC engine

7.8 Thermostat, showing temperature rating (arrowed) – OHC engine

3   Unscrew and remove the two thermostat housing cover bolts and remove the cover. This may need a little persuasion with a wooden or plastic-faced hammer (photo).
4   Remove the thermostat. If it is stuck, do not lever it out under its bridge piece, but cut around its edge with a sharp knife.
5   Remove the rubber ring(s) (if applicable) and clean the mating faces of the housing and cover.

6   If the thermostat is suspected of being faulty, suspend it in a container of water which is being heated. Using a thermometer, check that the thermostat starts to open at the specified temperature.
7   Remove the thermostat from the water and allow it to cool. The valve plate should close smoothly.
8   If the unit fails to operate as described or it is stuck open or shut, renew it with one of similar temperature rating (photo).

H.20122

Fig. 2.4 Thermostat, housing and associated fittings – OHV engine (Sec 7)

1 Bleed screw and washer	4 Coolant outlet housing and	6 Thermostat
2 End piece	gasset	7 Gasket
3 Temperature sender unit	5 Housing cover	

Fig. 2.5 Exploded view of the water pump – OHV engine (Sec 8)

1	Pulley retaining bolt	5	Drivebelt	9	Pump body	13	Impeller
2	Lockplate	6	Hub	10	Drain plug	14	Gasket
3	Plate	7	Shaft/bearing assembly	11	Drain plug seal	15	Assembled water pump
4	Pulley	8	Bolt	12	Seal		

9 Refitting is a reversal of the removal procedure. On OHV engine models ensure that the locating tab on the thermostat is correctly aligned and use a new cover gasket. On OHC engine models use new rubber sealing ring(s).
10 Do not overtighten the cover bolts when tightening them.
11 Reconnect the coolant hose and refill the system and bleed it as described in Section 4.

---

8 Water pump (OHV engines) – removal and refitting

1 Drain the cooling system as described in Section 4.
2 Jack up the front of the car and support it securely on safety stands.
3 Unbolt and remove the engine under shield and side shield.
4 Loosen the alternator mounting and adjusting arm bolts, move the alternator towards the engine and disengage the drivebelt.
5 Undo and remove the three retaining bolts and withdraw the water pump pulley from the pump flange (photo).
6 Disconnect the water hose from the outlet on the side of the pump.
7 Undo and remove the four retaining bolts and withdraw the water pump assembly from its location in the sump casting.
8 If the water pump is worn, noisy or leaks, it should be renewed by a new replacement unit. Although this type of water pump can be dismantled for inspection, any replacement parts may not be readily available and their cost may nearly equal that of a complete unit. Any repairs which may be possible should be entrusted to a Peugeot dealer who has the necessary experience and tools.
9 Refitting the water pump is the reverse sequence to removal, bearing in mind the following points:

  (a) Ensure that the sump face and water pump mating surfaces are thoroughly clean and free from any traces of old gasket
  (b) Use a new gasket lightly smeared on both sides with sealing compound (photo)
  (c) Tighten the pulley and water pump retaining bolts to the torque settings shown in the Specifications
  (d) Adjust the drivebelt tension as described in Chapter 12

9 Water pump (OHC engines) – removal and refitting

1 Drain the cooling system as described in Section 4.
2 Jack up the car at the front and support it securely on safety stands.
3 Unbolt and remove the engine undershield.
4 Detach and remove the radiator bottom hose.
5 Remove the camshaft drivebelt, as described in Chapter 1, followed by the tensioner.
6 Remove the plastic shield, noting the locations of the different types of bolt.
7 Unscrew the five mounting bolts and remove the water pump from the cylinder block. Remove the gasket.

8.5 Water pump pulley and retaining bolts – OHV engine

8.9 Refitting the water pump with new gasket located on body – OHV engine

8   If the water pump is worn, noisy or leaks coolant it must be renewed, as repair is not possible.
9   Refitting is a reversal of removal, but clean the mating faces and always fit a new O-ring or gasket, as applicable. Fill the cooling system, as described in Section 4.

10 Coolant temperature switch, gauge and level switch – general

1   The coolant temperature switch is located in the thermostat housing on OHV engines (photo) and in the coolant outlet housing (on the end of the cylinder head) on OHC engine models.
2   The coolant level switch is located in the side of the radiator.
3   To remove the temperature or level switch, first drain the cooling system, detach the wiring connector to the switch and then unscrew and remove the switch.
4   It is difficult to test a temperature switch without special equipment and the best method to use if a fault develops is to substitute a new switch, but only after the wiring to the gauge had been thoroughly checked.
5   When refitting the switch, make sure that the seal is in good condition and do not overtighten it.
6   If the switch is changed and the gauge still does not register, then the gauge should be checked by a competent auto-electrician. Access to the gauge is obtained after removing the instrument panel, as described in Chapter 12.
7   The coolant level switch is float operated and actuates a warning lamp in the event of a low coolant level. If the switch malfunctions it must be renewed as no repair is possible.

Fig. 2.6 Water pump – OHC engine (Sec 9)

1   Gasket   2   Pump unit

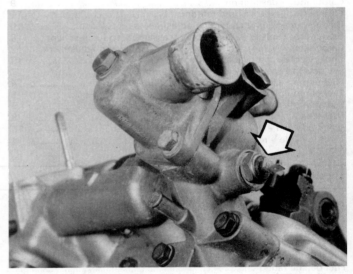

10.1 Coolant temperature switch location (arrowed) – OHV engine

11 Fault diagnosis – cooling system

Symptom	Reason(s)
Overheating	Insufficient coolant in system Radiator blocked either internally or externally Thermostat not opening Electric cooling fan or thermoswitch faulty Pressure cap faulty
Overcooling	Faulty, incorrect or missing thermostat Electric cooling fan thermoswitch not switching off
Loss of coolant	Damaged hoses or loose clips Leaking water pump O-ring or gasket, as applicable

Chapter 3 Fuel and exhaust systems

For modifications, and information applicable to later models, see Supplement at end of manual

Contents

Specifications

Part A: Carburettor models
General
Air cleaner .... Dry type with replaceable cartridge. Air temperature controlled inlet system

Fuel pump .... Mechanical diaphragm
Fuel octane rating .... 4-Star (97 RON)
Fuel tank capacity .... 55 litres (12.1 gal)

Carburettor
Type*:
   1118 cc engine .... Weber 32 IBSH 13 or Solex 32 BISA 9 (393)
   1294 cc engine .... Weber 32 IBSH 14 or Solex 32 BISA (392)
   1580 cc engine .... Weber 36 TLP 1/100
*Bressel carburettor .... A Bressel carburettor may be fitted. The Bressel unit is manufactured under licence from both Weber and Solex, and shares the same type numbers. They are in all respects otherwise identical to the equivalent Weber or Solex counterpart

Carburettor specifications:	Weber 32 IBSH 13	Weber 32 IBSH 14
Choke tube	25	26
Main jet	130	142
Air correction jet	155	175
Emulsion tube	F102	F102
Fuel enrichment jet	50	50
Econostat	75	110
Idle jet	46	46

Carburettor specifications (continued)	Weber 32 IBSH 13	Weber 32 IBSH 14
Idle air jet	185	175
Accelerator pump injector	40	40
Float valve	1.5	1.5
Float weight	11 g	11 g
Float level	7 mm	7 mm
Positive throttle opening	18° 30'	19°
Pneumatic opening	3.5 to 4.0 mm	4.0 to 4.5 mm
Idle speed	600 to 700 rpm	600 to 700 rpm
Idle mixture (CO)	1 to 2%	1 to 2%

Carburettor specifications:	Weber 36 TLP 1/110	
Choke tube	28	
Main jet	142	
Float valve	1.5	
Idle fuel jet	46	
Air correction jet	155	
Emulsion tube	F80	
Accelerator pump injector	50	
Econostat fuel jet	65 to 80	
Positive throttle opening	19° 30'	
Idle speed	650 to 750 rpm	
Idle mixture (CO)	1 to 2%	

Carburettor specifications:	Solex 32 BISA 9 (393)	Solex 32 BISA 9 (392)
Choke tube	25	26
Main jet	130±5	132±5
Air correction jet	170±5	165±5
Emulsion tube	EM	EM
Fuel enrichment	50±10	55±10
Econostat fuel	50±10	50±10
Econostat air	300	300
Idle fuel jet	48±5	48±5
Idle air jet	180±5	180±5
Progression slots	0.6x4.5	0.6x4.5
Accelerator pump injector	40±5	40±5
Accelerator pump bleed screw	35	35
Float valve	1.6	1.6
Float weight	5.7 g	5.7 g
Positive throttle opening	20° 10'	19° 40'
Pneumatic opening (high side)	4.3 mm	4.0 mm
Choke flap hole	8	5
Idle speed	600 to 700 rpm	600 to 700 rom
Idle mixture (CO)	1 to 2%	1 to 2%

Torque wrench settings	Nm	lbf ft
Fuel pump bolts	20	15
Carburettor bolts	15	11

Part B: Fuel injection models
General

System type	Rear-mounted fuel tank, Bosch LE2-Jetronic fuel injection system, electric fuel pump
Fuel tank capacity	55 litres (12.1 gallons)
Fuel octane rating	4-star (97 RON)
Idling speed	850 to 900 rpm
CO at idling	0.5%
CO_2 at idling	10% minimum
Fuel pressure	2.9 to 3.1 bar (42.1 to 45.0 lbf/in²)
Fuel pump delivery	540 cc/15 sec
Tachometric relay cut-out speed	6600 rpm
Fuel cut-off speed (decelerating)	Above 1600 rpm

Torque wrench setting	Nm	lbf ft
Fuel filter base banjo type union hollow bolt	35	26

PART A: GENERAL DESCRIPTION AND ROUTINE MAINTENANCE

1 General description

The fuel system comprises a rear-mounted fuel tank, and a single downdraught carburettor or a Bosch LE2-Jetronic fuel injection system on the XU5-JA engine variant.

On carburettor versions the fuel pump is a mechanical diaphragm type driven by an eccentric on the camshaft. On the fuel injection system the electric fuel pump is located in the fuel tank.

The air cleaner incorporates a dry element and the inlet air temperature is manually controlled.

2 Routine maintenance

Carry out the following procedures at the intervals given in Routine Maintenance at the beginning of the manual.
1 Check all fuel lines and hoses for damage and security, including those located on the underbody.

2.4 In-line fuel filter – carburettor engines

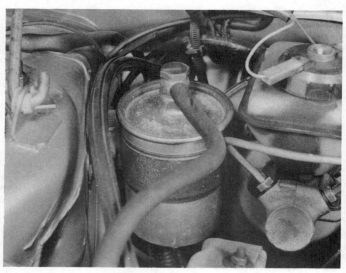

2.5 Fuel filter – fuel injection engines

2   Check the accelerator pedal operation and the throttle cable for the correct adjustment.

3   Renew the air filter element (Section 3 or 18).

4   On carburettor engines, clean the fuel pump filter (if applicable), as described in Section 4. Some models have an in-line fuel filter instead. This must be renewed at the specified intervals, by unclipping and detaching the unit. An arrow on the body of the filter indicates the direction of flow when fitting the new filter (photo).

5   On fuel injection engines, to renew the fuel filter first unscrew the union bolt from the top of the unit then place the bolt union and washers to one side and cover to prevent ingress of dirt. Unscrew the clamp bolt, then lift the filter and unscrew the bottom union. Fit the new filter using a reversal of the removal procedure; making sure that dust and dirt is prevented from entering the fuel lines (photo).

6   Lubricate the carburettor and choke cables.

PART B: CARBURETTOR ENGINES

3   Air cleaner – description and servicing

1   All models are fitted with a renewable paper element air filter housed in a plastic casing on top of the engine which is retained by a quick-release strap. The filter element must be renewed at the specified intervals if engine efficiency and fuel economy are to be maintained.

2   The temperature of the air entering the air cleaner can be controlled by means of a selector lever on the intake duct. In the 'summer' position cold air is drawn into the air cleaner assembly via a hose leading in from the front wing, while the 'winter' position allows air to be drawn in through a hot air duct fitted over the exhaust manifold. An intermediate position provides mixed hot and cold air (photo).

3   To renew the filter element, release the spring clips to release the end cover/filter element (photos). Loosen the intake hose retaining clips to the end cover and detach the hose. Withdraw the end cover/element from the filter body.

4   The end cover is integral with the filter element and the complete assembly must be discarded.

5   When fitting the new filter and end cover, ensure that the arrows on top of the cover and the filter housing are in alignment before fastening the clips and refitting the intake hose. Also ensure that the new filter is of the same make as the old; several different types have been fitted and not all are interchangeable (photo).

6   To remove the complete air cleaner assembly, undo the air cleaner-to-carburettor adaptor cover retaining nut(s) and detach the air intake hose from the air cleaner (photo).

7   Release the strap securing the air cleaner body, disengage the locating peg from its grommet and lift off the air cleaner assembly. Disconnect the vacuum hose(s) noting their connections (photos).

8   Refitting the air cleaner is the reverse of the removal procedure. When fitting the carburettor adaptor cover into position on the

3.2 Air cleaner inlet temperature control lever

3.3A Release the end cover retaining clips ...

3.3B ... to remove the cover/element

3.5 Align the arrows of the body and end cover

3.6 Air cleaner-to-carburettor adaptor cover showing the two retaining nuts (arrowed)

3.7A Disengage the air cleaner body retaining strap ...

3.7B ... and the cleaner body from the location peg

Fig. 3.1 O-ring seal location in the carburettor adaptor cover – OHV engine (Sec 3)

Fig. 3.2 O-ring seal locations in the carburettor adaptor cover – OHC engine (Sec 3)

carburettor, ensure that the O-ring seal(s) are correctly located (Fig. 3.1 or 3.2). Smear the ring seals with Vaseline to ease fitting.

4 Fuel pump – cleaning

This only applies to models with a fuel pump with an integral filter. Fully sealed units will have an in-line filter (see Section 2)

1   Detach the fuel supply hose from the pump and plug the hose to prevent loss of fluid.
2   Unscrew the top cover retaining screw(s) and carefully lift the cover off the pump.

3   Withdraw the filter gauze and wash it thoroughly in petrol. If it is badly contaminated it is best to renew it.
4   Remove all traces of dirt and sediment from the interior of the pump chamber.
5   Refit the filter to the pump body, place the cover gasket in position and refit the cover. Tighten but do not use excessive force on the retaining screw(s).
6   Reconnect the fuel hose, start the engine and check for leaks.

5 Fuel pump – testing

1   If the performance of the fuel pump is in doubt, first examine for fuel leaks and check that the fuel line connections are all sound.
2   Disconnect the fuel hose at the carburettor inlet connection and disconnect the high tension lead from the coil. Ensure that the tank contains fuel.
3   Direct the fuel feed hose into a suitable container and have an assistant operate the starter to crank the engine. A good spurt of fuel should be delivered on every second revolution of the engine. If not, check that the hose is not blocked. If that is clear the pump will need removal for examination or renewal.

6 Fuel pump – removal, overhaul and refitting

1   Disconnect the fuel hoses from the pump (photo). Plug the inlet hose.
2   Unscrew the pump mounting bolts/nuts and lift the pump away (photo).
3   An insulator block with a gasket each side is fitted between the pump flange and the mounting flange on the engine. The gaskets must be renewed when refitting the fuel pump.
4   Where applicable, withdraw the pump operating pushrod.
5   Further dismantling may not be possible on some types of pump. Even if it is, it should only be attempted if you have a repair kit. First mark the top and bottom halves of the pump for reassembly and then progressively loosen and remove the screws holding the two halves together. The diaphragm is connected to the operating mechanism beneath, and details will vary with different pumps. Note the sequence of assembly so that reassembly can be achieved in the same order.
6   Renew all defective parts; the kit will contain a variety of seals or gaskets which should automatically be fitted in place of the originals regardless of the fact that they may appear fit for further use.

6.1 Disconnect the fuel hoses ..

6.2 ... unbolt and remove the fuel pump (OHV engine)

7   Reassembly is the reverse of the dismantling sequence. Make sure that the upper and lower halves of the pump body are aligned and tighten the joint screws progressively and diagonally. Don't overtighten the top cover screws.

8   Before refitting the pump, check that the operating pushrod is in position (where applicable). Locate a new gasket each side of the insulator and refit the pump.

9   Tighten the securing bolts and make sure that the fuel hoses are reconnected to their correct pump connections.

7   Fuel level transmitter – removal and refitting

1   Disconnect the battery earth lead.
2   Fold the rear seat forwards and remove the insulator mat.
3   Prise free the circular plastic cover to expose the fuel level transmitter and disconnect the wiring from it (photo).

7.3 Fuel level transmitter unit (A) and fuel supply hose connector unit (B)

4   Before removing the transmitter from the fuel tank the safety precautions detailed in paragraph 2 in Section 8 should be observed.
5   Using a suitable tool, unscrew the transmitter mounting plate to release it from the securing tabs. Withdraw the transmitter unit.
6   Refitting is a reversal of removal, but use a new sealing ring if there is any doubt about the condition of the original one.

8   Fuel tank – removal and refitting

1   The fuel tank will normally only need removal from the vehicle if it is severely contaminated with sediment or other substance, or if it is to be renewed due to damage or for any repair work to the adjacent body or mechanical components.

2   As there is no drain plug incorporated in the tank, the best time to remove it is when it is nearly empty. If this is not possible, syphon as much fuel as possible from the tank into a container which can be sealed, but before doing so, observe the following precautions:
 (a)   Disconnect the battery
 (b)   Do not smoke or allow any naked lights near the working area
 (c)   Avoid placing the vehicle over an inspection pit as the fuel vapour is heavier than air; raise the vehicle at the rear and

support it on safety stands, supporting under the jacking point on the left-hand side and the rear crossmember on the right-hand side. Release the handbrake

3   From within the vehicle at the rear, disconnect the wiring from the fuel level transmitter (see previous Section).
4   Disconnect the fuel supply and return pipes from the fuel tank top face, but mark them for identification to ensure correct reconnection during refitting. Plug the pipes to prevent leakage and the ingress of dirt.
5   Remove the exhaust system (Section 16).
6   Unbolt and remove the heat shield(s).
7   Detach the fuel supply and vent hoses to the tank under the wheel arch.
8   Undo the two mounting strap bolts and carefully tilt the tank downwards at the rear. Detach the breather and bleed pipes on the right-hand side and further lower the fuel tank so that it rests on the handbrake cables.
9   The fuel tank can now be removed by passing it under the right-hand side of the vehicle. Get an assistant to help manoeuvre it free and support it as it is withdrawn.
10   If the tank is leaking or damaged it should be renewed or, if any repairs are possible, entrust them to your Peugeot dealer or a specialist.
11   If the tank contains sediment, remove the fuel level transmitter and wash out the tank using paraffin, then rinse it out with clean fuel. Refit in the reverse order of removal. Ensure that all hose connections are securely made. Renew the rubber mounting washers.

9   Carburettor – description

1   In production a Weber carburettor is fitted as standard, the type being in accordance with the engine fitted (see Specifications at the start of the Chapter).
2   The Solex carburettors listed are supplied as an alternative replacement unit for the original Weber. A third type of carburettor which may be fitted is the Bressel, which is a direct equivalent of the Weber or Solex counterpart.
3   In each case, the carburettor is of downdraught, single choke design, the main differences between the types being the jet sizes and the drillings in the carburettor body.
4   These carburettors comprise three main assemblies, namely the throttle block, the main body and the top cover. The throttle block embodies the throttle plate and control linkages and incorporates a water-heated jacket connected to the engine cooling system to provide pre-heating of the carburettor.
5   The main body incorporates the choke tube (sometimes known as the venturi or throttle barrel), the float chamber, accelerator pump and the jets, also the distributor vacuum and crankcase breather connections.
6   The top cover carries the choke plate, fuel inlet connection and needle valve.
7   The cold start enrichment device comprises a strangler type choke, which is operated manually by the driver. The choke plate is held open by a linkage when the control is pushed in; however, when the control is pulled out, the linkage is released and the choke plate is closed by a spring. When the engine starts, the depression in the carburettor overcomes the spring tension and automatically opens the choke plate slightly. Thus once the engine is running the mixture will be weakened by the additional air past the choke plate.
8   The accelerator pedal is connected via a cable to the linkage of the carburettor and operates the throttle plate. The depression created in the carburettor choke tube causes fuel to be drawn from the jets and out through the various drillings in the carburettor body. The fuel mixes with the incoming air to form a combustible mixture, the strength of which is controlled by the jet diameter.
9   When the accelerator is depressed quickly, a spring-loaded rod attached to the throttle spindle operates an accelerator pump which provides a jet of neat fuel into the choke tube. This creates the slightly richer mixture demanded by the engine during initial acceleration and eliminates flat spots.
10   Engine speed at tickover is adjustable by an idle speed control screw acting directly on the throttle control linkage.

Fig. 3.3 Exploded view of the Weber 32 IBSH carburettor fitted to OHV engines (Sec 9)

a	Air correction jet	Gg	Main jet	K	Choke tube	S	Emulsion tube
F	Float	i	Accelerator pump injector	P	Float valve	W	Idle mixture adjuster
g	Idle jet					Z	Throttle stop screw

Fig. 3.4 Throttle stop screw position (1) on the Weber 36 TLP carburettor – OHC engine (Sec 10)

Fig. 3.5 Mixture setting screw location (2) on the Weber 36 TLP carburettor – OHC engine (Sec 10)

10 Carburettor – tuning and idling adjustments

1   Adjustment of the carburettor should always be the last step in a complete engine tuning operation. Altering any of the carburettor settings will have little or no effect if any of the engine, ignition, fuel or exhaust system components are worn or incorrectly adjusted. These should all be checked first before making any carburettor adjustments.
2   Make sure that the engine is at normal working temperature, that the manual choke control is pushed fully in, and that the air cleaner assembly is in position on the carburettor. Adjustment of the various carburettors is as follows.
3   Connect a tachometer to the engine, following its manufacturer's instructions, then start the engine and allow it to idle.
4   Adjust the throttle stop screw until the correct engine rpm, as shown in the Specifications, is obtained. Refer to the photo or Fig. 3.4 for the location of the throttle stop screw.
5   Normally this is the only adjustment required. The mixture screw is set on production and should not need altering. If the idling is unsatisfactory, and all other engine variables described at the beginning of this Section are in order, the mixture may be adjusted as follows.
6   First break off the tamperproof cap on the end of the mixture screw, taking care not to bend the screw.
7   Start the engine and check that the idling speed is still at the specified rpm. Adjust the throttle stop screw if necessary.

8   Turn the mixture screw in or out until the highest possible idling speed is obtained (photo or Fig. 3.5).
9   Bring the idling speed back to the specified setting by adjusting the throttle stop screw.
10   Reduce the idling speed very slightly by screwing in the mixture screw, but without going so far as to cause uneven running.
11   Finally reset the idling speed again by altering the throttle stop screw. Switch off the engine and disconnect the tachometer.

11 Carburettor – removal and refitting

1   Disconnect the battery earth lead.
2   Unclip and detach the air ducting between the carburettor and the air cleaner unit.
3   Disconnect the wire from the idle cut-off solenoid.
4   Disconnect the fuel supply and return hoses from the carburettor. Plug the hoses (photo).
5   Detach the accelerator inner cable from the quadrant and the outer cable from its support at the carburettor and fold it back out of the way (photo).
6   Detach the choke cable by loosening the inner cable clamp screw. Unscrew the outer cable location clamp bolt and move the cable out of the way.
7   Where applicable, disconnect the vacuum hose from the carburettor.

10.4 Throttle stop screw adjustment – arrowed (Weber carburettor)

10.8 Mixture screw adjustment (Weber carburettor)

11.4 Weber carburettor showing hose connections (1.3 litre engine)

11.5 Disconnect the throttle (A) and choke (B) cables

12.5A Remove the carburettor top cover retaining screws

12.5B Throttle body separation from the carburettor main body. Note insulation spacer

8   Unscrew the carburettor retaining nuts and then lift it clear of the manifold. Retrieve the old joint gasket and place a piece of clean cloth over the aperture in the manifold to prevent dirt or anything from accidentally falling into it while the carburettor is removed.
9   Refitting the carburettor is the reverse of the removal procedure. Remove all traces of the old gasket and use a new one on installation. After fitting the carburettor, reconnect the accelerator cable and the choke cable. When the choke control cable is fitted and the choke knob is pushed fully in, the flap should be fully open and there should be a small amount of possible additional movement on the control knob. Check that the flap closes when the control is pulled.

12 Carburettor (Weber) – dismantling, reassembly and adjustment

1   The carburettor should not normally need to be dismantled except for cleaning and checking the float level.
2   If the carburettor is to be dismantled, remember that it is a relatively delicate instrument and therefore requires careful handling. Use the correct tools for the job and do not interchange jets or clean them out with wire or any similar item which could damage them and interfere with their calibration.
3   Before dismantling the carburettor, or any part of it, first clean the outside and prepare a clean work area. When taking anything mechanical apart, and this applies particularly to such components as carburettors, it is always sound policy to make sure that the individual parts are put back exactly where they came from, and even the same way round if it is possible to do otherwise, even though they may appear to be interchangeable.
4   To help in this procedure, mark or label items, put small parts in boxes or tins so that they don't get mixed up, and lay parts out in order of assembly on clean paper.
5   Undo the retaining screws and lift the carburettor top cover away from the main body (photo), and the main body from the throttle body – if required (photo).
6   The float can be removed by pushing out the hinge pin and then the needle valve assembly can be unscrewed from the cover. Unscrew the end bolt near the fuel inlet connection and remove the gauze filter. Examine the filter for contamination and blockage. Soak the filter in petrol to clean it (photos).
7   Carefully remove the accelerator pump valve, the main jet, the idle jet and the mixture adjustment screw; noting their respective fitting positions. When removing the idle jet and mixture setting adjusters, count the number of turns required to remove them so that they can be refitted in approximately the same position and give a provisional adjustment position (photo).
8   Do not disturb the choke flap and throttle butterfly valve or spindles. Their actuating mechanisms are external and normally require no attention unless excessively worn. If the spindles are worn in the carburettor body then serious consideration should be given to renewing the complete carburettor. Such wear is an indication that the carburettor is due for renewal and it would be false economy to refit

the original instrument. Air leaks around worn spindles make it impossible to tune the carburettor correctly and poor performance and impaired economy will inevitably result.
9   The respective chambers, passages and jet seats can be brush

Fig. 3.6 Weber 36 TLP 1/100 carburettor showing the main jet (1) and float valve (2) locations (Sec 12)

Fig. 3.7 Weber 36 TLP 1/100 carburettor showing positions of the idle fuel jet (3) air correction jet (4) and emulsion tube (5) (Sec 12)

12.6A Press out the hinge pin ...

12.6B ... and remove the float

12.7 View inside the carburettor main body showing location of jets, the accelerator pump injector and the emulsion tube

cleaned using clean fuel and they should then be blown dry, if an air supply is available, or allowed to dry naturally. Don't use rag or cloth. Clean and blow through the jets in a similar manner.

10 Reassembly is the reverse of the dismantling procedure. Whenever possible use new washers, gaskets, or seals wherever fitted. During reassembly check and adjust the float level.

11 Check the float level with the top cover removed and held vertically on its side with the float hanging down (photo). The cover gasket must be fitted on the flange face of the cover. With the tongue of the float arm in light contact with the ball of the needle valve, the dimension from the gasket bottom face to the lower part of the float is the float level. The correct dimension for the various carburettor types is given in the Specifications at the start of this Chapter (Fig. 3.8).

12 To adjust the float level setting, carefully bend the float arm as required.

13 On the Weber 36 TLP carburettor, the procedure for checking the float level differs slightly in that you will need to fabricate a check gauge to the shape and dimensions shown in Fig. 3.9. With the top cover removed and the gasket in position, support the carburettor with the top of the float chamber vertical and position the check gauge as shown in Fig. 3.10. The floats should just contact the gauge. If adjustment is necessary bend the tongue and/or the bars to suit (Fig. 3.11).

14 Another check which can be made on the Weber 36 TLP

carburettor is the positive throttle valve opening, but this is best entrusted to your Peugeot dealer.

15 Before refitting the carburettor, check that the filter is clean, insert it into its aperture and fit the retaining bolt (photos).

12.11 Float level check method

Fig. 3.8 Float level adjustment check – Weber 32 IBSH carburettor (Sec 12)

a   Float arm tongue (in contact with ball)
9   Gasket (must be fitted when checking)
X = 7 mm

Fig. 3.9 Float level check gauge required for the Weber 36 TLP carburettor showing shape and dimensions (in mm) (Sec 12)

Fig. 3.10 Float level check using gauge – Weber 36 TLP carburettor (Sec 12)

Fig. 3.11 Float level adjustment is made at tongue (2) or bars (3) – Weber 36 TLP carburettor (Sec 12)

12.15A Insert the filter ...

12.15B .. and fit the securing bolt

13 Carburettor (Solex) – dismantling, reassembly and adjustment

1   Refer to Section 12, paragraphs 1 to 3 inclusive for some general observations prior to dismantling the carburettor.
2   An exploded view of the Solex 32 BISA carburettor is shown in Fig. 3.12.
3   Remove the screws and lift off the float chamber cover.
4   Unscrew the air correction jet followed by the main jet and the idling fuel jet.
5   Unscrew the accelerator pump valve and remove the pump injector.
6   Remove the enrichment valve.
7   Unscrew the needle valve.
8   Clean the float chamber and removed components with fuel and blow through the internal channels using an air line if possible.
9   Obtain a repair kit of gaskets then reassemble the carburettor in reverse order. The float level is not adjustable.
10 The only adjustment possible is the fast idle setting of the throttle

valve, but this is best checked and if necessary adjusted by a Peugeot dealer.
11 When the carburettor is refitted to the car, check it for correct adjustment as described in Section 10.

14 Throttle cable – removal and refitting

1   Extract the spring retaining clip from the adjustment ferrule at the throttle cable support bracket at the carburettor.
2   Detach the throttle cable (inner) from the throttle quadrant of the carburettor (see photo 11.5).
3   Working inside the car, disconnect the cable end fitting from the top of the accelerator pedal arm (photo).
4   Release the cable from the bracket on the carburettor.
5   Withdraw the throttle cable through the bulkhead grommet.
6   Refitting is a reversal of removal, but adjust the cable at the ferrule to remove all but the slightest amount of play. Check that full throttle can be obtained with the accelerator pedal fully depressed.

Fig. 3.12 Exploded view of
the Solex BISA carburettor
(Sec 13)

1 Float chamber cover
2 Needle valve
3 Float
4 Accelerator pump injector
5 Air correction jet
6 Main body
7 Main jet
8 Idle mixture screw
9 Enricher device
10 Idling fuel jet
11 Throttle stop screw

H145812

14.3 Throttle pedal and cable end fitting
(arrowed)

15.3A Detach the inner cable nipple ...

15.3B ... and remove the cable from the
choke control

15 Choke cable – removal and refitting

1 At the carburettor end, undo the inner cable-to-choke lever
pinch-bolt and the outer cable support pinch-bolt (photo 11.5).
Disconnect the cable from the lever and support.
2 Working inside the car, reach up behind the choke control cable
lever and compress the clips to allow the control lever to be withdrawn
from the facia. It is advisable to remove the lower facia trim panel on
the drivers' side for access.
3 Detach the inner cable nipple from the control lever (photo) and
withdraw the cable from the control lever unit (photo). Remove the
cable.

4   Refitting is a reversal of removal, but adjust the cable at the carburettor end so that, when the control knob is pushed fully in, the choke valve plate is fully open.

16 Manifolds and exhaust system – general

1   The inlet and exhaust manifolds are located on opposite sides of the cylinder head.
2   The exhaust manifold is simply bolted into position with a common flange gasket for each port (photos).
3   The inlet manifold has coolant connections and before it can be

Fig. 3.13 Sectional view of the exhaust manifold-to-downpipe flange joint showing location for the insulating washers (11) (Sec 16)

removed, the cooling system should be at least partially drained to avoid any coolant running into the cylinder bores as the manifold is removed. Always renew the gasket when refitting the manifold (photos).
4   The exhaust system is in sections and the mountings are of the flexible rubber type (photo).
5   Even if only one section of the system is to be renewed, it is recommended that the complete system is removed from under the car with the car supported on axle stands.
6   When fitting the exhaust system tighten the flange mounting nuts evenly so that the special springs are compressed equally; the joint should be lubricated with grease (photo). Ensure that an insulating washer is positioned between each spring and the flange face (Fig. 3.13).

PART C: FUEL INJECTION ENGINE

17 Fuel injection system – general description and precautions

   Fuel injection system components are shown in Fig. 3.14 and 3.15. A roller type electric pump located in the fuel tank pumps fuel through the filter to the injectors via a distribution pipe. The electronic control unit which is triggered by the ignition circuit sends impulses to the injectors which operate simultaneously and inject fuel in the vicinity of the inlet valves. The electronic control unit is provided with sensors to determine engine temperature, speed and load, and the quantity of air entering the engine. This information is computed to determine the period of injection.
   For cold starting, additional fuel is provided and, to compensate for this, additional air is provided by a supplementary air device.
   The following Sections describe the procedures which can be

16.2A Exhaust manifold gasket in position on studs (1.3 litre engine)

16.2B Exhaust manifold in position (1.3 litre engine)

16.3A Inlet manifold gasket in position (1.3 litre engine)

16.3B Inlet manifold fitting (1.3 litre engine)

16.4 Typical exhaust system mounting

16.6 Exhaust manifold-to-downpipe connection view from underneath (1.3 litre engine)

Fig. 3.14 Fuel injection system component locations in the engine compartment (LH drive shown) (Sec 17)

A	Securing screw	2	Fuel pump
B	Securing screw	3	Fuel filter
C	Securing screw	4	Distribution pipe
D	ECU connector	5	Injectors
1	Fuel pump housing		

6	Fuel pressure regulator
7	Throttle switch unit
8	Airflow sensor
9	Supplementary air device

10	Temperature cover
11	Tachometric relay and engine speed limiter
12	Electric control unit
13	Connector

Fig. 3.15 Fuel injection system main components (Sec 17)

1 Fuel tank
2 Fuel pump (electric)
3 Fuel filter
4 Distribution pipe and injectors
5 Fuel pressure regulator

carried out by the home mechanic. Work involving the use of pressure gauges is not included.

In order to prevent damage to the electrical components of the system the battery must **never** be disconnected with the engine running, the electronic control unit must not be disconnected with the ignition on, and a test lamp must not be used for checking the circuits.

18 Air cleaner element – renewal

1 Disconnect the air duct from the end of the air cleaner.
2 Unscrew the nuts and remove the end cover (photo).
3 Extract the element (photo).

18.2 Filter end cover and retaining nuts (arrowed)

18.3 Removing the filter element

4   Discard the element and wipe the casing interior clean.
5   Insert the new element then refit the end cover and air duct.

19 Air cleaner – removal and refitting

1   Disconnect the inlet and outlet ducts.
2   Unscrew the mounting bolts and lift the air cleaner from the engine.
3   Refitting is a reversal of removal.

20 Throttle initial position – checking and adjustment

1   Run the engine to normal operating temperature – indicated when the electronic cooling fan has cut in and out twice. The ignition timing must be correctly adjusted, as described in Chapter 4.
2   Connect a vacuum gauge to the test point (Fig. 3.16) in the distributor vacuum advance line.
3   Check that the throttle movement is smooth.
4   Check that the vacuum reading at the test point does not exceed 50 mm Hg (65 mbar).
5   If adjustment is necessary, stop the engine then turn the air screw fully in (photo).
6   Prise the tamperproof cap from the throttle stop adjustment screw.
7   Loosen the two screws on the throttle switch unit (photo).
8   Unscrew the throttle stop adjustment screw then retighten it until it just touches the throttle lever. Tighten the screw a further four complete turns.
9   Adjust the idling speed and mixture, as described in the following Section.

21 Idle speed and mixture – adjustment

1   Connect a tachometer and an exhaust gas analyser to the engine.
2   With the throttle initial position set, as described in Section 20, run the engine at idle speed.
3   Turn the air (idle speed) adjustment screw to obtain an idle speed of 650 rpm. Check that the vacuum reading does not exceed 50 mmHg (65 mbar) and if necessary adjust the idle speed adjustment screw.
4   Stop the engine and adjust the throttle switch, as described in Section 22.
5   With the engine at normal operating temperature, unscrew the air screw to set the idling speed between 850 and 900 rpm.
6   Check that the CO reading is between 1 and 2% and the CO_2 reading is more than 10%.
7   If adjustment is necessary, prise out the tamperproof cap on the airflow sensor (photo) and use a 5 mm Allen key to adjust the mixture. Turn the screw in to richen the mixture and out to weaken it.
8   Blip the throttle two or three times and then recheck that the idle speed and mixture is correct.
9   If the Co_2 reading is less than 10% check that the air filter is clean and that there are no leaks in the inlet or exhaust systems.

Fig. 3.16 Vacuum gauge test point (1) (Sec 20)

22 Throttle switch – checking and adjustment

1   Pull the connector from the throttle switch (photo).
2   Connect a voltmeter between the middle terminal on the connector and earth.
3   Pull the connector from the ignition distributor then operate the starter motor and check that there is a reading of at least 9 volts.
4   Disconnect the air hose from the throttle housing.
5   Position a 0.30 mm (0.012 in) feeler blade between the throttle stop adjustment screw and the throttle lever (Fig. 3.17).
6   Loosen the two throttle switch screws.
7   Connect an ohmmeter between terminals 18 and 2 on the throttle switch, then rotate the switch until the internal contacts close and the reading is zero ohms. Tighten the screws with the switch in this position.
8   Remove the feeler blade and insert in its place a 0.70 mm (0.028 in) feeler blade. The internal contacts should now be separated and the reading on the ohmmeter infinity. If not, repeat the procedure in paragraph 7.
9   Remove the feeler blade.
10 Check the full throttle operation by connecting an ohmmeter between terminals 18 and 2, then fully opening the throttle so that dimension X (Fig. 3.18) is 4.0 mm (0.158 in). The internal contacts should close and the ohmmeter reading be zero.
11 If the switch does not operate correctly it should be renewed.

20.5 Throttle housing showing position of the (1) air screw (idle adjustment screw) and the throttle stop screw (2)

20.7 Throttle switch unit and retaining screw (arrowed)

21.7 Mixture adjustment using an Allen key

22.1 Disconnect the throttle switch wiring connector

Fig. 3.17 Adjusting the throttle switch (Sec 22)

3   Throttle stop screw   4   Throttle lever

Fig. 3.18 Full throttle dimension X (Sec 22)

4   Throttle lever   X = 4.0 mm (0.158 in)
7   Throttle housing

23 Air intake system – checking for leaks

1   For the correct operation of the airflow sensor there must be no air entering the system upstream of the sensor.
2   Check that there is no leakage at the points arrowed in Fig. 3.19 or at the inlet manifold gasket.
3   If an air line is available, disconnect the airflow sensor inlet hose and use an adaptor to blow air through the intake system while fully opening the throttle, blocking the exhaust pipe and pinching the crankcase breather hose. If the points indicated in paragraph 2 are then brushed with soapy water any bad seals will be immediately evident.

Fig. 3.19 Areas (arrowed) for checking air intake leakage (LH drive shown) (Sec 23)

1   Airflow sensor   4   Throttle housing   6   Fuel pressure regulator   10   Air distribution manifold
2   Cylinder head   5   Brake vacuum servo   7   Crankcase breather hose   11   Injectors

Fig. 3.20 Fuel pump connections (Sec 24)

1 *Wiring connector with wires R1 and U1*
2 *Fuel supply pipe*
3 *Fuel return pipe*
4 *Retaining screws*
5 *Fuel pump housing*

24 Fuel pump – removal and refitting

1 Remove the rear seat or tilt it forward, prise up the right-hand plastic cover then disconnect the wiring, and the fuel supply and return pipes, noting their location (Fig. 3.20).
2 Note the safety precautions given in Section 8 of this Chapter.
3 Unscrew the retaining screws and lift the fuel pump housing from the fuel tank.
4 Release the filter from the bottom of the housing, followed by the collar (Fig. 3.21).
5 Disconnect the wiring and release the fuel pump from the upper collar.
6 Refitting is a reversal of removal, but fit new collars and make sure that the wiring terminals are positioned away from the pump terminals. Always fit a new gasket between the pump housing and fuel tank.

25 Supplementary air device (cold start) – removal and refitting

1 The supplementary air device unit is located beneath the distributor and is attached to the flywheel end of the engine. Access is poor both from above and from underneath, but removal of the following will enable it to be inspected or removed.
2 Disconnect and remove the battery (Chapter 12).
3 Disconnect the air hoses then unbolt the airflow sensor and bracket. Disconnect the wiring (photos).

Fig. 3.21 Fuel pump components (Sec 24)

1 *Bleed tube*	4 *Collar*
2 *Bracket*	5 *Fuel pump*
3 *Collar*	6 *Filter*

25.3A Disconnect the wiring connector from the airflow sensor

25.3B Airflow sensor mounting bracket and retaining bolts

Fig. 3.23 Airflow sensor terminals (Sec 26)

Fig. 3.22 Supplementary air device and associated fittings
(Sec 25)

5	Mounting bracket screws	9	Coolant hoses
6	Hose clips	10	Air hose unions
7	Nuts	11	Retaining bolt
8	Connectors	12	Retaining bolt

4   Unscrew the supplementary air device bracket nuts and disconnect the wiring.
5   Tilt the assembly and coolant outlet housing (without disconnecting the coolant hoses) and remove the concealed mounting bolt (Fig. 3.22).
6   Disconnect the air hoses, then remove the remaining mounting bolt and withdraw the unit.
7   Refitting is a reversal of removal.

26 Fuel injection system – complete test

1   Pull the connector from the airflow sensor and connect a voltmeter between wire 18A and earth.
2   Disconnect the ignition control unit then operate the starter motor and check that a minimum of 9 volts is obtained.
3   Disconnect the battery negative lead.
4   Connect an ohmmeter between wire M18 and earth and check that the reading is less than 1 ohm.
5   Disconnect the airflow sensor inlet hose and use a screwdriver to open and close the sensor flap. The movement should be free. Clean the interior of the sensor if necessary.
6   Connect an ohmmeter between terminals 5 and 8 on the airflow sensor (Fig. 3.23) and check that a reading of 340 to 450 ohms is obtained.

Fig. 3.24 Checking the supplementary air device wiring
(Sec 26)

7   Connect the ohmmeter between terminals 9 and 8 and check that the reading is now between 160 and 300 ohms.
8   Connect the ohmmeter between terminals 5 and 7, then move the flap with a screwdriver. The resistance should vary between 60 and 1000 ohms.
9   Connect the ohmmeter between the terminal on the engine temperature sensor (above the supplementary air device) and earth. The reading should be less than 1 ohm.
10 Pull off the temperature sensor connector and connect the ohmmeter across the two terminals on the sensor. If the reading is infinity, renew the sensor.
11 Connect a voltmeter between wire 48 on the supplementary air device connector and earth (Fig. 3.24).
12 Disconnect the ignition control unit then operate the starter motor and check that the reading is at least 9 volts.
13 With the battery disconnected, connect an ohmmeter between wire M24 on the connector and earth. The reading should be less than 1 ohm.
14 Remove the supplementary air device (Section 25), and check that, at an ambient temperature of 20°C (68°F), the opening in the diaphragm is visible through the end of the unit.
15 Connect an ohmmeter across the terminals of the unit and check that a reading of 45 to 55 ohms is obtained at an ambient temperature of 20°C (68°F).
16 Connect a 12 volt supply to the terminals of the unit. After five minutes the diaphragm must completely block the airflow aperture.

27.3 Detach the injector wiring connection

30.2A The fuel tank vent valve

30.2B Fuel tank drain plug

27 Fuel injectors and distribution pipe – removal and refitting

1   Disconnect the battery earth lead.
2   Unbolt and disconnect the fuel pressure unit from the end of the distribution pipe.
3   Unclip and detach the wiring connectors from each injector. If they are not marked for identity, label them numerically as they are detached (photo).
4   Prise free the retaining clip from each injector connection (under the distribution pipe).
5   Unbolt and remove the feed pipe.
6   Pull free the injectors as required from the cylinder head.
7   When refitting the injectors and reconnecting the fuel feed lines and distribution pipe, ensure that no dirt is allowed to enter the system.
8   Refitting is a reversal of the removal procedure. Ease refitting of the injectors by lubricating the O-ring seals with a soapy solution. New O-ring seals must be fitted.

28 Fuel pressure regulator unit – removal and refitting

1   Disconnect the battery earth lead.
2   Detach the hoses from the regulator unit, allowing for fuel spillage. Plug the hoses to prevent excess leakage of fuel and the ingress of dirt.
3   Unbolt and remove the pressure regulator unit, noting how the hose bracket is attached to the upper bolt.
4   Refit in the reverse order of removal. Check for signs of fuel leakage on completion and when the engine is restarted.

29 Fuel level transmitter – removal and refitting

Refer to Section 7.

30 Fuel tank – removal and refitting

1   Disconnect the battery earth lead, then proceed as described in Section 8.
2   Note the following differences:

(a)   *There is an additional vent valve located separately and to the rear of the fuel tank near the rear towing eye (photo). This valve is secured by a clip.*
(b)   *The fuel tank has a drain plug (photo).*
(c)   *A baffle is fitted to the moulded stiffener within the tank, its purpose being to maintain the fuel level around the pump when the vehicle is cornering. The baffle is secured to the stiffener by clips. If the fuel tank is to be renewed the baffle will need to be transferred from the old tank to the new tank, together with the fuel level transmitter unit and pump. Fit and locate the baffle as shown in Figs. 3.25 and 3.26.*

Fig. 3.25 Fuel tank baffle replacement (Sec 30)

REMOVE PUMP AND LAY ON TOP DO NOT DISCONNECT INTERNAL FEED PIPE

REMOVE SENDER UNIT

INSERT BAFFLE WITH CLIP AND CUTOUT AS INDICATED

Fig. 3.26 Locate the baffle as shown (when fitted) (Sec 30)

31.1 Throttle cable and adjustment ferrule

31 Throttle cable – removal and refitting

The procedure is similar to that described in Section 14, but the adjustment ferrule is located beneath the inlet manifold (photo).

32 Manifolds and exhaust system – general

Inlet manifold

1 Removal of the inlet manifold necessitates access from underneath as well as from above and the engine undershield should therefore be removed.
2 From the underside, disconnect the crankcase breather hose and unbolt and remove the support bracket and arm.
3 From above, remove the injection distribution pipe (Section 27) together with the pressure valve. Detach the throttle switch wire connector and the throttle cable, also the vacuum and air hoses.

4 The manifold retaining bolts can now be removed and the manifold withdrawn from the cylinder head. Remove the old gasket.
5 Renew the gasket when refitting the manifold. Refitting is otherwise a reversal of the removal procedure.

Exhaust system

6 The exhaust system is similar to that fitted to carburettor models, combining a manifold and sectional pipe system (see Section 16).
7 When removing the manifold, remove the air filter unit to gain access to the upper retaining nuts and remove the engine undershield to provide access to the lower manifold retaining nuts from underneath.
8 Removal is relatively easy and it is therefore recommended that the complete system is removed, at least from the manifold flange, whenever any work or repairs to the exhaust system are necessary. Ensure that the vehicle is securely supported when raised for working underneath the vehicle.
9 Always renew the manifold-to-cylinder head flange gasket, and refer to Section 16 when reconnecting the downpipe to the manifold.

PART D: FAULT DIAGNOSIS (ALL ENGINES)

33 Fault diagnosis – fuel and exhaust systems

Symptom	Reason(s)
Difficult starting from cold	Choke control inoperative (carburettor)
	Fuel pump fault
	Blocked fuel line or filter
	Needle valve sticking (carburettor)
	Supplementary air device fault (fuel injection)
	Temperature sensor faulty or disconnected (fuel injection)
Difficult starting when hot	Choked air filter
	Choke control sticking (carburettor)
	Fuel pump faulty
Excessive fuel consumption	Mixture setting incorrect
	Excessive fuel pressure (fuel injection)
	Temperature sensor faulty (fuel injection)
	Airflow sensor faulty (fuel injection)
Uneven idling	Mixture setting incorrect
	Air leak in intake system
	Throttle switch out of adjustment (fuel injection)
	Loose electronic control unit connector (fuel injection)
Hesitation after cornering	Displaced baffle in fuel tank (fuel injection)

Chapter 4 Ignition system

For modifications, and information applicable to later models, see Supplement at end of manual

Contents

Specifications

System type .... 12 volt, electronic (breakerless) system

Distributor
Make .... Ducellier or Bosch
Firing order .... 1–3–4–2 (No 1 cylinder at flywheel end)
Rotation:
    OHV engines .... Clockwise
    OHC engines .... Anti-clockwise

Ignition coil
Make and type .... Bosch or Ducellier, BTR01

Ignition control unit
Make and type .... Bosch or Ducellier, MTR01

Ignition timing
Vacuum hose disconnected (and plugged):
    OHV engines .... 8° BTDC at 650 rpm
    OHC engines .... 10° BTDC at 700 rpm

Spark plugs
OHV engines .... Eyquem FC 52 LS, Champion C9YC or equivalent
OHC engines .... Eyquem C 62 LJS, Champion S9YC or equivalent
Electrode gap .... 0.6 mm (0.024 in)

Torque wrench settings
	Nm	lbf ft
Spark plugs:		
OHV engines	20 to 30	15 to 22
OHC engines	17	13

1 General description

On all models the ignition system is of electronic breakerless type, which provides a high degree of reliability combined with the minimum of service requirements.

The system components comprise the ignition control unit module, ignition coil, distributor (incorporating a pulse generator) and the spark plugs (photo).

It should be noted that the spark plugs used on the OHC engine variants have a tapered seat with no sealing washers fitted.

In order that the engine may run correctly it is necessary for an electrical spark to ignite the fuel/air mixture in the combustion chamber at exactly the right moment in relation to the engine speed and load.

Basically the ignition system functions as follows. Low tension voltage from the battery is fed to the ignition coil, where it is converted into high tension voltage. The high tension voltage is powerful enough to jump the spark plug gap in the cylinder many times a second under high compression, providing that the ignition system is in good working order.

The ignition system consists of two individual circuits known as the low tension (LT) circuit and high tension (HT) circuit.

The low tension circuit (sometimes known as the primary circuit) comprises the ignition switch, primary ignition coil windings, and control module. The high tension circuit (sometimes known as the secondary circuit) comprises the secondary ignition coil windings, distributor cap, rotor arm, spark plugs and HT leads.

The primary circuit is initially switched on by the control module and a magnetic field is formed within the ignition coil. At the precise point of ignition the pulse generator causes the control module to switch off the primary circuit, and high tension voltage is then induced in the secondary circuit and fed to the spark plug via the distributor cap and rotor arm.

The ignition is advanced and retarded automatically by centrifugal weights and a vacuum capsule to ensure that the spark occurs at the correct instant in relation to engine speed and load.

Note: *When working on the ignition system remember that the high tension voltage can be considerably higher than on a conventional system and in certain circumstances could prove fatal.*

2 Routine maintenance

Carry out the following procedures at the intervals given in Routine Maintenance at the beginning of the manual.

1 Remove the spark plugs and renew them, with reference to Section 9. Do not forget to set the electrode gaps on the new plugs.
2 Check and, if necessary, adjust the ignition timing, as described in Section 6.
3 Periodically inspect the ignition system HT and LT wiring for security at their connection points and their general condition.
4 Periodically the condition of the distributor cap and rotor should be checked.

5 Remove the protective boot from around the distributor cap, release the two spring clips or unscrew the two retaining screws and lift off the cap.
6 Clean the inside and outside of the cap with a clean cloth and check the centre contact and four segments on the inside of the cap for excessive wear or burning. If evident the cap should be renewed.
7 Carefully lift the rotor off the distributor shaft and check the end of the brass segment for burning. Renew if necessary.
8 The air gap between the vane tips and the magnetic pick-up point is preset. It cannot be adjusted and requires no maintenance.
9 Apply a few drops of clean engine oil to the felt pad in the top of the distributor shaft.
10 Refit the rotor and distributor cap followed by the protective boot.

3 Distributor (OHV engine) – removal and refitting

1 Release the retaining clips and detach the distributor cap and leads from the distributor (photo).
2 Disconnect the vacuum hose from the distributor vacuum advance unit.
3 Disconnect the low tension wires at the in-line connector.
4 Using a small sharp screwdriver or similar instrument, carefully scribe an alignment mark between the distributor body and the crankcase mounting bracket (photo).
5 Undo the distributor clamp bolt, remove the clamp and lift out the distributor from the engine (photo).
6 To refit the distributor, enter it into the crankcase mounting bracket and then turn the distributor rotor until the tongue on the distributor shaft engages with the slot in the driveshaft (photo).
7 Rotate the distributor body to line up the previously made scribe marks, refit the clamp and tighten the securing bolt.
8 Refit the remaining distributor components using the reverse sequence to removal. After completing the installation it is advisable to check the ignition timing as described in Section 6.
9 If a new distributor is being fitted or if for any reason the alignment marks scribed between the distributor body and mounting bracket have been lost, it will be necessary to time the distributor to the engine, before fitting, as described below.
10 Pull off the HT lead and remove No 1 spark plug (nearest the flywheel end of the engine).
11 Place a finger over the spark plug hole and rotate the engine until pressure is felt, indicating that the piston is on the compression stroke. (Rotate the engine by means of a large socket on the crankshaft pulley bolt, or put the car in gear and move it forwards). The direction of engine rotation is clockwise viewed from the timing cover end.
12 With the No 1 cylinder at TDC on its firing stroke, the slot in the distributor drive collar on the distributor driveshaft will be set at the angle shown in Fig. 4.1 (three teeth anti-clockwise from the vertical). The TDC position can be further checked by observing the position of the timing notch in the crankshaft pulley. The notch should be aligned with the 0 (TDC) mark on the timing case (photos). This check will require the removal of the engine side cover from the right-hand wheel arch for access.

1.2 Ignition module unit

3.1 Distributor showing cap retaining clips (arrowed) – OHV engine

3.4 Scribe alignment marks on distributor body and mounting bracket – OHV engine

3.5 Remove distributor clamp bolt (arrowed) – OHV engine

3.6 Refitting the distributor – OHV engine

N°4

A
0

N°1

X

**Fig. 4.1 Distributor refitting requirements – OHV engine
(Sec 3)**

Slot angle X = 3 teeth from vertical

3.12A Flywheel timing mark and timing scale marks on the clutch housing – OHV engine

3.12B Align the pulley notch with appropriate timing mark (shown at TDC) – OHV engine

13 Temporarily place the distributor cap in position on the distributor and make a mark on the distributor body, with pencil or crayon adjacent to the No 1 HT segment of the cap.

14 Remove the cap and turn the distributor rotor so that it is pointing toward the mark.

15 Refit the distributor to the crankcase mounting bracket and engage the offset drive dog of the distributor with the slot in the drive collar. When in position the vacuum advance unit should be positioned on the underside of the distributor (towards the sump).

16 Relocate the distributor retaining clamp and bolt, but only hand tighten the bolt at this stage. Full tighten the bolt when the timing has been checked.

17 Check and adjust the timing as described in Section 6.

4 Distributor (OHC engine) – removal and refitting

1 Where necessary, remove the air cleaner and/or the intake duct to provide access to the distributor (refer to Chapter 3).

2 Identify the HT leads for position then disconnect them from the spark plugs.

3 Slide off the ignition coil cover and disconnect the HT lead from the coil.

4 Pull back the plastic cover then unclip and remove the distributor cap (photo).

5 Disconnect the wiring at the connector, where necessary pulling out the spring clip first.

6 Pull the hose from the vacuum advance unit.

7 Mark the relative positions of the distributor and mounting flanges for positional reference when refitting.

8 Unscrew the mounting nuts, remove the small plates, and withdraw the distributor.

9 Check the condition of the O-ring on the mounting flange and renew it if necessary.

10 Refitting is a reversal of removal, but turn the rotor arm as required to align the lugs with the offset slot in the camshaft. If the old distributor is being refitted, align the previously made marks before tightening the mounting nuts. If fitting a new distributor, initially set the distributor in the middle of the slotted holes or follow the procedure given in Section 6, then finally adjust the ignition timing (Section 6).

5 Distributor – overhaul

1 Clean the exterior of the distributor.

2 Pull off the rotor arm and remove the plastic cover, where fitted.

Ducellier

3 Extract the screw and remove the clamp and wiring plug (photo).

4 Extract the three body screws. The lugs are offset so the body sections cannot be misaligned when reassembled. Separate the body sections (photo).

5 Invert the body upper section, pull out the plastic ring and lift out the magnetic coil (photos).

6 From the body upper section, extract the circlip and the thrust washer (photo).

7 Extract the vacuum unit screw and then lift out the baseplate at the same time unhooking the vacuum link (photos).

8 Extract the circlip and shim from the body lower section (photo).

9 Lift out the counterweight assembly.

10 The drive dog is secured to the shaft by a pin.

11 Reassembly is a reversal of dismantling, but note that one baseplate hole is marked by engagement of the vacuum unit link rod (photo).

4.4 Distributor removal sequence – SRi engine shown

1	Withdraw the cover	5	Mark relative positions of flanges
2	Release cap clips		
3	Detach wiring connector	6	Remove retaining nuts and flat plate washers
4	Detach vacuum advance hose		

Fig. 4.2 Exploded view of
the Ducellier distributor
(Sec 5)

1   Lower body
2   Plastic ring
3   Circlip
4   Magnetic coil
5   Upper body
6   Vacuum unit
7   Clips
8   Wiring plug
9   Cover
10 Rotor arm
11 Distributor cap

H145816

5.3 Clamp and wiring plug (Ducellier)

5.4 Separating the body sections
(Ducellier)

5.5A Remove the plastic ring ...

5.5B ... and the magnetic coil (Ducellier)

5.6 Remove the circlip and thrust washer
(Ducellier)

5.7A Vacuum unit and screw (Ducellier)

5.7B Baseplate removal (Ducellier)

5.8 View showing reluctor, centrifugal weights and securing circlip – arrowed (Ducellier)

5.11 Hole marked for engagement of vacuum unit link (Ducellier)

5.12A General view of the Bosch distributor fitted to 1.1 and 1.3 litre models
1   Wiring connector plug and retaining screw
2   Vacuum advance/cap clip retaining screw

5.12B Vacuum advance unit removal from Bosch distributor (1.1 and 1.3 litre models)

5.12C Bosch distributor showing bearing plate (SRi model)

Bosch
12 The procedure is similar to that for the Ducellier distributor but the body is in one piece. Refer to Fig. 4.3 (photos).

6 Ignition timing – checking and adjustment

Note: *Where necessary, first remove the air cleaner intake duct to allow access to the timing aperture in the top face of the clutch housing/gearbox casing.*

Static ignition timing
1 To set the ignition timing statically so that the engine can be started, first remove No 1 spark plug (nearest clutch) and turn the engine in the normal rotational direction until pressure is felt – indicating that the piston is commencing the compression stroke. The pressure can be felt using a suitable wooden rod or piece of cork placed over the spark plug hole.
2 While looking into the timing aperture in the clutch housing/gearbox casing, continue turning the crankshaft until the single mark on the flywheel is opposite the BTDC mark on the timing plate (see photo 3.12A or 6.2).
3 Check that the distributor rotor arm is facing the No 1 HT lead segment position in the distributor cap. To do this, remove the cap and mark the outside in line with the segment, then put it back on the distributor noting which way the rotor arm is facing.
4 If necessary, loosen the mounting nuts and turn the distributor body to bring the segment and rotor arm in line, then tighten the nuts. Refit No 1 spark plug. The ignition timing should now be checked dynamically as described below. For this you will need a stroboscopic timing light. Alternatively the ignition timing may be checked and

adjusted using the engine diagnosis socket, but the special Peugeot instrument necessary will not normally be available to the home mechanic.

Dynamic ignition timing
5 Because the distributor only gives a timing signal when the shaft is rotating, a stroboscopic timing light must be used with the engine running at idling speed. The timing light must be suitable for use with electronic ignition systems.
6 First disconnect the vacuum advance pipe from the distributor and connect the timing light between No 1 spark plug (nearest the flywheel end of the engine) and its associated HT lead, or as instructed by the maker of the timing light.
7 Remove the plug from the clutch housing aperture (where fitted). Clean the appropriate flywheel and housing timing marks with a piece of rag and mark them with a spot of white paint. For the correct degree mark, refer to the Specifications at the beginning of this Chapter.
8 Start the engine and adjust the engine idling speed (refer to Chapter 3 if necessary) to the correct setting as shown in the Specifications. If a tachometer is not fitted to the car, it will be necessary to obtain a unit that is suitable for use on electronic ignition systems. Some timing lights have a tachometer incorporated.
9 Aim the timing light at the clutch housing aperture and observe the timing marks. They will appear stationary, and if the timing is correct, the mark on the flywheel will be adjacent to the appropriate degree mark on the scale. If this is not the case, slacken the clamp bolt at the base of the distributor and then turn the distributor slowly in the desired direction (clockwise to retard the timing, anti-clockwise to advance it) until the mark on the flywheel is in line with the appropriate mark on the scale. Tighten the clamp bolt and recheck that the marks are still in alignment.

Fig. 4.3 Exploded view of the Bosch distributor (Sec 5)

1	Wiring plug	10	Ring
2	Connector	11	Circlip
3	Clip	12	Reluctor
4	Body	13	Magnetic coil
5	Vacuum unit	14	Stator
6	Distributor cap	15	Baseplate
7	Rotor arm	16	Clip
8	Cover	17	Shaft assembly
9	Bearing plate		

H145817

6.2 Flywheel timing mark and timing marks on plate – OHC engine

10 To check the centrifugal advance, increase the engine speed and note whether the white mark on the flywheel moves away from the mark on the scale. If it does, the centrifugal advance is functioning.

11 To check the vacuum advance, reconnect the vacuum pipe to the distributor. If the unit is functioning, this should also cause the timing marks to move away from each other slightly.

12 When all checks are completed, readjust the engine idling speed if necessary and then switch off and disconnect the timing light and tachometer (where applicable). Refit the air cleaner intake duct (where applicable).

13 If the centrifugal advance is suspected of malfunction, have it checked by a Peugeot dealer using the necessary diagnostic equipment.

7 TDC sensor – removal and refitting

1 The TDC sensor (photo) is for use with the diagnostic socket located on the clutch housing. As a special instrument and adaptor are required it will normally be used only by a Peugeot garage.

2 To remove the sensor, unscrew the mounting screw or release the clamp (as applicable).

3 The sensor forms part of the diagnostic socket assembly so, if it is to be completely removed, the socket must be unclipped from its bracket and the remaining wiring and earth leads disconnected.

4   Refitting is a reversal of removal, but the adjustment procedure for new and used sensors differs. New sensors have three extensions on the inner face and the unit should be inserted through the clamp until the extensions just touch the flywheel (photo). The clamp screw is then tightened and clearance is provided as the flywheel rotates and wears the ends of the extensions. This method should not be used when refitting a used sensor. In this case, cut off the extensions completely then temporarily insert the sensor until it touches the flywheel, remove it and reposition it in the clamp 1.0 mm (0.04 in) further out.

8   Ignition coil – general

1   The maintenance of the coil is minimal and is limited to periodically wiping its surfaces clean and dry and ensuring that the lead connectors are secure. High voltages generated by the coil can easily leak to earth over its surface and prevent the spark plugs from receiving the electrical pulses. Water repellent sprays are now available to prevent dampness causing this type of malfunction (photo).
2   Wipe clean and spray the HT leads and distributor cap also.
3   Special equipment is required to test a coil and is best left to an auto-electrician. Substitution of another coil is an alternative method of fault tracing.

9   Spark plugs, HT leads and distributor cap – general

1   The correct functioning of the spark plugs is vital for the correct running and efficiency of the engine, and is therefore important to keep them clean and correctly gapped.
2   To remove the plugs, first open the bonnet and pull the HT leads from them. Grip the rubber end fitting not the lead otherwise the lead

connection may be fractured. Also remove the extensions (photo).
3   The spark plugs are recessed in the cylinder head and it is recommended that dirt is removed from the recesses using a vacuum cleaner or compressed air, before removing the plugs, to prevent dirt dropping into the cylinders.
4   Unscrew the plugs using a suitable box spanner, such as the Peugeot type shown (photo). On some models, it will be necessary to remove the air filter intake duct to allow the No 1 spark plug to be removed. As each plug is removed, examine it before cleaning it.
5   Examination of the spark plugs will give a good indication of the condition of the engine. If the insulator nose of the spark plug is clean and white, with no deposits, this is indicative of a weak mixture, or too hot a plug (a hot plug transfers heat away from the electrode slowly, a cold plug transfers heat away quickly). The plugs fitted as standard are specified at the beginning of this Chapter.
6   If the top and insulator nose are covered with hard black-looking deposits, then this is indicative that the mixture is too rich. Should the plug be black and oily, then it is likely that the engine is fairly worn, as well as the mixture being too rich.
7   If the insulator nose is covered with light tan to greyish brown deposits, then the mixture is correct and it is likely that the engine is in good condition.
8   If there are any traces of long brown tapering stains on the outside of the white portion of the plug, then the plug will have to be renewed, as this shows that there is a faulty joint between the plug body and the insulator, and compression is being allowed to leak away.
9   Before cleaning a spark plug, wash it in petrol to remove oily deposits.
10 Although a wire brush can be used to clean the electrode end of the spark plug this method can cause metal conductance paths across the nose of the insulator. It is therefore to be preferred that an abrasive powder cleaning machine is used. Such machines are available quite cheaply from motor accessory stores or you may prefer to take the plugs to your dealer who will not only be able to clean them, but also

7.1 TDC sensor location in the clutch housing closing (belly) plate

7.4 TDC sensor showing the three extensions on the inner face

8.1 Ignition coil and connections – SRi model

9.2 Spark lead removal – grip and pull on the insulator/end fitting – not the lead

9.4 Spark plug removal using Peugeot box spanner

Measuring plug gap. A feeler gauge of the correct size (see ignition system specifications) should have a slight 'drag' when slid between the electrodes. Adjust gap if necessary

Adjusting plug gap. The plug gap is adjusted by bending the earth electrode inwards, or outwards, as necessary until the correct clearance is obtained. Note the use of the correct tool

Normal. Grey-brown deposits, lightly coated core nose. Gap increasing by around 0.001 in (0.025 mm) per 1000 miles (1600 km). Plugs ideally suited to engine, and engine in good condition

Carbon fouling. Dry, black, sooty deposits. Will cause weak spark and eventually misfire. Fault: over-rich fuel mixture. Check: carburettor mixture settings, float level and jet sizes; choke operation and cleanliness of air filter. Plugs can be re-used after cleaning

Oil fouling. Wet, oily deposits. Will cause weak spark and eventually misfire. Fault: worn bores/piston rings or valve guides; sometimes occurs (temporarily) during running-in period. Plugs can be re-used after thorough cleaning

Overheating. Electrodes have glazed appearance, core nose very white – few deposits. Fault: plug overheating. Check: plug value, ignition timing, fuel octane rating (too low) and fuel mixture (too weak). Discard plugs and cure fault immediately

Electrode damage. Electrodes burned away; core nose has burned, glazed appearance. Fault: pre-ignition. Check: as for 'Overheating' but may be more severe. Discard plugs and remedy fault before piston or valve damage occurs

Split core nose (may appear initially as a crack). Damage is self-evident, but cracks will only show after cleaning. Fault: pre-ignition or wrong gap-setting technique. Check: ignition timing, cooling system, fuel octane rating (too low) and fuel mixture (too weak). Discard plugs, rectify fault immediately to check the sparking efficiency of each plug under compression.

11 The spark plug gap is of considerable importance as, if it is too large or too small, the size of the spark and its efficiency will be seriously impaired. For the best results the spark plug gap should be set in accordance with the Specifications at the beginning of this Chapter.

12 To set it, measure the gap with a feeler gauge, and then bend open, or close, the outer plug electrode until the correct gap is achieved. The centre electrode should never be bent, as this may crack the insulation and cause plug failure, if nothing worse.

13 Special spark plug electrode gap adjusting tools are available from most motor accessory shops.

14 Before refitting the spark plugs check that the threaded connector sleeves are tight and that the plug exterior surfaces and threads are clean.

15 Screw in the spark plugs by hand where possible, then tighten them to the specified torque. Take extra care to enter the plug threads correctly as the cylinder head is of aluminium.

16 The OHC engine variants use a taper seat type spark plug which do not use washers. When tightening this type of plug, take care not to overtighten them. If a torque wrench is not available, tighten them as much as possible by hand, then a further $1/16$ th of a turn using the box wrench. Overtightening of this plug type will make them difficult to remove and damage would easily result.

17 Refit the extensions followed by the HT leads, making sure that the latter are in their correct order of 1-3-4-2 (No 1 nearest the clutch end of engine) in relation to the normal rotation of the rotor arm.

18 The HT leads and their connections should always be kept clean and dry and arranged neatly in the special holder. If any lead shows signs of cracking or chafing of the insulation it should be renewed.

19 Check the distributor cap whenever it is removed. If there are any very thin black lines running between the electrodes this indicates tracking and a new cap should be fitted. Check the rotor arm in a similar way. Where applicable check that the spring-tensioned carbon brush in the centre of the cap is free to move and is not worn excessively.

10 Fault diagnosis – ignition system

Symptom	Reason(s)
Starter turns but engine will not start	Faulty or disconnected leads Faulty spark plug Fault in ignition coil Fault in pick-up/starter unit
Engine starts but runs erratically	Incorrect timing Fouled spark plug Incorrectly connected HT leads Crack in distributor cap or rotor Poor battery, engine and earth connections

Chapter 5 Clutch

Contents

Specifications

General

Type	Single plate with diaphragm spring. Cable operation
Driven plate clutch disc outer diameter:	
OHV engines	181 mm (7.13 in)
OHC engines	200 mm (7.87 in)
Adjustment:	
Clutch pedal travel	140 mm (5.5 in)

Torque wrench settings

	Nm	lbf ft
Clutch cover bolts:		
OHV engines	15	11
OHC engines	25	18

1 General description

The clutch is of diaphragm spring, single dry plate type with cable actuation.

The clutch pedal pivots in a bracket mounted under the facia and operates a cable to the clutch release arm (or fork). The release lever operates a thrust bearing (clutch release bearing) which bears on the diaphragm spring of the pressure plate, and releases the clutch driven plate from the flywheel. The driven plate (or disc) is splined to a shaft which transmits the drive to the gearbox.

The clutch release mechanism consists of a fork and bearing which are in permanent contact with release fingers on the pressure plate assembly. The fork pushes the release bearing forwards to bear against the release fingers, so moving the centre of the diaphragm spring inwards. The spring is sandwiched between two rings which act as fulcrum points. As the centre of the spring is pushed in, the outside of the spring is pushed out, so moving the pressure plate backwards and disengaging it from the clutch driven plate.

When the clutch pedal is released, the diaphragm spring forces the pressure plate into contact with the friction linings on the driven plate and at the same time pushes the driven plate a fraction of an inch

forwards on its splines so engaging it with the flywheel. The driven plate is now firmly sandwiched between the pressure plate and the flywheel, so the drive is taken up.

As wear takes place on the driven plate friction linings the diaphragm fingers move outwards and the pedal stroke decreases; the cable mechanism incorporates an adjustment to compensate for this wear.

2 Routine maintenace

Carry out the following procedures at the intervals given in Routine Maintenance at the beginning of the manual.

1 Depress the clutch pedal fully three times then, using a rule, measure the total stroke of the pedal pad.

2 If the stroke is not as given in the specifications it will be necessary to adjust the clutch cable.

3 To make the adjustment, loosen the locknut at the gearbox end of the cable, turn the adjusting nut as required, then retighten the locknut.

4 Before checking the adjustment, fully operate the clutch pedal three times.

Fig. 5.1 Clutch pedal stroke (X) adjustment diagram (Sec 2)

1   Adjustment nut and locknut

3 Clutch cable – removal and refitting

1   Working in the engine compartment, loosen the locknut and slacken the cable adjustment (photo).
2   Release the cable end fitting from the intermediate lever. Recover the pushrod (where applicable).
3   Remove the metal clip which secures the clutch cable to the underside of the car.
4   Working inside the car, remove the lower facia panel from the steering column.
5   Pull off the spring clip and remove the clevis pin from the top of the pedal to disconnect the cable end.
6   Release the cable from the bulkhead by twisting the plastic grommet through a quarter of a turn and withdraw it into the engine compartment.
7   Refitting is a reversal of removal, but finally adjust the pedal stroke, as described in Section 2.

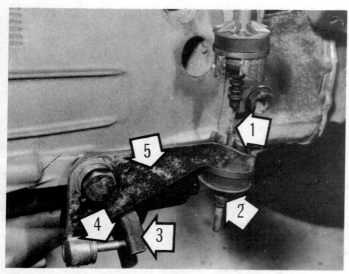

3.1 Clutch cable and associated fittings at the transmission end
1   Clutch cable   4   Pushrod (where applicable)
2   Adjustment and locknuts   5   Relay lever
3   Release lever

4 Clutch pedal – removal and refitting

1   Working in the engine compartment, loosen the locknut and slacken the cable adjustment.
2   Working inside the car, remove the lower facia panel from the steering column.
3   Pull off the spring clip and remove the clevis pin from the top of the pedal to disconnect the cable end.
4   Unhook the cable tension spring from the pedal.
5   Unscrew the nut from the pivot bolt, pull out the bolt and lower the clutch pedal from the bracket.
6   Examine the pedal bushes for wear and renew them if necessary.
7   Refitting is a reversal of removal, but lightly grease the bushes and clevis pin, finally adjust the pedal stroke, as described in Section 2.

5 Clutch – removal

1   Remove the gearbox only leaving the engine and clutch unit *in situ* as described in Chapter 6, or remove the engine and gearbox units combined, then separate as described in Chapter 1.
2   Mark the clutch pressure plate in relation to the flywheel then progressively loosen the bolts. If necessary hold the flywheel stationary using a screwdriver engaged with the starter ring gear.
3   With all the bolts removed lift the pressure plate assembly from the location dowels followed by the driven plate. Note the orientation of the driven plate to ensure correct refitting.

6 Clutch – inspection and renovation

1   The clutch driven plate should be inspected for wear and for contamination by oil. Wear is gauged by the depth of the rivet heads

Fig. 5.2 Clutch pedal components (Sec 4)

1   Pivot bolt   6   Clevis pin
2   Bush   7   Pedal
3   Spacer   8   Bush
4   Tension spring (circular type   9   Nut
    on some models)   10 Pad
5   Clip

below the surface of the friction material. If this is less than 0.6 mm (0.024 in) the linings are worn enough to justify renewal.

2   Examine the friction faces of the flywheel and clutch pressure plate. These should be bright and smooth. If the linings have worn too much it is possible that the metal surfaces may have been scored by the rivet heads. Dust and grit can have the same effect. If the scoring is very severe it could mean that even with a new clutch driven plate, slip and juddering and other malfunctions will recur. Deep scoring on the flywheel face is serious because the flywheel will have to be removed and machined by a specialist, or renewed. If the pressure plate is worn excessively it must be renewed. If the driven plate friction linings are contaminated with oil, the plate must be renewed and the source of the oil traced and rectified.

3   Replacement of the crankshaft rear oil seal is possible after removing the flywheel and is described in Chapter 1. If the oil leak is from the gearbox, renew the input shaft oil seal as described in Chapter 6. If in doubt, renew both the crankshaft rear oil seal and the gearbox input shaft seal.

4   If the reason for removal of the clutch has been because of slip and the slip has been allowed to go on for any length of time, it is possible that the heat generated will have adversely affected the diaphragm spring in the cover with the result that the pressure is now uneven and/or insufficient to prevent slip, even with a new driven plate. Where this occurs, the friction surfaces on the flywheel and pressure plate will often show a blue discoloration necessitating the renewal of the pressure plate.

5   With the clutch removed, the release bearing should be checked for excessive wear and noise, and renewed if necessary. Also check the spigot bush in the crankshaft rear flange for wear and, if necessary, renew it.

7   Clutch – refitting

1   Ensure that the friction surfaces are clean of dirt and free from grease then commence refitting by offering the driven plate to the flywheel (photo), making sure it is the right way round. It will only fit one way. Retain the disc in position by inserting a centering mandrel. Various proprietary centering tools are available, or alternatively one can be made from a piece of dowel or bar built up with tape.

2   Fit the pressure plate, observing the alignment marks made when dismantling if the old plate is being refitted. Insert the six bolts and just nip them up so that the driven plate is lightly nipped.

3   Make sure that the driven plate is accurately centred, either by visual inspection or by inserting an old gearbox input shaft. If the plate is not centred it will not be possible to refit the gearbox.

4   With the centering mandrel in position, tighten the pressure plate securing bolts progressively to the special torque. Remove the centering mandrel (photo).

5   Prior to refitting the gearbox, lubricate the clutch mechanism components (release bearing tube, fork balljoint and fingers, and shaft splines) with Molykote 321R, but take great care not to get any lubricant onto the clutch friction surfaces.

6   Refit the gearbox referring to Chapter 1 or 6 as applicable.

8   Clutch release mechanism – overhaul

1   Remove the gearbox, as described in Chapter 6.
2   Release the spring clips and slide the bearing from the guide sleeve.
3   Withdraw the release fork from the ball-stud.
4   Where applicable, the pivot bush may be removed as follows. First drill out the rivets which secure the old bush. Remove the bush and discard it. Position the new bush on the fork and pass its rivets through the holes. Heat the rivets with a cigarette lighter or a low powered blowlamp, then peen over their heads while they are still hot.
5   Lightly coat the bush with grease, then refit the release fork. Press it onto the ball-stud until it snaps home.
6   If the ball-stud requires renewal, remove it with a slide hammer having a suitable claw. Support the casing and drive in the new stud using a soft metal drift.
7   Refit the remaining components using a reversal of the removal procedure.

7.1 Locating the driven plate – note direction of fitting

Fig. 5.3 Clutch disc centralizing tool showing dimension requirements (in mm) (Sec 7)

7.4 Centralising the driven plate and tightening the clutch cover bolts

H.20124

Fig. 5.4 Clutch release mechanism and associated components (Sec 8)

1	Guide sleeve	4	Protective boot	7	Locking plate	10 Seal cap
2	Plug – OHC engine	5	Gasket	8	Fork lever	11 Plug
3	Lower plug – OHC engine	6	Gasket	9	Ball-stud	12 Release fork gaiter

9 Fault diagnosis – clutch

Symptom	Reason(s)
Judder when taking up drive	Loose engine/gearbox mountings Badly worn friction linings or contaminated with oil Worn splines on input shaft or driven plate hub Worn spigot bush in crankshaft flange
Clutch drag (failure to disengage so that gears cannot be meshed)	Incorrect cable adjustment Rust on splines (may occur after vehicle standing idle for long periods) Damaged or misaligned pressure plate assembly Cable stretched or broken
Clutch slip (increase in engine speed does not result in increase in vehicle road speed – particularly on gradients)	Incorrect cable adjustment Friction linings worn out or oil contaminated
Noise evident on depressing clutch pedal	Dry, worn or damaged release bearing Excessive play between drive plate hub splines and shaft splines
Noise evident as clutch pedal released	Distorted driven plate Broken or weak driven plate cushion coil springs Release bearing loose on retainer hub

Chapter 6 Transmission

For modifications, and information applicable to later models, see Supplement at end of manual

Contents

Specifications

General

Type	Manual gearbox with 4 or 5 forward speeds plus reverse. All forward speeds have synchromesh

Identification codes:
4-speed	BE1/4
5-speed	BE1/5

Ratios:
	BE1/4	BE1/5
1st	3.31:1	3.31:1
2nd	1.88:1	1.88:1
3rd	1.15:1	1.28:1
4th	0.80:1	0.97:1
5th	–	0.76:1
Reverse	3.33:1	3.33:1

Final drive ratios:
1.1 litre	4.43:1
1.3 litre	4.06:1
1.6 litre	3.81:1

Lubrication

Oil type/specification	Multigrade engine oil, viscosity SAE 10W/40 (Duckhams QXR, Hypergrade, or 10W/40 Motor Oil)
Capacity	2.0 litre (3.5 pints)

Torque wrench settings

	Nm	lbf ft
Rear cover bolts (use thread locking compound)	12	9
Input and output shaft nuts	50	37
Rear bearing retainer bolts	15	11
Selector rod backplate bolt	15	11
End casing to main casing bolts	12	9
Reverse idler spindle bolt	20	15
Selector shaft spring bracket	15	11
Reverse selector spindle nut	20	15
Breather	15	11
Reversing lamp switch	25	18
Drain plug (gearbox)	9	7
Drain plug (final drive)	30	22
Speedometer pinion adaptor	12	9
Final drive extension housing bolts	15	11
Crownwheel securing bolts	65	48
Final drive half housing bolts, 10 mm	41	30
Final drive half housing bolts, 7 mm	12	9
Clutch release bearing guide tube bolts	12	9
Mounting stud nut	100	74

1 General description

A four or five-speed gearbox will be fitted depending on the vehicle model. The 5th speed gears of the BE1/5 gearbox are located on the primary and secondary shafts, but otherwise both gearbox types are similar in construction.

The transmission is of conventional two shaft constant-mesh layout. There are four pairs of gears, one for each forward speed. The gears on the primary shaft are fixed to the shaft, while those on the secondary or pinion shaft float, each being locked to the shaft when engaged by the synchromesh unit. The reverse idler gear is on a third shaft.

Fig. 6.1 Sectional view of the BE1/5 transmission (Sec 1)

1	Input shaft	8	5th gear (driving)	14	1st gear (driven)
2	Release bearing guide tube	9	5th synchro	15	Output shaft
3	Casings	10	5th gear (driven)	16	Crownwheel
4	Reverse idler gear	11	3rd/4th gears (driven)	17	Differential gear
5	3rd gear (driving)	12	2nd gear (driven)	18	Side gear
6	3rd/4th synchro	13	1st/2nd synchro	19	Differential carrier
7	4th gear (driving)				

20	Speedo driving gear
21	Extension housing
a	Selective shim – input shaft bearing preload
b	Selective shim – differential bearing preload

On five-speed units, the 5th speed gears are of fixed type with an extra synchromesh assembly.

The gear selector forks engage in the synchromesh unit; these slide axially along the shaft to engage the appropriate gear. The forks are mounted on selector shafts which are located in the base of the gearbox.

The helical gear on the end of the pinion shaft drives directly onto the crownwheel mounted on the differential unit. The latter differs from normal practice in that it runs in shell bearings and the end play is taken up by thrust washers in a similar manner to the engine crankshaft.

2 Routine maintenance

1   The only regular maintenance required is to change the transmission oil at the specified intervals. The oil level, drain and filler plug locations differ in accordance with the model year and are shown in Figs. 6.2 and 6.3.

2   On earlier models there is no transmission level plug, and to check the level the oil must be drained completely by removing the gearbox and final drive drain plugs, then measuring the total amount drained to see if it complies with the amount specified.

3   When draining later models, the removal of the differential unit

Fig. 6.2 Oil drain and filler plug positions – early 1986 models (Sec 2)

a	Gearbox drain plug	c	Oil filler plug
b	Final drive drain plug		

Fig. 6.3 Gearbox/final drive level plug location (arrowed) – 1986 on (Sec 2)

A

B

Fig. 6.4 Early (A) and late (B) type gearboxes (Sec 2)

1 Breather	2 Reverse lock mechanism	3 Breather

drain plug drains both the differential and gearbox housing oils. As a combined level/filler plug is fitted to later models, draining is only necessary when removing the transmission unit or when renewing the transmission oil.

4   When checking the oil level in the transmission on later models with a combined level/filler plug, the oil level must be up to the base of the plug hole.

5   On earlier models, a differential level plug was fitted, but this was deleted with the introduction of the reverse lock mechanism (in early 1986), when the breather location was also changed (Fig. 6.4).

6   Access to the oil drain and filler/level plugs may necessitate the removal of the engine undertray and the side shields.

7   Do not overfill the transmission and use only the specified grade of oil. On completion ensure that the drain and filler plugs are secured to the specified torque wrench settings.

8   On earlier models, where the oil filler plug does not act as a level gauge as well, measure out the required amount of oil before filling.

9   Apart from the regular oil change at the specified intervals the oil should be changed in a new or reconditioned unit after the first 1000 to 1500 miles, and in any unit after detection and rectification of an oil leak.

3   Gearchange linkage – general

1   The gearchange linkage assemblies are shown in Figs. 6.5 and 6.6.

2   The gear selector and engagement rods have balljoint connections. The balljoints can be detached by prising them free from the lever balls, using an open-ended spanner.

3   The balljoints are 'long-life' types and as such require no maintenance, but if gear selection becomes difficult, the joints should be checked for excessive wear, and if necessary renewed.

4   The balljoint at one end of the selector and engagement rod is screwed onto the rod and secured by a locknut. If the balljoint is to be removed at any time, first measure the length of the rod between the balljoint centres and make a note of it. When refitting the balljoint to the rod set it at the distance noted to retain the adjustment and secure with the locknut. When reconnecting the balljoints, the use of self-locking pliers will facilitate the job.

5   Access to the gearlever can be obtained after removing the floor console and gaiter.

6   The gearchange rods should be set to the following lengths (centre-to-centre of ball end fittings)

Engagement rod	283.0 to 285.0 mm
Selection rod	110.0 to 113.0 mm

H.20125

Fig. 6.5 Gearchange selector rods and associated components (Sec 3)

1 Layshaft (pivot bolt)	5 Bush	8 Lever (gearshift passage)	11 Heat shield
2 Bush	6 Snap ring	9 Countershaft	12 Engagement rod
3 Spring	7 Lever (gear selection)	10 Protector cap	13 Gear selection rod
4 Ball-head screw			

Fig. 6.6 Gear lever and associated components (Sec 3)

1	Gear selector lever	6	Plate	10	Reverse stop cable	14	Half-bearing
2	Gear lever knob	7	Rubber dowel	11	Bearing support	15	Lever bush
3	Half-bearing	8	Upper sleeve	12	Gearshift passage bar	16	Lever shaft
4	Boot	9	Lower sleeve	13	Gear selector bar	17	Cable support clip
5	Gasket						

4 Gearbox removal methods

1 The gearbox can be removed together with the engine as described in Chapter 1, or on its own leaving the engine in position.
2 Whichever method is employed, the gearbox will have to be withdrawn from underneath the vehicle and requires the vehicle to be raised at the front end to allow sufficient working clearance.
3 Safety stands will be required to support the vehicle at the front end and the manufacturers recommend that the front suspension be retained with special cables as described in Chapter 9, Section 4.

5 Gearbox – removal and refitting

1 Disconnect the battery earth lead, then the positive lead and remove the battery.
2 Remove the engine undertray and the side shield under the left-hand wheel arch.
3 Drain the transmission oil, with reference to Section 2, then refit the drain plug(s). The oil should be drained into a suitable container for disposal.
4 Retain the suspension strut each side at the front using the Peugeot special tool (see Chapter 9, Section 4).
5 Undo the driveshaft hub nut each side, then raise and support the front end of the vehicle on safety stands.
6 Working underneath the vehicle, undo the retaining nuts and detach the exhaust downpipe from the manifold flange.
7 Disconnect the gearchange rod and selector rod from the gearbox by prising free the balljoints (photo).

5.7 Gear selector rod viewed from underneath. Note the heatshield (arrowed)

8 Disconnect the speedometer cable and the reverse stop cable at the gearbox.
9 Remove the starter motor as described in Chapter 12.
10 Unbolt and remove the clutch housing closing (belly) plate together with the TDC sensor and cable.
11 Disconnect the suspension arm from the steering knuckle at the balljoint each side, referring to Chapter 10 for details.
12 Remove the balljoint protectors but take care not to damage the balljoint boots – protect with a cloth.
13 Remove the left-hand driveshaft as described in Chapter 7.
14 Unbolt and remove the torque reaction link.
15 Remove the right-hand driveshaft with reference to Chapter 7.
16 Remove the fuel system air cleaner and ducting with reference to Chapter 3.
17 On fuel injection models, remove the airflow sensor unit (see Chapter 3).

18 Disconnect the clutch cable from the operating lever and transmission (see Chapter 5).
19 Disconnect the earth cable from the transmission unit (noting its connection point) and also the reversing light switch wire connector.
20 On models with the ignition coil mounted on top of the clutch housing, disconnect the coil leads and unclip the wiring harness from the battery tray. Unbolt and remove the coil support bracket and refit one of the bolts.
21 Undo and remove the clutch housing-to-engine lower retaining bolts.
22 Support the weight of the engine using a sling and hoist.
23 Remove the upper nut from the flexible engine mounting on the left-hand side, then remove the mounting.
24 Lower the power unit a little so that the battery tray bolts are accessible. Undo the bolts and remove the tray.
25 Support the weight of the gearbox from underneath, then unscrew and remove the upper transmission-to-engine mounting bolts.
26 Check that all attachments are disconnected and out of the way then withdraw the transmission from the engine. If possible get an assistant to lend a hand here to help steady the engine and/or gearbox as necessary as the two are separated. Do not allow the weight of the gearbox to be supported by the input shaft as it is withdrawn. Keep the two units parallel until they are disengaged, then lower the transmission and withdraw it from under the vehicle.
27 Refitting is a reversal of the removal procedure but note the following special points.

> (a) Ensure that all mating surfaces are clean
> (b) Renew the drain plug washers, Nylstop nuts, lockwashers and the final drive oil seals
> (c) Lubricate the input shaft with a liberal amount of Molykote 321R grease, but do not get grease onto or near the clutch friction surfaces
> (d) Tighten all fastenings to their specified torque wrench settings (where given)
> (e) Do not remove the engine support hoist until the engine and transmission units are securely located
> (f) Refer to Chapter 7 when refitting the driveshafts
> (g) Refer to Chapter 10 when refitting the lower suspension arm to the left-hand steering knuckle

28 On completion top up the gearbox/final drive oil level with the specified grade and quantity of oil (see Section 2).

6 Gearbox – preliminary overhaul notes

Although the transmission system employed is relatively simple, a few words of warning must be stressed before any inexperienced dismantlers start work to make sure that they know what they are letting themselves in for.

First of all decide whether the fault you wish to repair is worth the time and effort involved. Secondly bear in mind that, if the transmission is well worn, then the cost of the necessary component parts could well exceed the cost of an exchange factory unit and, furthermore, you will get a guaranteed job without the bother of having to do it yourself. Thirdly, if you are intent on doing it yourself, make sure that you understand how the transmission works.

Special care must be taken during all dismantling and assembly operations to ensure that the housing is not overstressed or distorted in any way. When dismantled, check the cost and availability of the parts to be renewed and compare this against the cost of a replacement unit, which may not be much more expensive and therefore would be a better proposition.

On reassembly, take careful note of the tightening procedures and torque wrench settings of the relevant nuts and bolts. This is most important to prevent overtightening, distortion and oil leakage, and also to ensure smooth, trouble-free running of the unit.

7 Gearbox – dismantling into major assemblies

1 Remove the eight bolts and washers which secure the end cover. Remove the cover (photo).

7.1 Removing the gearbox end cover

7.3 Alignment mark for 5th gear synchro-hub and sleeve

7.5 5th gear selector fork and roll pin (arrowed)

7.7 Unscrewing the input shaft nut

7.9 Unscrewing the output shaft nut

7.12 Remove the selector rod lockplate bolt

Four-speed transmission

2   On four-speed units, release the nuts on the input and output shafts. In order to prevent the shafts from rotating, engage a gear by moving a selector fork and then hold the input shaft using a tool made up from an old clutch driven plate to which a lever has been welded (Fig. 6.7). Do not grip the shaft splines with a tool.

Five-speed transmission

3   On five-speed units, use a dab of quick drying paint to mark the alignment of the 5th speed gear synchro-hub and its sleeve (photo).
4   Engage 5th gear by moving the selector fork.
5   Drive out the roll pin which secures 5th gear fork to its selector rod (photo).
6   Hold 5th gear selector fork in the engaged position and return the gear selector to neutral so that the selector passes through the fork.
7   Engage any other gear to lock up the shafts, then unscrew and remove the 28 mm nut from the end of the input shaft. If the nut is staked in position it may be necessary to relieve the staking (photo).
8   Remove 5th gear synchro-hub, sliding sleeve and selector fork from the input shaft. Be prepared for the ejection of the detent ball from the selector fork.
9   Refit the 5th gear sliding sleeve and hub and engage 5th gear again. Relieve the staking from the output shaft nut and remove the nut. Remove the sliding sleeve and hub again (photo).
10 Remove from the input shaft the 5th gear, its bush and the spacer.

Four- and five-speed transmissions

11 Remove the two bolts and washers which secure the output shaft rear bearing. Remove the circlip from the output shaft rear bearing by prising up its ends. The circlip should be renewed anyway, so do not be afraid of breaking it. Raise the output shaft if the circlip is jammed in its groove.
12 Extract its securing bolt and remove the selector rod lockplate (photo).

H14558

Fig. 6.7 Typical tool for locking the input shaft on the 4-speed gearbox (Sec 7)

A   Lever   *B   Old clutch driven plate*

7.15 Selector arm, spring, circlip, washer and O-ring

7.17 Selector shaft cover and reverse lamp switch (arrows)

7.19 Removing the reverse idler spindle

13 Remove the bolt which retains the reverse idler gear spindle. The belt location is on the lower side face of the end case.

14 Remove the thirteen bolts and washers which secure the end casing to the main casing. Withdraw the end casing; it is located by dowels, and may need striking with a wooden or plastic mallet to free it. Do not use a metal hammer, nor lever in between the joint faces.

15 Remove the selector arm and spring from the gear selector shaft. Remove the circlip and washer, push the shaft in and recover the O-ring (photo).

16 Drive out the roll pins which secure the selector finger and the interlock bracket to the selector shaft.

17 Use pliers or a self-gripping wrench to remove the cover from the end of the selector shaft (if required) (photo).

18 Press the selector shaft from the casing so that the circlip can be removed then push it back in reverse and out of the casing.

19 Screw the reverse idler spindle retaining bolt back into the spindle and use it as a lever to extract the spindle. Remove the reverse idler gear itself (photo).

20 Remove the swarf-collecting magnet from the casing (photo).

21 Carefully lift out the two geartrains with their shafts, the selector forks and the selector rods.

22 Remove the selector rod spring support bracket from inside the main casing.

23 Extract the lubrication jet, using a wire hook.

24 Unscrew and remove the reversing lamp switch.

25 Remove the nut and washer which secure the reverse selector fork spindle. Remove the spindle and selector fork. Recover the detent plunger and spring.

26 Unscrew and remove the breather from the main casing.

27 Turning to the clutch housing, remove the clutch release bearing (if not already done). Pull off the release fork.

28 Unbolt and remove the release bearing guide tube.

29 From behind the tube remove the preload shim and the outer track of the input shaft front bearing.

30 To remove the final drive unit, first unbolt and remove the speedometer pinion and its adaptor.

31 Unbolt and remove the extension housing. Recover the speedometer driving gear and the bearing preload shim (if fitted).

32 Unbolt the final drive half housing. Remove the half housing and final drive unit. Note the location of the gearchange pivot bracket.

33 Identify the final drive bearing outer tracks; if they are to be re-used they must be refitted on the same sides.

34 Remove the selector lever from the main casing. It is retained by a circlip and a washer.

35 If it is wished to remove the clutch release lever balljoint, do so with a slide hammer having a suitable claw. (A new gearbox will not necessarily be fitted with a balljoint).

36 The gearbox is now dismantled into its major assemblies.

8 Input shaft – dismantling

1 Remove the 3rd and 4th gear components from the input shaft by supporting the assembly under the 3rd gear and pressing or driving the shaft through. Protect the end of the shaft. Once the rear bearing is free, the other components can be removed from the shaft in order: 4th gear and its bush, 3rd/4th synchro sleeve and hub and 3rd gear (photos).

2 Mark the synchro sleeve and hub relative to each other and to show which side faces 4th gear (Fig. 6.8).

3 Remove the front bearing from the shaft, preferably with a press or a bearing puller. As a last resort it may be possible to support the bearing and drive the shaft through; be sure to protect the end of the shaft if this is done.

4 Once the input shaft bearings have been removed, they must be renewed. Press the rear bearing outer track from the end casing and press in the new track, making sure it enters squarely.

7.20 Withdraw the casing magnet

8.1A Input shaft bearing

8.1B 4th gear on the input shaft

8.1C 4th gear bush

8.1D 3rd/4th synchro sleeve on input shaft

8.1E 3rd/4th synchro-hub on input shaft

8.1F 3rd gear on input shaft

8.1G Input shaft stripped except for front bearing

Fig. 6.8 Input shaft components (Sec 8)

1   4th gear bush
2   4th gear
3   Sliding sleeve and hub
4   3rd gear

Note alignment marks across hub and sleeve faces (arrowed)

9   Output shaft – dismantling

1   Remove 5th gear (when applicable) and the rear bearing from the output shaft. Use a puller or bearing extractor if they are a tight fit on the shaft (photo).
2   Remove 3rd/4th gear assembly, 2nd gear and its bush (photos).

3   Make alignment marks between the 1st/2nd synchro-hub and sleeve, then remove them from the shaft (photo).
4   Remove 1st gear and the thrust bearing. Remove the bearing circlip (photos).
5   Press or drive the shaft out of the pinion end bearing, protecting the end of the shaft.

9.1 Output shaft rear bearing

9.2A 3rd/4th gear assembly on output shaft

9.2B 2nd gear on output shaft

9.2C 2nd gear bush

9.3 1st/2nd sychro sleeve on output shaft

9.4A 1st gear on output shaft

9.4B Needle thrust bearing

9.4C Output shaft bearing circlip (arrowed)

Fig. 6.9 Output shaft components (Sec 9)

3 5th gear (driven)   5 3rd/4th gear (driven)   7 Bush (2nd gear)
4 Bearing   6 2nd gear

Fig. 6.10 Differential components (Sec 10)

1   *Crownwheel (ring gear)*
2   *Pinion shaft (spindle)*
3   *Pinion gear*
4   *Friction cup*
5   *Centering tube*
6   *Pinion gears (planet)*
7   *Housing*
8   *Crownwheel bolt*
9   *Bearing*
A   *Roll pin (secured pinion shaft)*

10 Differential – dismantling

1   Unbolt the crownwheel from the differential housing (Fig. 6.10).
2   Remove the side gears by pushing them round inside the housing until they can be removed (photo).
3   Drive out the roll pins which secure the differential gear spindle.
4   Remove the spindle, the differential gears and their washers (photo).
5   Use a press or bearing extractor to remove the bearings.

11 Selector mechanism – dismantling

1   On early models the selector mechanism assembly is as shown in Fig. 6.11, whilst later models (from about April 1986 on) have the type shown in Fig. 6.12.

2   With both types, the detent springs and balls are located in the selector forks and are secured by roll pins (photos).
3   If the detent balls and springs are to be removed, support the selector fork so that it will not be damaged or distorted, then drive out the roll pin, but catch the spring and ball as they are released. Keep them with their respective selector fork.
4   If removing the selector forks from their shafts note their orientation and fitting position prior to separation to avoid confusion when reassembling.

12 Gearbox components – examination and renovation

1   Having removed and dismantled the transmission unit, the various components should be thoroughly washed with a suitable solvent or with petrol and paraffin, and then wiped dry. Take care not to mix to lose identification of where they fit and which way round they should be fitted. Don't use hard scrapers or emery cloth to clean

10.2 Removing a differential side gear

10.4 Differential spindle, gears and thrust washer removal

11.2A 1st/2nd and 3rd/4th selector rod and fork assembly (later type)

11.2B Detent spring and ball port in the selector showing the retaining pin (arrowed)

11.2C View showing roll pin, detent spring and ball – 5th gear selector

Fig. 6.11 Selector mechanism – early type (Sec 11)

1   1st/2nd fork   3   Rod with 5th gear fork dog
2   3rd/4th fork   4   Selector rod (fixed)

Fig. 6.12 Selector mechanism – late type (Sec 11)

1   1st/2nd fork   3   Rod with 5th gear fork dog
2   3rd/4th fork   4   Selector rod (fixed)

the housing mating faces as the surface must be kept perfectly flat and undamaged.

2   Inspect the transmission housing and the differential unit housing for cracks or damage, particularly near bearings or bushes. The transmission housing, differential housing and the mainshaft centre bearing cap are all machined after assembly and none of these parts must be renewed separately.

3   Components requiring special attention will have been noted as a result of the performance of the transmission when installed in the car or will have been noted during dismantling.

4   Examine the teeth of all gears for signs of uneven or excessive wear or chipping. If you find a gear in a bad state have a close look at the gear it engages with – this may have to be renewed as well. All gears should run smoothly on their bushes or in their bearings with no sign of rocking or sloppiness.

5   A not so obvious cause of noise and trouble is bearing wear. Wash

and dry the bearings thoroughly and examine them closely for signs of scoring, pitted tracks or blueing. Rotate the races and feel for smooth movement with no grittiness or abnormal noise. A new ball-bearing will show no perceptible axial movement between the inner and outer races. As the bearing wears, some play will be evident but if this is excessive the bearing must be renewed. After examining bearings they should be lubricated with engine oil to prevent corrosion, and wrapped to avoid contamination with dust and dirt.

6 Carefully inspect the synchromesh units for excessive wear or damage. If weak or ineffective synchromesh action has been experienced, renew the units as complete assemblies.

7 Check the selector forks for wear in the areas which contact the synchromesh units. Any wear evident should be minimal; if in doubt renew the forks.

8 Inspect the selector shafts and detents for wear which can cause imprecise gear changing, and renew where necessary.

9 All remaining components such as the speedometer gears, locking plungers, springs, balls, and so on, should be inspected for signs of wear or damage and, where necessary, renewed.

10 It is now worth reviewing the total requirements needed to restore the transmission unit to full serviceability, not forgetting the new lockwashers, circlips, roll pins, seals and gaskets. Compare the cost with that of an overhauled or good condition secondhand unit as it may be more economical to go for one of these alternatives.

11 If new input shaft or differential bearings are to be fitted, a selection of preload shims will be required. Read through the relevant procedures before starting work.

13 Input shaft – reassembly

1 Before commencing reassembly, make sure that the input shaft is free from burrs and wear marks. Lubricate all parts as they are fitted.

2 Fit a new front bearing to the shaft, using a suitable tube to press or drive it home.

3 Fit 3rd gear, 3rd/4th synchro-hub and sleeve, 4th gear and its bush. Take care not to get 3rd and 4th gears mixed up, they are similar in appearance (4th gear has more teeth). If the original synchro components are being refitted, observe the mating marks made during dismantling.

4 Fit a new rear bearing to the shaft, again using a piece of tubing.

5 The input shaft is now reassembled (photo).

14 Output shaft – reassembly

1 Before commencing reassembly, make sure that the shaft is free from burrs or wear marks. Lubricate all parts as they are fitted.

2 Fit the pinion end bearing to the shaft, using a piece of tubing to drive or press it home.

3 Fit the thrust bearing into position against the pinion end bearing then slide 1st gear onto the shaft and up to the thrust bearing.

4 Refit the 1st/2nd synchro unit, observing the mating marks made when dismantling. The chamfer on the external teeth must face towards 1st gear.

5 Fit 2nd gear and its bush.

6 Fit the 3rd/4th gear assembly, making sure it is the right way round.

7 Fit the rear bearing, with the circlip groove nearest the tail of the shaft.

8 On five-speed units, fit the 5th gear so that the boss on the gear is towards the shaft bearing (photo).

9 On four-speed units, fit the shaft spacer (Fig. 6.13).

10 Screw on a nut, but do not tighten at this stage.

15 Differential – reassembly

1 Fit the bearings, using a piece of tube to press or drive them home.

2 Fit the spindle with the differential gears and washers. Secure the spindle with new roll pins, which should be driven in until they are centrally located in their holes (photo).

3 Fit the side gears, one at a time, and work them into their proper positions.

4 Fit the crownwheel with its chamfer towards the differential housing. Secure with the bolts, tightening them in diagonal sequence to the specified torque (photos).

16 Selector mechanism – reassembly

1 Reassemble the selector forks to the rods, ensuring that their orientation is correct as noted during removal. Lubricate the shafts with oil to ease assembly.

2 Insert the detent ball and spring into the selector fork and, compressing the spring with a suitable rod, drive the new roll pin into position in the fork. Once the pin is retaining the spring, the rod used to compress the spring can be removed, and the roll pin fully fitted.

3 Check that the forks move on the shaft and lock into their detent positions.

17 Gearbox – reassembly

1 The only difference in reassembling the four-speed transmission apart from the obvious absence of 5th gear components, lies in the

13.5 Input shaft assembly

14.8 Output shaft assembly

H14561

Fig. 6.13 Shaft spacer (A) on four-speed gearbox (Sec 14)

casing. Make sure that the locating dowel is in position in the final drive housing mating face.

4 Apply jointing compound to the mating face, then fit the differential assembly with its bearing tracks.

5 Before proceeding further it must be noted that the preload procedure for the differential bearings differs according to the type of extension housing fitted. On earlier models the extension housing shoulder protrusion is 8.65 mm (0.341 in) and shims are used to set the bearing preload. On later models the extension housing shoulder protrusion is 10 mm (0.394 in) and in this instance no preload shims are required. To clarify which type is being fitted measure the shoulder protrusion of the extension housing. For the earlier type extension housing, proceed as described in paragraphs 6 to 12 inclusive. For the later type extension housing proceed as described in paragraphs 6, 11 and 12 but ignore the reference to preload shims in paragraph 12. As the extension housing bolts are tightened, turn the differential to seat the bearings.

6 Fit the final drive half housing and the extension housing, but only tighten their securing bolts finger tight at this stage (photo).

7 Fit a new oil seal, lips well greased, to the other side of the final drive housing from the extension (photo).

8 Remove the extension housing, fit a preload shim 2.2 mm thick to the bearing outer track and refit the extension housing (without its O-ring). Rotate the crownwheel while tightening the extension housing bolts until the crownwheel *just* starts to drag. This operation seats the bearings.

9 Remove the extension housing and the preload shim. With an accurate depth gauge, measure the distance from the final drive housing joint face to the bearing outer track. Call this dimension A. Similarly measure the protrusion of the spigot on the extension housing above the joint face. Call this dimension B (photos).

10 The thickness S of preload shim required is determined by the formula:

$$S = (A-B) + 0.10 \text{ mm}$$

The extra 0.10 mm is the preload factor for the bearings. Shims are available in thicknesses of 1.1 to 2.2 mm in steps of 0.1 mm.

11 Tighten the final drive half housing securing bolts to the specified torque (photo).

12 Fit the preload shim just determined (where applicable), and the speedometer driving gear and the extension housing with a new O-ring. Tighten the securing bolts to the specified torque. Make sure that the crownwheel is still free to rotate (photos).

13 Fit a new oil seal, lips well greased, into the extension housing.

14 Fit a new gear selector shaft oil seal in the main casing.

15 From the clutch housing side, fit the clutch release bearing guide tube. Do not use a gasket under the guide tube flange, and only tighten the bolts finger tight. Invert the casing and fit a preload spacer (any size) and the input shaft bearing outer track (photos).

16 Fit the gear selector shaft spring bracket and tighten its securing bolts to the specified torque (photo).

17 If removed, fit the two locating dowels in the main casing mating face.

18 Fit and tighten the breather.

19 Refit the lubrication jet (photo).

20 Fit the reverse detent spring and plunger. Depress the plunger and

method of locking the geartrains when tightening the input and output shaft nuts.

2 Refer to Section 7, paragraph 2 and use the method described there. Remember to stake the nuts after tightening.

3 Commence reassembly by fitting the selector lever into the main

15.2 Differential spindle roll pin

15.4A View showing crownwheel and retaining bolts

15.4B General view of the reassembled differential unit

Fig. 6.14 Sectional view of the extension housing and differential (Sec 17)

Measure distance at X to see if preload shims (1) are required

17.6 Refit the final drive unit and housing

17.7 Locate a new oil seal

17.9A Measure the bearing outer track recess depth ...

17.9B ... and the extension housing spigot projection

17.11 Tighten the bolts to the specified torque

17.12A Locating the O-ring seal

17.12B Fitting the extension housing

17.15A Locate a preload spacer ...

17.15B ... and the input shaft bearing track

17.16 Refit the selector shaft spring bracket

17.19 Fit the lubrication jet

fit the reverse selector fork and its spindle. Tighten the spindle securing nut to the specified torque (photo).

21 Fit the reversing lamp switch using a new copper washer. Tighten it to the specified torque.

22 Assemble the geartrains and the selector forks and rods. Offer the whole assembly to the gearcase (photo).

23 Fit the reverse idler spindle and gear, with the chamfer towards the rear of the gearbox. Make sure the 5 mm pin in the shaft is correctly located (photo).

24 Refit the swarf-collecting magnet (photo).

25 Insert the spring and washers into the bracket (photo).

26 Enter the selector shaft into the casing, passing it through the compressed spring and washers inside the casing. Also engage the shaft with the spacer washer, selector finger and the interlock bracket. It may be helpful to keep the finger and the bracket together with a short length of rod (maximum diameter 14 mm) which can be withdrawn as the selector shaft enters (photos).

27 Make sure that the flat on the shaft (if applicable) and the roll pin hole are correctly orientated, also the selector key (Fig. 6.15). Secure the selector finger and interlock bracket with two new roll pins. The slots in the roll pins should be 180° away from each other and in line with the longitudinal axis of the shaft (photo).

28 Fit the circlip to the groove on the end of the selector shaft bush (photo). Early models may also have an O-ring seal and washer fitted.

17.20 Reverse selector fork and spindle

17.22 Refit the geartrains with selectors

17.23 Reverse idle spindle and gear

17.24 Locate the magnet

17.25 Selector spring and nylon washers located in bracket

17.26A Insert the selector shaft ...

17.26B ... passing it through the spring and fitting the spacer washer

17.26C Fit and engage the 5th gear rod

29 Refit the selector shaft end cover (photo).
30 Apply jointing compound to the main casing/end casing mating face. Fit the end casing, making sure that the input and output shafts and the selector rod pass through their respective holes. Fit the thirteen securing bolts and tighten them progressively to the specified torque (photo).
31 Fit the reverse idler spindle bolt, using a new washer. Tighten the bolt to the specified torque (photo).

Fig. 6.15 Selector shaft fitting details – early type (Sec 17)

1   Cover
2   Flat on shaft
3   Selector finger and interlock bracket

17.27A Drift the new roll pins into position ...

17.27B ... with slots as shown. Interlock bracket key orientation must be as shown

17.28 Selector shaft and circlip

32 Fit the drain plugs, using new washers, and tighten them to the specified torque.
33 Fit the selector rod lockplate. Secure it with its bolt and washer, tightening the bolt to the specified torque (photo).
34 Fit the output shaft bearing circlip, making sure it is properly located in the groove (photo).
35 Fit the output shaft rear bearing retaining washers and bolts. Tighten the bolts to the specified torque (photo).

36 On four-speed units, lock up the gearshafts as described in Section 7, paragraph 22, tighten the shaft nuts to the specified torque and stake the nuts into the shaft grooves.
37 On five-speed units, fit the spacer (shoulder to bearing) then 5th gear bush and 5th gear to the input shaft followed by the sliding sleeve and hub, but not the selector fork (photos).
38 Lock up the geartrains by engaging 5th gear with the sliding sleeve and any other gear with the selector shaft. Fit the output shaft nut and

17.29 Fit the selector shaft end cover

17.30 Refit the main casing to the end casing

17.31 Refit the reverse idler spindle bolt (with a new washer)

17.33 Fit the selector rod lockplate

17.34 Locate the output shaft bearing circlip into its groove ...

17.35 ... and fit the bearing retaining washers and bolts

17.37A Fit the spacer over the input shaft (5-speed models) ...

17.37B ... the 5th gear bush ...

17.37C ... and 5th gear

17.38 Tighten the output shaft nut to the specified torque

17.39 Fitting the 5th gear sliding sleeve, hub and selector fork

tighten it to the specified torque, then lock it by staking its skirt into the groove (photo).

39 Remove the 5th gear sliding sleeve and hub, then refit them with the selector fork. If the original components are being refitted, observe the mating marks made when dismantling. As the fork is being lowered into position insert the detent ball into its hole (Fig. 6.16). Alternatively

Fig. 6.16 Alternative method of fitting 5th gear selector fork detent spring and ball (Sec 17)

As the fork is lowered (arrows), insert the detent ball

extract the roll pin and insert the detent ball and spring from the other end (photo).

40 Engage two gears again, then fit the input shaft nut and tighten it to the specified torque. Lock the nut by staking.

41 Secure 5th gear selector fork to its rod with a new roll pin (photo).

42 Coat the mating faces with jointing compound, then refit the rear cover. Use thread locking compound on the securing bolts and tighten them to the specified torque.

43 Turn to the clutch housing and remove the release bearing guide tube. If a new release lever balljoint is to be fitted, do so now; put thread locking compound on its splines and drive it in.

44 Refit the clutch release bearing guide tube with a spacer 2.4 mm thick and without a gasket. Insert the retaining bolts and tighten them progressively, at the same time rotating the input shaft. Stop tightening when the shaft *just* starts to drag: the bearings are then correctly seated.

45 Remove the guide tube and the shim. Using a depth gauge, accurately measure the distance from the bearing outer track to the joint face on the casing. Call this dimension C. Similarly measure the protrusion of the spigot on the guide tube flange above the joint face. Call this dimension D (photos).

46 The thickness T of the endfloat shim required is given by the formula:

$$T = (C-D) + 0.03 \text{ mm}$$

47 Fit a new oil seal, lips well greased, to the guide tube (photo).

48 Fit the shim (of calculated thickness), a new gasket and the guide tube. Secure with the bolts and tighten them to the specified torque (photos).

49 Refit the clutch release fork and release bearing.

50 If not already done, refit the gearchange levers, making sure that they are in the correct neutral position. Also refit the clutch bellcrank (if removed) and the gearchange pivot bracket.

51 Reassembly of the transmission is now complete. Do not refill it with oil until the driveshafts have been engaged.

17.41 Drive the roll pin into position to secure the selector fork to the shaft

17.45A Measure the input shaft front bearing outer track recess ...

17.45B ... and the guide tube spigot projection

17.47 Fit a new oil seal into the guide tube

17.48A Locate the selected shim against the front of the bearing

17.48B ... then fit the guide sleeve

18.1 Reverse stop cable removal from the gearbox

18.3 Reverse stop cable nipple and outer cable clip on gear lever (arrowed)

18 Reverse stop cable – removal and refitting

1   At the gearbox end of the cable, undo the black plastic retainer and detach the cable from the gearbox (photo).
2   Working within the car, undo the two screws and remove the floor console away from the gear lever, (tilt it to one side).
3   Disconnect the reverse stop cable from the gear lever by detaching the nipple (photo).
4   Loosen the nuts securing the lower support plate to the floor, lift the plate and remove the cable by pulling it through into the engine compartment.
5   Refit in reverse, passing the cable under the floor carpet and support plate and attach it to the gearbox reverse stop release sleeve. Screw the front end of the cable into the gearbox and then check for satisfactory operation before refitting the console.

Fault diagnosis overleaf

19 Fault diagnosis – transmission

Symptom	Reason(s)
Weak or ineffective synchromesh	Synchromesh units worn, or damaged
Jumps out of gear	Gearchange mechanism worn Synchromesh units badly worn Selector fork badly worn
Excessive noise	Incorrect grade of oil or oil level too low Gearteeth excessively worn or damaged Intermediate gear thrust washers worn allowing excessive end play Worn bearings
Difficulty in engaging gears	Clutch pedal adjustment incorrect Worn selector components Worn synchromesh units

Chapter 7 Driveshafts

For modifications, and information applicable to later models, see Supplement at end of manual

Contents

Specifications

Type .... Open, with constant velocity joint at each end. Right-hand driveshaft has intermediate bearing

Torque wrench settings	Nm	lbf ft
Front hub nut	265	196
Lower suspension balljoint	35	26
Right-hand intermediate bearing bolt	18	13

1 General description

Drive to the front wheels is transmitted from the final drive unit to the front hubs by two driveshafts. The driveshafts incorporate inner and outer joints to accommodate suspension and steering angular movement.

The inner ends of the driveshafts are splined to the final drive/differential side gears, and the outer ends are splined to the front hubs.

The right-hand driveshaft is longer than the left-hand driveshaft and it has additional support by means of an intermediate bearing carried in a support bracket bolted to the engine.

2 Routine maintenance

Carry out the following procedures at the intervals given in Routine Maintenance at the beginning of the manual.

1 Jack up the front of the car and support on axle stands. Apply the handbrake.
2 Thoroughly examine the rubber bellows at each end of the driveshafts for splitting, damage and grease leakage (photo). If evident the bellows will need renewal, refer to Chapter 13.
3 Check the right-hand driveshaft intermediate housing for excessive wear by attempting to move the driveshaft up and down. Also turn the right-hand wheel and listen for excessive noise which would indicate pitted tracks or balls. Renew the bearing if necessary.
4 If the driveshaft joints are excessively noisy, perhaps more noticeable when turning corners, renew the driveshaft or obtain an exchange unit.

2.2 Examine the driveshaft rubber bellows

3 Driveshafts – removal and refitting

1 Unclip and remove the engine/gearbox undershield.
2 Place a container beneath the gearbox and final drive casing then remove the drain plug(s) and drain the oil. Clean the drain plugs then refit and tighten them (refer to Section 2 in Chapter 6).

3   Fully apply the handbrake then remove the roadwheel trim on the side concerned and loosen the hub nut. Do not apply the footbrake when loosening the hub nut as damage can occur to the brake disc retaining screws.

4   If available fit Peugeot special retaining cables to the front suspension strut(s), as described in Chapter 9. Although not absolutely necessary they do ease the driveshaft removal and refitting procedures by restraining the suspension movement when the vehicle is raised.

5   Raise the car so that the roadwheels are clear of the ground and to provide a suitable working clearance underneath. Support the vehicle on safety stands.

6   Unscrew the clamp bolt securing the front suspension lower balljoint to the bottom of the hub carrier then pull the lower suspension arm down from the carrier. **Do not** lever the clamp slot open to separate the suspension arm from the carrier. As they are separated, take care not to damage the driveshaft bellows (gaiters). If the Peugeot retaining cables mentioned in paragraph 4 were not fitted, it may be necessary to unbolt the suspension arm at its inner pivot to allow the lower arm balljoint clamp to be separated from the carrier.

7   Unbolt the balljoint guard plate from the hub carrier.

Left-hand driveshaft

8   Turn the front wheels to full right-hand lock, and remove the hub nut.

9   Pull the hub carrier outwards and at the same time withdraw the outer end of the driveshaft from the hub.

10   Withdraw the inner end of the driveshaft from the final drive unit.

11   Note that the weight of the car **must not** be taken by the front wheels with the driveshaft(s) removed otherwise damage may occur to the hub bearings.

Right-hand driveshaft

12   Loosen the two nuts retaining the intermediate bearing in the bracket bolted to the rear of the cylinder block, then turn the bolts so that their heads move through 90° (photo).

13   Turn the front wheels to full left-hand lock, and remove the hub nut.

14   Pull the hub carrier outwards and at the same time withdraw the outer end of the driveshaft from the hub (photo).

15   Withdraw the inner end of the driveshaft from the final drive unit and guide it through the intermediate bearing bracket.

16   Note the caution given in paragraph 11.

Both driveshafts

17   With the driveshafts removed, the opportunity should be taken to renew the oil seal in the final drive housing. To do this, prise out the old seal and wipe clean the recess. Fill the space between the new oil seal lips with grease then use a suitable block of wood to tap it into the housing. The right-hand oil seal should be flush with the housing, but the left-hand oil seal recessed. Fit the special protector to the right-hand oil seal (Fig. 7.1).

18   Refitting is a reversal of removal, but tighten all nuts and bolts to

Fig. 7.1 Special oil seal protector for use when renewing the final drive housing right-hand oil seal (Sec 3)

the specified torque. When refitting the right-hand driveshaft, make sure that the lugs on the intermediate bearing bolt heads are located over the bearing outer track, and after tightening the nuts remove the special protector from the oil seal. After tightening the hub nut lock it by staking the shoulder into the groove on the end of the driveshaft (photo).

19   Remove the strut retainer(s) (if fitted).

20   Check that the gearbox/final drive drain plug(s) are securely fitted, then top up the gearbox and final drive oil with reference to Section 2 in Chapter 6.

___

4   Driveshaft intermediate bearing – renewal

___

1   Refer to the previous Section and remove the right-hand driveshaft.

2   Undo the retaining bolts and remove the torque reaction link.

3   Unbolt and remove the engine mounting/intermediate bearing carrier. If the bearing did not come away with the driveshaft, press it and its sealing ring out of the carrier.

4   Fit the new bearing and sealing ring, refit the carrier and the driveshaft. Tighten all fastenings to the specified torque, using new nuts on the steering and suspension balljoints.

5   Refit the torque reaction link.

3.12 Right-hand driveshaft intermediate bearing and retaining nuts (arrowed)

3.14 Right-hand driveshaft removal from the wheel hub

3.18 Stake punch the hub nut to lock it

Fig. 7.2 Driveshaft intermediate bearing components (Sec 4)

1   Oil seal
2   Bearing mounting bracket
3   Bearing
4   End cover
5   Bolts

HI45829

---

5 Fault diagnosis – driveshafts

Symptom	Reason(s)
Knocking noise, particularly on full lock	Worn driveshaft joints
Metallic grating, varying with roadspeed	Worn intermediate bearing on the right-hand driveshaft

Chapter 8 Braking system

For modifications, and information applicable to later models, see Supplement at end of manual

Contents

Specifications

Type .... Front disc brakes, rear drum brakes, (self-adjusting). Servo assistance on all models. Rear brake compensator. Cable-operated handbrake on rear wheels

Brake fluid type/specification .... Hydraulic fluid to SAE J1703C (Duckhams Universal Brake and Clutch Fluid)

Disc brakes
Disc diameter .... 247 mm (9.72 in)
Disc thickness .... 10 mm (0.39 in)
Minimum disc thickness (after regrind) .... 8.5 mm (0.335 in)
Maximum disc run-out .... 0.07 mm (0.0028 in)
Caliper type .... DBA (IV) or Girling
Front brake cylinder diameter .... 48 mm (1.89 in)
Disc pad wear limit .... 2 mm (0.08 in)

Rear drum brakes
Drum diameter .... 180 mm (7.09 in)
Maximum drum internal diameter (after regrind) .... 181.0 mm (7.13 in)
Lining width .... 40 mm (1.57 in)
Lining thickness:
    New .... 5 mm (0.20 in)
    Wear limit .... 1 mm (0.04 in)
Rear wheel cylinder diameter:
    OHV engine models .... 17.5 mm (0.69 in)
    OHC engine models .... 22.0 mm (0.87 in)
Brake compensator type .... DBA or Automotive Products (fixed)

Master cylinder
Type .... DBA Bendix or ATE Teves
Bore diameter .... 19 mm (0.75 in)
Stroke .... 30 mm (1.18 in)

Servo unit

Pushrod-to-master cylinder mounting face .... 22.3 mm (0.88 in)
Pushrod length – servo-to-clevis eye (at brake pedal) .... 88.0 mm (3.46 in)
Servo unit diameter .... 177.8 mm (7.00 in)

Torque wrench settings

	Nm	lbf ft
Rear wheel hub nut	215	159
Caliper mounting bolts:		
Girling	97	72
DBA	120	88

1 General description

The braking system is of hydraulic type with discs on the front and drums on the rear. The handbrake is cable-operated on the rear wheels.

The hydraulic circuit is of two independent sections so that, in the event of the failure of one section, the remaining section is still functional. The master cylinder has a primary and secondary barrel; the primary operating the rear brakes, the secondary the front brakes, thus splitting the hydraulic circuit operation front and rear.

A compensating valve fitted to some models reduces the hydraulic pressure to the rear brakes under heavy applications of the brake pedal in order to prevent rear wheel lock-up.

A vacuum servo unit is fitted to all models, and is mounted between the master cylinder and engine compartment bulkhead.

Precautions

All work undertaken on the braking system, including routine maintenance, must be to the highest standard. It is vitally important to maintain the integrity of the system and to use the right fasteners with correct locking devices where appropriate. Adjustments must be within specified limits where these apply and spare parts must be new or in faultless condition. Absolute cleanliness when assembling hydraulic components is essential. New seals and fresh hydraulic fluid must be used and any fluid drained or removed from the system must

be discarded. Remember that your life and possibly the lives of others could depend on these points; if you are in any doubt at all concerning what to do or how to do it, get professional advice or have the job done by an expert.

If the brake system tell-tale warning light comes on and the handbrake is not applied, immediately check the level of the brake fluid. If the level is satisfactory check the setting of the handbrake warning switch.

2 Routine maintenance

Carry out the following procedures at the intervals given in Routine Maintenance.

1 Thoroughly clean the external surfaces of the reservoir and its filler cap. The reservoir is made of semi-transparent plastic and the fluid can be seen without removing the cap. However, you should only rely on this check once you have satisfied yourself that an accurate indication of the fluid level is possible. If necessary top up with fresh fluid, but make allowances for the change in level that will occur when the cap, with its switch and float, is refitted. The level in the reservoir will rise to some extent due to displacement by the switch assembly. Check **that** the vent hole in the filler cap is clear. Any need for regular topping-up must be viewed with suspicion and the whole hydraulic system

Fig. 8.1 Braking system layout (LH drive model) (Sec 1)

inspected for signs of leaks. A *small*, slow fall in the level as the disc pads wear is normal.

2   Inspect the front disc pads for wear (see Section 3). The wear indication grooves in the pads should be visible, indicating that adequate pad material remains.

3   Remove the rubber inspection plugs in the rear brake backplates and inspect the shoe linings for wear. All four shoes will need renewing if the thickness of any one lining is below 1.0 mm (0.04 in) (photo).

4   Check the operation of the handbrake. The brakes should lock the wheels when the lever has been moved six to eight notches.

5   Check the clearance between the brake foot pedal and the floor when the brakes are applied, to make sure that the pedal is not bottoming.

6   Examine the hydraulic circuit lines and hoses for damage and deterioration, and for any signs of leakage. There is no need to retighten union nuts as this may distort the sealing faces.

7   Renew the brake fluid at the specified intervals.

---

3   Disc pads – inspection and renewal

1   Jack up the front of the car and support on axle stands. Apply the handbrake and remove the roadwheels.

2   If the friction material has worn down to 2.0 mm (0.08 in) (this is indicated if the groove in the pad has disappeared) then the pads must be renewed as an axle set. The removal and refitting operations will vary according to the type of caliper, but first reduce the fluid level in the reservoir to allow for displacement of fluid when the pistons are pushed back into their calipers. Syphon a small amount of fluid from the reservoir but do not spill the hydraulic fluid on paintwork or fittings. Wipe any spillage of fluid clean. Do not allow the fluid reservoir to be emptied.

DBA Bendix disc caliper

3   Remove the clip from the end of the upper sliding key (photo). Disconnect the pad wear wiring as necessary (photo).

4   Pull out the upper sliding key (photo).

5   Using a lever against the front suspension strut, push the cylinder towards the brake disc so that the outer pad can be withdrawn from the caliper (photo).

2.3 Inspection plug location in rear brake backplate (arrowed)

6   Push back the caliper and withdraw the inner pad (photo).

7   Clean away all dust and dirt from the caliper. **Do not** inhale the dust, as it may be injurious to health. Check for brake fluid leakage around the piston dust seal and, if evident, overhaul the caliper, as described later in the Chapter. Check the brake disc for wear and also check that the rubber bellows on the cylinder sliding rods are in good condition.

8   Clean the backs of the disc pads and apply a little anti-squeal brake grease. Also apply the grease to the lower pad locating lip of the caliper (photo).

9   With the caliper pushrod inwards, insert the inner pad then push the caliper outwards and insert the outer pad.

3.3A Pad sliding key clip-arrowed (DBA Bendix type)

3.3B Disconnecting the pad wear wiring (DBA Bendix type)

3.4 Remove the pad sliding key (DBA Bendix type)

3.5 Remove the outer pad

3.6 Remove the inner pad

3.8 Applying anti-squeal brake grease to the pad locating lip on the caliper

3.10 Correct location of the anti-rattle clips on the disc pads (DBA Bendix type)

10 Check that the pads are correctly located on the caliper lip (photo) then tap in the upper sliding key to lock them. Fit a new sliding key clip.

Girling disc caliper
11 Extract the spring clips and tap out the pad retaining pins. Disconnect the pad wear wiring as necessary. Release the pad anti-knock spring (photos).
12 Lever the cylinder outwards and withdraw the outer pad then push in the caliper and withdraw the inner pad (photos).

13 Clean and check the caliper, as described in paragraph 7, then clean the backs of the disc pads and apply a little anti-squeal brake grease.
14 With the caliper pushed inwards, insert the inner pad then push the caliper outwards and insert the outer pad.
15 Tap in the pad retaining pins and fit the spring clips (photo).
16 Where fitted, hook the anti-knock spring on the lower pad retaining pin (Fig. 8.2).

3.11A Disconnecting the pad wear wiring (Girling type)

3.11B Withdraw the pad retaining pins (Girling type)

3.12A Remove the outer pad (Girling type)

3.12B Remove the inner pad (Girling type)

3.12C Pads, springs and retaining pins removed for inspection (Girling type)

3.15 Reassembled brake pads (Girling type)

Fig. 8.2 Method of fitting anti-knock spring to Girling inner disc pad (Sec 3)

1   Loop for rivet
2   Loop for lower retaining pin
3   Anti-knock spring

DBA Bendix and Girling disc calipers
17 Repeat the operations on the opposite disc caliper.
18 Apply the footbrake several times to position the pads against the discs.
19 Top up the master cylinder reservoir to its correct level.
20 Refit the roadwheels and lower the car to the ground.
21 The new pads supplied by Peugeot are special in that they have an abrasive top surface skin. The object of the thin abrasive coating is to clean the surface of the discs and remove any minor imperfections in their friction surfaces during the initial braking applications. These brake pads require careful running in, ideally as follows:-

(a) For the first three miles (5 km), drive at low speeds and apply the brakes intermittently under a light pressure
(b) During the first 120 miles (200 km) of use, avoid (where possible) any heavy or prolonged braking

4   Rear brake shoes – inspection and renewal

DBA or Girling type rear brakes may be fitted. The two types are shown in Figs. 8.3 and 8.4. The photos which accompany this Section show the DBA type. The inspection and renewal procedures for both types are similar, but where differences occur they are described.
1   Jack up the rear of the car and support it on axle stands. Chock the front wheels and release the handbrake.
2   The lining thickness may be checked without removing the

Fig. 8.3 Diagram of the DBA Bendix type rear brake (Sec 4)

Arrow indicates wheel rotation

Fig. 8.4 Diagram of the Girling type rear brake (Sec 4)

Arrow indicates wheel rotation

4.4A Prise free the grease cap ...

4.4B ... then unscrew the staked nut ...

4.4C ... and remove the washer

4.4D Inner end of rear stub axle (arrowed) which can be held with a splined key

4.5A Insert a screwdriver through the wheel bolt hole ...

4.5B ... and push the handbrake lever behind the shoe (DBA Bendix type)

drums/hubs. Pull out the rubber plugs from the backplates by the handbrake cables and use a torch, if necessary, to check the lining thickness (photo 2.3). If it is at or near the specified minimum remove the drums and make a more thorough inspection.

3   Remove the rear roadwheels.

4   Tap off the grease cap, taking care not to damage its outer lip, then unscrew the staked nut from the end of the stub axle and remove the washer (photos). Should the stub axle rotate within the trailing arm, hold it stationary with a 12 mm splined key on the inner end (photo).

5   Withdraw the hub/drum from the stub axle. If difficulty is experienced, due to the shoes wearing grooves in the drum, proceed as follows according to type.

DBA: Insert a screwdriver through one of the wheel bolt holes and depress the handbrake lever on the rear brake shoe so that it slides back behind the shoe (photos).

Girling: Insert a punch through one of the wheel bolt holes and drive out the roll pin from the handbrake lever (Fig. 8.5). With the brake shoes retracted the hub/drum can be withdrawn. Lay the drum down so that the hub oil seal faces upwards (if faced downwards it could be damaged).

6   Brush the dust and dirt from the shoes, backplate and drum. **Do not** inhale it, as it may be injurious to health.

7   It is now possible to inspect both shoe linings for wear. If either is worn down the specified minimum amount, renew them both.

8   Note the position of each shoe and the location of the return and steady springs (photos).

9   Unhook and remove the upper return spring (photo).

10   Remove the steady springs using pliers to depress the outer cups and turn them through 90° (photo). Remove the pins from the backplate.

11   On DBA type brakes, move the serrated automatic adjuster lever quadrant against spring tension (photo), move the lever forwards and release the strut from the top of the shoes. On Girling type brakes, prise the shoes apart and remove the pushrod.

Fig. 8.5 Roll pin removal from the handbrake lever on the Girling drum brake (Sec 4)

12   Expand the shoes over the wheel cylinder then release them from the bottom anchor.

13   Unhook the lever return spring and the handbrake cable.

14   If necessary, position a rubber band over the wheel cylinder to prevent the pistons coming out. Should there be evidence of brake fluid leakage from the wheel cylinder, renew it or overhaul it, as described in Section 7.

15   Transfer the handbrake and automatic adjuster levers to the new

4.8A Rear brake assembly – DBA type

4.8B Rear brake assembly – Girling type

4.9 Upper return spring location

4.10 Shoe steady spring (arrowed)

4.11 Automatic adjuster lever (arrowed) and bottom return spring location

4.24A Tighten the rear hub nut ...

4.24B ... then stake it to the stub axle

shoes as required. Note that the levers and strut on each rear wheel are different, and that the leading and trailing shoes are fitted with different grade linings. On Girling types, ensure that the roll pin is refitted to the handbrake operating lever (the pin acts as a stop).

16 Place the shoes on the bench in their correct location and fit the lower return spring.

17 Apply brake grease sparingly to the metal contact points of the shoes, then position them on the backplate and reconnect the handbrake cable. Locate the shoe ends on the bottom anchor.

18 Engage the strut with the slots at the top of the shoes, making sure it is located correctly on the automatic adjuster lever. Engage the upper shoe ends on the wheel cylinder pistons.

19 Insert the steady spring pins in the backplate and through the shoe webs, then fit the springs and outer cups.

20 Fit the upper return spring.

21 Move the serrated automatic adjuster lever quadrant against the spring tension to set the shoes at their minimum diameter.

22 Check that the handbrake lever on the rear brake shoe is positioned with the lug on the edge of the shoe web and not behind the shoe.

23 Fit the hub/drum on the stub axle and retain with the washer and nut. Always renew the nut.

24 Tighten the nut to the specified torque then lock it by staking the nut flange into the groove on the stub axle (photos).

25 Tap the grease cap into the hub/drum.

26 Repeat all the operations on the opposite rear brake then refit the roadwheels and lower the car to the ground.

27 Apply the footbrake several times to set the shoes in their adjusted position.

28 Adjust the handbrake, as described in Section 14.

5 Disc caliper – removal, overhaul and refitting

1   Remove the disc pads, as described in Section 3.

2   Fit a brake hose clamp to the flexible hose connected to the caliper. Alternatively remove the brake fluid reservoir filler cap and tighten it down onto a piece of polythene sheeting to reduce the loss of fluid when disconnecting the caliper.

3   Loosen the flexible hose union connection at the caliper.

4   Unscrew the two mounting bolts, withdraw the caliper from the disc then unscrew the caliper from the flexible hose. Plug the hose to prevent loss of fluid.

5   Clean the exterior of the caliper.

6   On the DBA type, unbolt the caliper frame from the cylinder.

7   Prise the dust cover and ring from the end of the piston.

8   Withdraw the piston from the cylinder. If necessary use air pressure from a foot pump in the fluid inlet to force the piston out.

9   Prise the seal from inside the cylinder, taking care not to damage the cylinder wall.

10 If required, dismantle the sliding guides. On the DBA type, unbolt the endplate from the guides and remove the rubber dust covers. Keep the guides identified for location.

11 Clean all the components using methylated spirit or clean brake fluid then examine them for wear and damage. Check the piston and

Fig. 8.6 Bendix type disc caliper components (Sec 5)

1	Mounting bolt	3	Sliding key kit	5	Retaining plate	7	Repair kit with grease
2	Caliper assembly	4	Bleed screw	6	Sliding guide kit with grease		

Fig. 8.7 Girling type disc caliper components (Sec 5)

1   *Mounting bolt*   4   *Bleed screw*
2   *Caliper assembly*   5   *Repair kit*
3   *Pad retaining pin and spring*

cylinder surfaces for scoring, excessive wear and corrosion, and if evident renew the complete caliper assembly. Similarly check the sliding guides. If the components are in good condition obtain a repair kit which will contain all the necessary rubber seals and other renewable items.
12 Dip the new seal in fresh brake fluid then locate it in the cylinder groove using the fingers only to manipulate it.
13 Dip the piston in brake fluid and insert it in the cylinder, twisting it as necessary to locate it in the seal.
14 Fit the dust cover and ring over the end of the piston and cylinder.
15 Lubricate the sliding guides with the grease supplied and refit them, together with the new seals. On the DBA type, refit the endplate and tighten the bolts.
16 On the DBA type, refit the caliper frame and tighten the bolts.
17 To refit the caliper, first screw it onto the flexible hose and locate it over the brake disc so that the hose is not twisted.
18 Clean the mounting bolt threads and apply locking fluid. Insert the mounting bolts and tighten them to the specified torque.
19 Tighten the flexible hose union on the caliper. Check that the hose is clear of the strut and surrounding components and, if necessary, loosen the rigid pipe union on the body bracket, reposition the hose and retighten the union.
20 Refit the disc pads, as described in Section 3.
21 Remove the brake hose clamp or polythene sheeting and bleed the hydraulic system, as described in Section 12. It is only necessary to bleed the front circuit.

6   Brake disc – inspection, removal and refitting

1   Remove the disc pads, as described in Section 3.
2   Using a dial gauge or feelers and a fixed block, check that the disc

6.3 Disc retaining screws (arrowed)

run-out is within the specified limit. Do not confuse wheel bearing endfloat with disc wear. Also check the condition of the disc, for scoring. Light scoring is normal, but if excessive either renew the disc or have it ground.
3   To remove the disc, unscrew the two cross-head screws (where fitted) and withdraw the disc at an angle from the caliper and hub (photo).
4   Refitting is a reversal of removal, but make sure that the disc-to-hub mating surfaces are clean and that the cross-head screws are tightened fully. Refer to Section 3 when refitting the disc pads.

7   Rear brake wheel cylinder – removal, overhaul and refitting

1   Jack up the rear of the car and support on axle stands. Chock the front wheels and remove the relevant rear wheel.
2   Remove the hub/drum, as described in Section 4.
3   Note the location of the brake shoe upper return spring then unhook and remove it.
4   Pivot the brake shoes away from the wheel cylinder and wedge them in this position. If a suitable wedge, or sufficient clearance between each shoe and the brake wheel cylinder pistons cannot be obtained, the brake shoes will need to be removed as described in Section 4. Avoid damage or distortion to the brake components.
5   Fit a brake hose clamp to the flexible hose supplying the rear brakes. Alternatively remove the brake fluid reservoir filler cap and tighten it down onto a piece of polythene sheeting to reduce the loss of fluid when disconnecting the wheel cylinder.
6   Unscrew the hydraulic pipe union nut from the rear of the wheel cylinder.
7   Unscrew the two mounting bolts and withdraw the wheel cylinder from the backplate. Take care not to spill any brake fluid on the brake shoe linings.
8   Clean the exterior surfaces of the wheel cylinder before dismantling it. The cylinder will be of Girling or DBA Bendix manufacture (see Figs. 8.8 or 8.9).
9   Pull off the dust excluders.
10 Extract the pistons, seals and return spring; keeping each component identified for location.
11 Check the surface of the cylinder bore and pistons for scoring and corrosion and, if evident, renew the complete wheel cylinder. If the components are in good condition discard the seals and obtain a repair kit which will contain all the necessary renewable components.
12 Clean the pistons and cylinder with methylated spirit or clean brake fluid then dip each component in fresh brake fluid and reassemble in reverse order, making sure that the lips of the seals face into the cylinder. When completed, wipe clean the outer surfaces of the dust excluders.

Fig. 8.8 Exploded view of the DBA Bendix type rear wheel cylinder (Sec 7)

1   Cylinder
2   Retaining bolt
3   Bleed screw and dust cap
4   Cylinder components (repair kit parts indicated)

13   Clean the backplate and refit the wheel cylinder using a reversal of the removal procedure. Refer to Section 4 when refitting the hub/drum.
14   Make sure that the brake hose clamp or polythene sheeting is removed then bleed the hydraulic system, as described in Section 12; noting that it is only necessary to bleed the rear circuit (if only the rear brakes have been disturbed).

8   Rear brake drum – inspection and renovation

1   Whenever the hub/brake drum is removed to check the linings, take the opportunity to inspect the interior of the drum.
2   If the drum is grooved, owing to failure to renew worn linings or after a very high mileage has been covered, then it may be possible to regrind it, provided the maximum internal diameter is not exceeded.
3   Even if only one drum is in need of grinding both drums must be reground to the same size in order to maintain even braking characteristics.
4   Judder or a springy pedal felt when the brakes are applied can be

Fig. 8.9 Exploded view of the Girling type rear wheel cylinder (Sec 7)

1   Cylinder
2   Retaining bolt
3   Washer
4   Bleed screw and dust cap
5   Cylinder components (repair kit parts indicated)

caused by a distorted (out-of-round) drum. Here again it may be possible to regrind the drums, otherwise a new drum will be required.

9   Master cylinder – removal, overhaul and refitting

1   Unscrew the filler cap from the brake fluid reservoir and draw out the fluid using a syringe.
2   Prise the reservoir from the master cylinder and remove the seals.

Fig. 8.10 Master cylinder components (Sec 9)

3   Body
4   Mounting nut
5   Secondary piston components
6   Primary piston components
7   Servo unit

Fig. 8.11 Master cylinder, servo unit and brake pedal assembly (Sec 9)

a   Clevis pin in lower hole
A = 184.0 mm (7.244 in)
B = 114.0 mm (4.488 in)
C = 3.5 mm (0.138 in)

3   Unscrew the union nuts securing the rigid brake lines to the master cylinder and pull out the lines. Cap the pipe ends to prevent loss of fluid.
4   Unscrew the mounting nuts and withdraw the master cylinder from the servo unit.
5   Clean the exterior of the master cylinder.
6   Using circlip pliers, extract the circlip from the mouth of the cylinder.
7   Remove the primary and secondary piston components noting their locations. If necessary tap the cylinder on a block of wood.
8   Clean all the components in methylated spirit. Check the surfaces of the cylinder bore and pistons for scoring and corrosion, and if evident renew the complete master cylinder. If the components are in good condition remove and discard the seals and obtain a repair kit which will contain all the necessary renewable components.
9   Dip the new seals in fresh brake fluid and fit them to the pistons using the fingers only to manipulate them.
10 Reassemble the master cylinder in reverse order to dismantling and make sure that the circlip is fully engaged with the groove in the mouth of the cylinder.
11 Refitting is a reversal of removal. Take care to align the brake line unions correctly or cross threading may occur. On completion, bleed the complete hydraulic system as described in Section 12.

10 Brake compensator – description, removal and refitting

1   The OHC engine models have a brake compensator fitted in the rear brake hydraulic system and it is located under the car floor just forward of the rear suspension. Its purpose is to maintain equal braking effect on the front and rear wheels and prevent the rear brakes fom locking up (photo).
2   If you find that, on applying the brakes, the effect is mainly on the front wheels and that it is impossible to lock the rear brakes without using the handbrake or, alternatively, if you find that the rear brakes

invariably lock under heavy braking, it is likely that the compensator is defective.
3   A Peugeot agent will have to test the component if its performance is in doubt as pressure test equipment is necessary. No attempt must be made to dismantle the unit.
4   Renewal of a brake compensator is a straightforward removal and refitting procedure followed by bleeding of the hydraulic system. Ensure that the unit is correctly orientated when fitted.

11 Flexible and rigid hydraulic lines – inspection and renewal

1   Examine all the unions for signs of leaks. The look at the flexible hoses for signs of fraying and chafing (as well as for leaks). This is only a preliminary inspection of the flexible hoses as exterior condition does not necessarily indicate interior condition which will be considered later.
2   The steel pipes must be examined equally carefully. They must be thoroughly cleaned and examined for signs of dents or other percussive damage, rust and corrosion. Rust and corrosion should be scraped off and, if the depth of pitting in the pipes is significant, they will need renewal. This is most likely in those areas underneath the chassis and along the rear suspension arms where the pipes are exposed to the full force of road and weather conditions.
3   Rigid pipe removal is usually quite straightforward. The unions at each end are undone and the pipe drawn out of the connection. The clips which may hold it to the car body are bent back and it is then removed. Underneath the car exposed unions can be particularly stubborn, defying the efforts of an open-ended spanner. As few people will have the special split ring spanner required, a self-grip wrench is the only answer. If the pipe is being renewed, new unions will be provided. If not then one will have to put up with the possibility of burring over the flats on the union and use a self-grip wrench for replacement also.

10.1 Rear brake compensator (AP type)

11.4 Rear brake pipe-to-hose junction and rigid support bracket on rear suspension arm

11.5 Method of clamping brake hose using two sockets and clamp to prevent damaging the hose

4   Flexible hoses are always fitted to a rigid support bracket where they join a rigid pipe, the bracket being fixed to the chassis or rear suspension arm (photo). The rigid pipe unions must first be removed from the flexible union, then the retaining plate must be pulled out and the flexible hose and fitting released from the bracket.

5   Whenever a part of the hydraulic system is disconnected, clamp the hose (photo) or plug the pipe end connections to prevent leakage of fluid and the possible ingress of dirt.

6   Depending upon the make of the particular caliper, the flexible hose may be connected simply by screwing it into its tapped hole or by using a hollow bolt with banjo end fitting. Use a new copper sealing washer on each side of the banjo union.

7   Once the flexible hose is removed, examine the internal bore. If clear of fluid it should be possible to see through it. Any specks of rubber which come out, or signs of restriction in the bore, mean that the inner lining is breaking up and the hose must be renewed.

8   Rigid pipes which need replacement can usually be purchased at any local garage where they have the pipe, unions and special tools to make them up. They will need to know the pipe length required and the type of flare used at the ends of the pipe. These may be different at each end of the same pipe.

9   Installation of the pipes is a reversal of the removal procedure. The pipe profile must be preset before fitting. Any acute bends must be put in by the garage on a bending machine, otherwise there is the possibility of kinking them and restricting the fluid flow.

10 All hose and pipe threads and unions are to metric standards. Screw in new components by hand initially to ensure that the threads are compatible.

11 Remember that a metric hose end fitting seals at the tip of its threaded section and will leave a gap between the hexagon of the end fitting and the surface of the component. Do not attempt to overtighten the hose end fitting in order to eliminate the gap.

12 The hydraulic system must be bled on completion of hose or rigid pipe renewal.

12 Hydraulic system – draining and bleeding

1   To renew the hydraulic fluid, remove the filler cap from the reservoir and use a syringe to remove the fluid. Fill the reservoir with new hydraulic fluid and bleed the complete system as described later. If the master cylinder or connecting pipes have been removed, the complete hydraulic system must be bled, but if only a caliper or wheel cylinder has been removed then only that particular circuit need be bled.

2   If the complete system is being bled, the sequence of bleeding should be as follows:

LH rear wheel and brake compensator (if fitted)
RH rear wheel
LH front wheel
RH front wheel

3   Unless the pressure bleeding method is being used, do not forget to keep the fluid level in the master cylinder reservoir topped up to prevent air from being drawn into the system which would make any

work done worthless. Before commencing operations, check that all system hoses and pipes are in good condition with unions tight and free from leaks.

4   Take great care not to allow hydraulic fluid to come into contact with the vehicle paintwork as it is an effective paint stripper. Wash off any spilled fluid immediately with cold water.

5   To dissipate any vacuum assistance from the brake system, apply the brake pedal several times in quick succession (with the engine switched off).

Bleeding – two man method

6   Gather together a clean jar and a length of rubber or plastic tubing which will be a tight fit on the brake bleed screws.

7   Engage the help of an assistant.

8   Push one end of the bleed tube onto the first bleed screw and immerse the other end in the jar which should contain enough hydraulic fluid to cover the end of the tube.

9   Open the bleed screw one half a turn and have your assistant depress the brake pedal fully then slowly release it. Tighten the bleed screw at the end of each pedal downstroke to obviate any chance of air or fluid being drawn back into the system.

10 Repeat this operation until clean hydraulic fluid, free from air bubbles, can be seen coming through into the jar.

11 It is important to dislodge air trapped in the inertia compensator (if fitted). To do this, open the bleed screw again and have your assistant fully depress and release the brake pedal rapidly 4 or 5 times, finally keeping the pedal depressed before tightening the bleed screw.

12 With the bleed screw tightened, remove the bleed tube and proceed to the next wheel (photo).

12.12 Bleeding the front brake disc caliper

Bleeding – using one-way valve kits

13 There are a number of one-man, one-way brake bleeding kits available from motor accessory shops. It is recommended that one of these kits is used wherever possible as it will greatly simplify the bleeding operation and also reduce the risk of air or fluid being drawn back into the system, quite apart from being able to do the work without the help of an assistant. To use the kit, connect the tube to the bleed screw and open the screw one half a turn.

14 Depress the brake pedal fully then slowly release it. The one-way valve in the kit will prevent expelled air from returning at the end of each pedal downstroke. Repeat the operation several times to be sure of ejecting all the air from the system. Some kits include a translucent container which can be positioned so that the air bubbles can actually be seen being ejected from the system.

15 Tighten the bleed screw, remove the tube and repeat the operations on the remaining brakes, but first carry out the procedure described in paragraph 11.

16 On completion, depress the brake pedal. If it still feels spongy, repeat the bleeding operations as air must still be trapped in the system.

Bleeding – using a pressure bleeding kit

17 These kits are available from motor accessory shops and are usually operated by air pressure from the spare tyre.

18 By connecting a pressurised container to the master cylinder fluid reservoir, bleeding is then carried out simply by opening each bleed screw in sequence and allowing the fluid to run out, rather like turning on a tap, until no air is visible in the expelled fluid.

19 By using this method, the large reserve of hydraulic fluid provides a safeguard against air being drawn into the master cylinder during bleeding which may occur if the fluid level in the reservoir is allowed to fall too low.

20 Pressure bleeding is particularly useful when bleeding the complete system at time of routine fluid renewal.

All methods

21 When bleeding is completed, check and top up the fluid level in the master cylinder reservoir.

22 Check the feel of the brake pedal. If it feels at all spongy, air must still be present in the system and the need for further bleeding is indicated. Failure to bleed satisfactorily after a reasonable repetition of the bleeding operations may be due to worn master cylinder seals.

23 Always discard brake fluid which had been bled from the system. It is almost certain to be contaminated with moisture, air and dirt, making it unsuitable for further use.

24 Clean fluid should always be stored in an airtight container as it absorbs moisture readily which lowers its boiling point and could affect braking performance under severe conditions.

Testing

7 With the engine switched off, depress the brake pedal several times. The distance by which the pedal moves should now alter over all applications.

8 Depress the brake pedal fully and hold it down then start the engine. The pedal should be felt to move downward slightly.

9 Hold the pedal depressed with the engine running, switch off the ignition and continue to hold the pedal depressed for 30 seconds during which period the pedal should neither rise nor drop.

10 Start the engine whilst the brake pedal is released, run it for a minute and switch off. Give several applications of the brake pedal. The pedal travel should decrease with each application.

11 Failure of the brake pedal to act in the way described will indicate a fault in the servo unit.

12 The servo unit should not be serviced or overhauled beyond the operations described in this Section and in the event of a fault developing, renew the servo complete.

13 Periodically check the condition of the vacuum hose and security of the clips.

14 Renew the hose if necessary.

15 If the servo hose right-angled non-return valve is loose in its sealing grommet, or if the grommet shows evidence of cracking or perishing, renew it. Apply some hydraulic fluid to the rubber to facilitate fitting.

Air filter – renewal

16 Although not a specified operation, the air filter through which the pushrod passes at the rear of the servo can become clogged after a high mileage. Disconnect the rod from the pedal, cut the filter diagonally having slipped the dust excluder off the rod. Fit the new filter.

Removal and refitting

17 Remove the master cylinder, as described in Section 9. Disconnect the servo vacuum hose. On fuel injection models it ia also necessary to remove the fuel filter unit (see Chapter 3).

18 Working inside the car, disconnect the pushrod from the brake pedal; noting that it is on the lower hole.

19 Unscrew the mounting nuts behind the pedal bracket then withdraw the servo unit into the engine compartment. Remove the gasket.

20 Before fitting a servo unit, check the pushrod dimensions shown in Fig. 8.12 and adjust where possible.

21 Refitting is a reversal of removal, but fit a new gasket and fully tighten the mounting nuts. Refer to Section 9 when refitting the master cylinder. Finally, with the brake pedal released, check that the clearance between the stop-lamp switch threaded shank and pedal is 3.5 mm (0.138 in). If necessary loosen the locknuts, adjust the switch and tighten the locknuts (photo).

---

13 Vacuum servo unit – description, testing, maintenance, removal and refitting

Description

1 The vacuum servo unit is fitted into the brake hydraulic circuit in series with the master cylinder to provide power assistance to the driver when the brake pedal is depressed.

2 The unit operates by vacuum obtained from the engine induction manifold and consists of, basically, a booster diaphragm and non-return valve.

3 The servo unit and the master cylinder are connected so that the servo piston rod acts as the master cylinder pushrod.

4 The driver's braking effort is transmitted from the brake pedal to the servo unit piston and its integral control system.

5 The forward chamber of the servo unit is held under vacuum at all times whilst the rear chamber is held under vacuum conditions only when the brake pedal is in the released position. When the pedal is depressed, the rear chamber opens to atmospheric pressure which causes the servo piston to move forward and so operate the master cylinder pushrod.

6 It is emphasised that a servo unit provides assistance only and, should a fault occur, the normal hydraulic braking system is unaffected except that the need for higher pedal pressure will be noticed.

13.21 Brake stop-lamp switch (arrowed)

Fig. 8.12 Cross-section of the vacuum servo unit showing pushrod adjustment dimensions (Sec 13)

1   Adjustment screw

A = 22.2 to 22.4 mm (0.874 to 0.882 in)   B = 86.5 to 89.5 mm (3.406 to 3.524 in)

14 Handbrake – adjustment

1   The handbrake is normally kept adjusted by the action of the automatic adjusters on the rear brake shoes. However, in due course the cables will stretch and will have to be adjusted in order to fully apply the handbrake.
2   Access to the adjuster is obtained after removing the handbrake cover. To do this unbolt and remove the driver's seat, pull free the fuel filler cap release handle from its shaft, then undo the retaining screws and remove the cover from the handbrake.
3   Jack up the rear of the car and support it on axle stands. Chock the front wheels.
4   Release the handbrake then move the lever to the third notch position. Loosen the adjuster locknut.
5   Turn the adjustment nut on the rear of the cable equaliser so that both rear wheels are just binding on the brake shoes (photo).
6   The number of notches through which the handbrake lever should be able to be pulled from fully-off to fully-on should be as follows:

   With rear drums 5 to 7
   With rear discs 6 to 8

7   On no account adjust the handbrake to operate over fewer notches, or the automatic brake adjusters will not operate.
8   Fully apply the handbrake lever, and then check that both rear wheels are locked.
9   Fully release the handbrake, then check that the rear wheels rotate freely. With the adjustment satisfactory, retighten the locknut.
10 Refit the handbrake cover, fuel filler release handle and driver's seat then lower the car.

15 Handbrake cables – renewal

1   Remove the rear brake shoes as described in Section 4.
2   Remove the handbrake cover as described in paragraph 2 of Section 14.
3   Undo the handbrake lever retaining nuts and bolts and lift the lever to gain access to the handbrake cable and equaliser. Unhook the cables from the equalizer (photo).
4   Release the cable(s) from the retaining clips, the floor, the fuel tank, and the rear brake backplate(s) and withdraw from under the car (photos).
5   If renewing both cables, note that the right-hand cable is longer than the left.
6   Fit the new cable(s) using a reversal of the removal procedure with reference also to Section 4. Finally adjust the cable(s) as described in Section 14.

16 Handbrake warning light switch – removal and refitting

1   Remove handbrake cover as described in Section 14, paragraph 2.
2   With the handbrake applied, remove the mounting screw,

14.5 Adjusting the handbrake

withdraw the switch and disconnect the wiring (photo).
3   Refitting is a reversal of removal.

17 Handbrake lever – removal and refitting

1   Remove the handbrake cover as described in paragraph 2 of Section 14.
2   Undo the handbrake lever retaining nuts and bolts. Move the fuel filler release lever to one side (photo).
3   Disconnect the handbrake cables from the equalizer and then remove the handbrake lever.
4   Refit in the reverse order of removal. Adjust the handbrake as described in Section 14, paragraphs 5 to 7.

18 Brake pedal – removal and refitting

1   Remove the lower trim panel on the driver's side to gain access to the brake pedal assembly.
2   Remove the clevis pin and disconnect the pushrod from the brake pedal. Note that the pushrod is on the lower hole (photo).
3   Unscrew the self-locking nut from the pivot bolt, pull out the bolt and lower the brake pedal.
4   Examine the pedal bushes for wear and renew them if necessary.
5   Refitting is a reversal of removal, but lightly grease the bushes and clevis pin and renew the self-locking nut.

15.3 Unhook the handbrake cable(s) from the equaliser

15.4A Handbrake cable removal from retaining clip – remove clip to release cable

15.4B Pull cable(s) through the floor from the underside

16.2 Handbrake warning light switch

17.2 Handbrake lever/fuel filler release lever retaining bolts and nut

18.2 Pushrod to brake pedal clevis pin – arrowed (note location of clevis pin hole used)

19 Fault diagnosis – braking system

Before diagnosing faults from the following chart, check that any braking irregularities are not caused by:
   (a) Uneven and incorrect tyre pressures
   (b) Incorrect mix of radial and crossply tyres
   (c) Wear in the steering mechanism
   (d) Misalignment of the chassis geometry

Symptom	Reason(s)
Pedal travels a long way before the brakes operate	Brake shoes set too far from the drums due to faulty self-adjusting mechanism
Stopping ability poor, even though pedal pressure is firm	Linings/pads and/or drums/disc badly worn or scored One or more wheel hydraulic cylinders or caliper pistons seized resulting in some brake shoes/pads not pressing against the drums/discs Brake linings/pads contaminated with oil Wrong type of linings/pads fitted (too hard) Brake shoes/pads wrongly assembled Faulty servo unit
Car veers to one side when the brakes are applied	Brake linings/pads on one side are contaminated with oil Hydraulic wheel cylinder/caliper on one side partially or fully seized A mixture of lining materials fitted between sides Unequal wear between sides caused by partially seized wheel cylinders/pistons
Pedal feels spongy	Air in the hydraulic system
Pedal feels springy when the brakes are applied	Braking linings/pads not bedded into the drums/discs (after fitting new ones) Master cylinder or brake backplate mounting bolts loose Out-of-round drums or discs with excessive run-out
Pedal travels right down with little or no resistance and brakes are virtually non-operative	Leak in hydraulic system resulting in lack of pressure for operating wheel cylinders/caliper pistons If no signs of leakage are apparent the master cylinder internal seals are failing to sustain pressure
Binding, juddering, overheating	One or a combination of causes given in the foregoing sections Handbrake over-adjusted Handbrake cable(s) seized
Lack of servo assistance	Vacuum hose leaking Non-return valve defective or leaking grommet Servo internal fault

Chapter 9 Suspension, hubs, wheels and tyres

For information applicable to later models, see Supplement at end of manual

Contents

Specifications

Front suspension

Type	Independent, MacPherson struts, coil springs and anti-roll bar
Front suspension geometry	*Refer to Chapter 10*
Anti-roll bar diameter	20 mm, 22 mm or 23 mm (dependent on model)

Rear suspension

Type	Independent, trailing arms, torsion bars, inclined shock absorbers. Anti-roll bar on OHC engine models
Rear suspension geometry:	
Toe-in	0.5 ± 1 mm (0.02 ± 0.04 in)
Camber	−1° ± 30′
Rear suspension ride height	436 to 450 mm (17.2 to 17.7 in)
Maximum allowable difference in ride height, side to side ...	10 mm (0.4 in)

Roadwheels and tyres

Wheels:

GE	4^1/$_2$B steel
GL	5B steel
GR and GR Profile	5B steel
SR	5B steel
SRi	5^1/$_2$J alloy

Tyres:

GE	145 SR 13
GL	165/70 SR 13
GR	165/70 SR 13
GR Profile	145 SR 13
SR	165/70 SR 13
SRi	175/65 HR 14

Tyre pressures (cold):	Front	Rear
All models except SR Injection	28 lbf/in² (1.9 bar)	30 lbf/in² (2.1 bar)
SR Injection	29 lbf/in² (1.9 bar)	26 lbf/in² (1.8 bar)

Torque wrench settings

Front suspension	Nm	lbf ft
Top mounting	12	9
Shock absorber piston rod	45	33
Crimped nuts	70	52
Strut clamp bolt	58	43
Anti-roll bar clamp	35	26
Anti-roll bar end	75	55
Bottom balljoint	35	26
Lower suspension arm pivot bolt	35	26
Front hub nut	265	195

Rear suspension		
Suspension to body mountings	45	33
Suspension front mounting pivot	80	59
Hub nut	215	159
Cable support bracket bolt	35	26

Roadwheels		
Roadwheel bolts (steel or alloy wheels)	85	63

1 General description

The front suspension is of independent type; incorporating McPherson struts with coil springs and integral shock absorbers. An anti-roll bar is fitted to all models.

The rear suspension is also of independent type; incorporating a cross-tube with trailing arms set in each end and supported on needle or plain bearings. Torsion bars are fitted to the trailing arms and, on certain models, an anti-roll bar located inside the cross-tube stabilizes the car when cornering. The telescopic shock absorbers are inclined with their top mountings attached to the suspension side-members. A

Fig. 9.1 Front suspension assembly showing the subframe (1) and mounting points (2) with silentbloc mounting at 3 (Sec 1)

Fig. 9.2 Rear suspension assembly (Sec 1)

rubber cone bump stop is provided on each side for times of excessive movement of the trailing arms (photo).

2   Routine maintenance

Carry out the following procedures at the intervals given in Routine Maintenance at the beginning of the manual.
1   Check and adjust the tyre pressures and make sure that the caps are securely fitted to the valves.
2   Thoroughly examine the tyres for wear, damage and deterioration. When making this check, raise the vehicle so that each wheel in turn is clear of the ground so that a complete check can be made.
3   Check the hub bearings for excessive wear. With the wheels clear of the ground, grip the top and bottom and attempt to rock the wheel. Any excessive play indicates wear in the hub bearings although, on the front wheels, check that the movement is not due to a worn lower suspension balljoint.
4   Place the car on ramps or jack it up and support on axle stands, then check the front and rear shock absorbers for leakage of fluid. If

evident, renew the shock absorber or strut as necessary. The efficiency of the shock absorbers can be checked as described later in this Chapter.

3   Front anti-roll bar – removal and refitting

1   Detach and remove the engine undershield.
2   Measure and note the distance 'X' between the subframe and guide bar bush shown in Fig. 9.3, then remove the lower suspension arm from one side, as described in Section 5.
3   Unscrew the nut securing the remaining end of the anti-roll bar to the other suspension arm and recover the washer.
4   Unbolt the guide bar from the subframe (photo).
5   Unscrew the mounting clamp bolts (photo) and withdraw the anti-roll bar over the subframe.
6   Examine the nylon mounting bushes and the rubber bushes in the suspension arms for damage or excessive wear and renew them as necessary. The bushes in the suspension arms can be prised or driven out.

1.3 Rear suspension bump stop

3.4 Anti-roll bar guide bar bolt (arrowed)

3.5 Anti-roll bar mounting clamp bolts (arrowed)

Fig. 9.3 Top view of front suspension showing measuring points for anti-roll bar guide dimension (X) (Sec 3)

7   Refitting is a reversal of removal, but delay fully tightening the clamp bolts until the full weight of the car is on the suspension. The guide bar bolts should also remain loosened until after the bearing clamp bolts have been tightened and its length should be suitably set (see Fig. 9.3, as noted during removal).

4   Front suspension strut – removal, overhaul and refitting

1   Before raising the car it is recommended that a retaining tool is fitted to the coil spring to enable easier removal of the strut. Peugeot garages use two special cables inserted through the holes at the top of the front suspension tower and engaged with further holes in the bottom coil spring seat (Fig. 9.4). If available use these, otherwise fit universal coil spring compressors. **Do not** attempt to use any makeshift tool, as considerable damage could occur if the spring breaks free. To fit either type of tool it will be necessary to turn the front wheel to full lock in alternate directions.
2   Loosen, but do not remove, the three top strut mounting nuts (photo).
3   Jack up the front of the car and support on axle stands. Apply the handbrake and remove the roadwheel on the relevant side.
4   Unscrew the clamp bolt securing the hub carrier to the bottom of the strut (photo).

Fig. 9.4 Front suspension strut showing Peugeot special retaining cables (1), upper cable locations (a and b) and the strut securing nuts (2) (Sec 4)

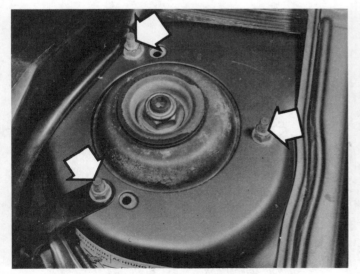

4.2 Front suspension top mounting nuts (arrowed)

4.4 Hub carrier-to-strut clamp bolt

5 In order to prevent any damage to the driveshaft joints, fit a length of wire from the top of the hub carrier to the subframe.
6 Drive a suitable wedge into the slot on the hub carrier and slide the carrier from the bottom of the strut. If available, use the special Peugeot tool which consists of a cranked rod inserted in the slot and turned through 90°.
7 Support the strut then unscrew the top mounting nuts and withdraw it from under the wing. Recover the washers.
8 Clean away all external dirt from the strut and coil spring.
9 Fit spring compressors to the coil spring (if applicable) and tighten them evenly until the spring is released from the upper mounting. If applicable, remove the Peugeot cables.
10 Unscrew the piston rod nut, if necessary using a 7 mm Allen key to hold the rod stationary.
11 Remove the washer and upper mounting, followed by the coil spring. The spring may remain in the compressed state ready for refitting to the strut. If the spring is to be renewed, release the compressors very gently and evenly until they can be removed and fitted to the new spring.
12 If necessary, remove the gaiter and bump stop from the piston rod. Note the location of each component to ensure correct refitting.
13 Check the strut for signs of fluid seepage at the piston rod seal. Temporarily refit the upper mounting to the piston rod and, with the bottom of the strut gripped in a vice, fully extend and retract the piston rod. If the resistance is not firm and even in both directions, or if there are signs of leakage or damage, the strut must be renewed.
14 Refitting is a reversal of removal, but note that the bump stop must be fitted with the largest diameter uppermost. Renew the piston rod nut and tighten it to the specified torque. Make sure that the strut fully enters the hub carrier; if there is any doubt about this loosen the clamp bolts with the full weight of the car on the suspension and the strut will be forced fully home. Retighten the bolt to the specified torque.

5 Front lower suspension arm – removal, overhaul and refitting

1 Loosen the front roadwheel bolts on the side concerned, then jack up the car and support it on safety stands. Check that the handbrake is fully applied, then remove the roadwheel.

Fig. 9.5 Front suspension strut components (Sec 4)

1	Top mounting nut	7	Cap
2	Piston rod nut	8	Stop
3	Washer	9	Coil spring
4	Spacer	10	Bump stop
5	Top mounting	11	Piston rod
6	Pad	12	Strut

Fig. 9.6 Front lower suspension arm components (Sec 5)

1	Arm	4	Bush (spindle)
2	Spindle (pivot) bolt	5	Bushes (anti-roll bar)
3	Clamp bolt	6	Balljoint protector shield

5.2 Suspension arm-to-hub carrier clamp bolt and balljoint protector shield (arrowed)

5.3 Suspension arm inner pivot bolt and nut

6.6 Unbolt the brake caliper from the hub carrier

2   Unscrew the hub carrier-to-arm clamp bolt and withdraw it from the front. Remove the balljoint protector shield (photo).
3   Unscrew the retaining nut from the suspension arm inner pivot bolt, remove the washer, then withdraw the pivot bolt (photo).
4   Turn the hub onto full left-hand lock, then lever down on the suspension arm to separate it from the hub carrier. If necessary drive a suitable wedge into the slot in the carrier to ease separation.
5   Undo the anti-roll bar nut and withdraw the suspension arm from the anti-roll bar.
6   Check the inner pivot and anti-roll bar bushes for wear and deterioration. Check the lower balljoint on the outer end of the arm for excessive wear indicated by up and down movement of the ball in the socket. Check the arm for damage or deterioration. The bushes may be renewed using a simple puller consisting of a metal tube and washers, together with a long bolt and nut, It is not possible to renew the balljoint separately.
7   Refitting is a reversal of removal, but delay tightening the inner pivot bolt until the full weight of the car is on the suspension.

6   Front suspension hub carrier – removal and refitting

Before removing the hub, it should be noted that a new bearing must always be fitted whenever the hub is removed and refitted. If available, use the special Peugeot tools referred to in the text.
1   Detach the wheel trim from the wheel concerned, then undo the driveshaft nut.
2   Fit the Peugeot restraining cables or a suitable retaining tool to the strut coil spring, as described in paragraph 1 of Section 4.
3   Loosen the roadwheel bolts, raise the front of the car and support it on safety stands. Remove the front roadwheel.
4   Unscrew and remove the bolt securing the hub carrier to the bottom of the strut.
5   Drive a suitable wedge into the slot on the hub carrier and slide the carrier from the bottom of the strut. If available use the Peugeot special tool which consists of a cranked rod inserted in the slot and turned through 90°. As the stub axle is lowered, disconnect the driveshaft from it. Tie up or rest the driveshaft on something for support.
6   Unbolt and remove the brake caliper as described in Chapter 8. The hydraulic hose can be left attached providing the caliper is supported (photo).
7   Unscrew the two retaining screws and remove the brake disc.
8   The hub bearings can be checked or renewed at this stage, or the hub carrier fully detached and the bearings removed later, as required (see Section 1).
9   Unscrew the nut and use a balljoint removal tool to separate the track rod arm from the steering arm.
10   Unscrew and remove the lower suspension arm-to-hub carrier clamp bolt and detach the lower suspension arm from the hub carrier (see Section 5).
11   Refitting is a reversal of the removal procedure but refer to Chapters 7 and 8 respectively when refitting the driveshaft, and brake disc and caliper.

7   Front hub and bearing – renewal

1   Remove the hub carrier, as described in Section 6. Note that the hub and bearing can be renewed with the hub carrier attached to the track rod and lower suspension arm.
2   Clean away all external dirt with a wire brush.
3   Using circlip pliers, extract the bearing retaining circlip from the inner side of the hub carrier (photo).
4   The hub must now be pressed or driven from the bearing using force from the inner side of the hub carrier. If available, use the Peugeot bearing removal tool for your model (Fig. 9.7) which locates in the circlip groove, otherwise use a suitable soft metal drift. Note that the bearing becomes unsuitable for further use after removal of the hub.
5   Using a puller, remove the bearing inner track half from the hub and refit it to the outside of the bearing.
6   Press or drive the bearing from the hub carrier. It is possible that the bearing is so tight that it cannot be removed with hand tools, in which case have your dealer remove it on a press.
7   Clean the hub and bearing recess in the carrier. Do not attempt to remove the seals or plastic ring from the new bearing.
8   Smear a little grease on the bearing recess in the carrier.
9   Press or drive the new bearing into the hub carrier using force on the outer track only, then refit the circlip in the groove.
10 Press the hub into the bearing inner tracks using the special Peugeot tool shown in Fig. 9.8 or a similar tool made from metal tubing, washers, a long bolt and nut. Note that the tube must locate on the inner track and there must be a space provided to receive the plastic ring which is pushed out by the hub.
11 Refit the hub carrier with reference to Section 6.

7.3 Front hub bearing and circlip

Fig. 9.7 Using Peugeot tool to remove the front hub (Sec 7)

OHV engine models – tool no 0613
OHC engine models – tool no 0606

Fig. 9.8 Using Peugeot tool to refit the front hub (Sec 7)

8.5 Gearchange selector rod to subframe connection – withdraw the retaining clip to detach

8 Front suspension assembly – removal and refitting

1   Loosen the front roadwheel bolts, then raise the car at the front end and support it on safety stands each side. Chock the rear wheels then unbolt and remove the front roadwheels.

2   Referring to Chapter 8, disconnect the brake caliper unit each side from the hub carrier. The calipers can remain attached to the hydraulic lines providing they are supported to prevent the weight of the caliper straining the hydraulic hose.
3   Disconnect the driveshaft each side from the hub carrier as described in Chapter 7. The driveshafts can be left engaged with the transmission, but suspend them to support their weight.
4   Undo and remove the steering pinion-to-column shaft coupling bolt (see Chapter 10).
5   Disconnect the gearchange selector rod unit from the subframe after extracting the retaining clip (photo).
6   Position a trolley jack centrally under the subframe to support it. Prior to undoing the subframe retaining bolts, enlist the aid of a pair of assistants and have them support the suspension assembly on each side during the detachment and lowering of the unit.
7   Undo and remove the two rear subframe-to-floor mounting bolts each side (photo).
8   Undo and remove the self-locking nut and special washer securing the subframe to the chassis member stud each side.
9   Unscrew and remove the three suspension strut top mounting nuts each side. Remove the flat washers and the harness location bracket on the left-hand side. Detach the earth leads from the spade connectors on the top of each strut.
10 With an assistant steadying the suspension assembly each side, slowly lower the jack under the subframe and, as the unit is lowered, check that the brake lines are clear. Withdraw the unit from under the car (photos).
11 Refitting is a reversal of the removal procedure.
12 When the assembly is initially raised into position, loosely fit the various mounting nuts and bolts, then when they are all located, tighten them to the specified torque settings.

8.7 Subframe-to-floor mounting bolts

8.10A Lowering the front suspension assembly

8.10B Front suspension assembly removed from the car and cleaned for inspection

Fig. 9.9 Cross-sectional view of the rear suspension (Sec 9)

1 Cross tube
2 Trailing arm
3 Left-hand torsion bar
4 Right-hand torsion bar
5 Housing
6 Anti-roll bar (if fitted)
All measurements in mm

13 Reconnect the driveshafts with reference to Chapter 7.
14 Refit the brake calipers with reference to Chapter 8.
15 Refit the steering couplings with reference to Chapter 10.
16 When the car is lowered to the ground check the brakes and steering for satisfactory action. If any of the steering and/or suspension components were removed or renewed, check the steering geometry with reference to Chapter 10.

Fig. 9.10 The shoulder at the left-hand end of the rear anti-roll bar (arrowed) (Sec 9)

9 Rear anti-roll bar – removal and refitting

1 Jack up the rear of the car and support on axle stands. Chock the front wheels and remove the rear wheels.
2 Working on the right-hand side, unscrew the bolt securing the anti-roll bar lever and bracket to the trailing arm. Move the bracket down, leaving it still attached to the handbrake cable.
3 Unscrew the plug from the end of the anti-roll bar then insert a well oiled bolt into the lever and tighten it until the lever is forced off. If available use the bolt included in the Peugeot tool kit 70908.
4 Working on the left-hand side, unscrew the bolt securing the anti-roll bar lever and bracket to the trailing arm, then move the bracket down leaving it still attached to the handbrake cable.
5 Withdraw the anti-roll bar to the left.
6 Mount the anti-roll bar in a vice with the lever uppermost then remove the lever using the procedure described in paragraph 3.
7 Before refitting the anti-roll bar, clean the splines both on the bar and levers and coat them with Esso Norva 275 grease.
8 Mount the anti-roll bar in the vice with its left-hand end uppermost. Note that the left-hand end has an additional shoulder, as shown in Fig. 9.10.
9 Fit a new sealing ring to the left-hand lever. The left-hand lever has a single identification line on its inner face. Locate the ring with the curved end facing inwards and apply some Kluber Proba grease to its outer surface.
10 Slide the lever on the bar with the identification line aligned with the line on the bar shoulder.
11 Press the lever fully onto the splines using Peugeot tool 70908 or a suitable nut, bolt and washer. If the lever is particularly tight it is permissible to drive it on with a length of metal tube.

12 Remove the tool and fit a temporary bolt in the bar to ensure the lever does not move in subsequent work.
13 Where the lever incorporates a 2 mm recess, fit a new seal; otherwise apply some sealant to the lever shoulder.
14 Insert the anti-roll bar into the left-hand side of the suspension tube then position the handbrake lever bracket, insert the bolt and tighten it to the specified torque.
15 Fit a new sealing ring to the right-hand lever. The right-hand lever has three identification lines at 120° intervals on its inner face. Locate the ring with the curved end facing inwards and apply some Kluber Proba grease to its outer surface.
16 Slide the lever on the bar so that the bolt holes in the lever and trailing arm are aligned.
17 Locate a 1.0 mm (0.039 in) spacer between the lever and trailing arm, as shown in Fig. 9.11, then press on the lever using the method described in paragraph 11. If a metal tube is used, the left-hand lever must be suitably supported.
18 Remove the tool and spacer, then position the handbrake lever bracket, insert the bolt, and tighten it.
19 Remove the temporary bolt fitted in paragraph 12.
20 Apply sealing compound to the threads and collars of the end plugs and screw them into the levers.
21 Refit the rear wheels then lower the car to the ground.

Fig. 9.11 Using feeler blades to check the rear anti-roll bar end gap (Sec 9)

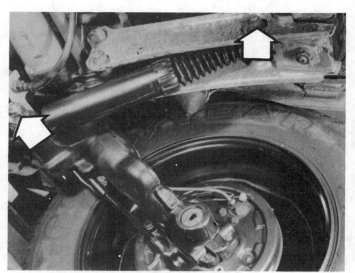

10.3 General view of the rear suspension assembly with the shock absorber upper and lower mounting bolts indicated (arrowed)

10 Rear shock absorber – testing, removal and refitting

1   The efficiency of a rear shock absorber can be checked by depressing the rear corner of the car then releasing it quickly. If the body rises then stabilises, the shock absorber is good, but if there are several oscillations it should be renewed.
2   Position the rear of the car on ramps or alternatively jack it up and support it beneath the wheels. Apply the handbrake.
3   Unscrew the shock absorber bottom mounting nut and tap the bolt outwards until it clears the shock absorber (photo). If the bolt head fouls the handbrake cable bracket, loosen the bracket bolt on the side of the trailing arm and lift the bracket as required. Do not forget to tighten the bolt after refitting the shock absorber.
4   Unscrew the upper mounting nut, remove the washer, and tap out the bolt.
5   Withdraw the shock absorber from under the car.
6   A more thorough check of the shock absorber may now be made by gripping the bottom mounting in a vice and attempting to extend and retract it. If the resistance is not firm and even in both directions, or if there are signs of leakage or damage, the shock absorber must be renewed.
7   Refitting is a reversal of removal, but renew the self-locking nuts. The nuts must be tightened when the distance between the mounting bolt centres is 288.0 mm (11.339 in). The Peugeot tool 80911 for this operation consists of a bar and adjustable bolt located beneath the lifting ramp and hooked on the suspension tube; however, loading the rear of the car by trial and error will produce the same result.

11 Rear torsion bar – removal and refitting

The removal of the rear torsion bar will necessitate the use of a suitable slide hammer, if available use Peugeot tool 0316 and adaptor 0908.
1   Jack up the rear of the car and support on axle stands under the body. Chock the front wheels and remove the rear wheels.
2   Remove the rear anti-roll bar, as described in Section 9.
3   Remove the shock absorber on the side being worked on, with reference to Section 10.
4   In order to retain the suspension ride height it is necessary to hold the trailing arm stationary with the torsion bar relaxed. Note that the arm itself must be slightly raised to eliminate the effect of its own weight. If available use Peugeot tool 0908 fitted in place of the shock absorber, otherwise firmly support the trailing arm and record the distance between the shock absorber mounting bolt centres (Fig. 9.12).

5   Unscrew and remove the nut and washer from the torsion bar end fitted to the suspension tube.
6   Unscrew the bolt and remove the seal and thrust washer from the torsion bar end fitted to the trailing arm.
7   Using a centre punch, mark the torsion bar and trailing arm in relation to each other.
8   Support the trailing arm then extract the torsion bar using a slide hammer and adaptor screwed into the end of the bar. When removing the left-hand side torsion bar take care not to damage the hydraulic brake line by supporting the suspension arm.
9   Unscrew the shouldered stud from the end of the bar.
10 Note that the right and left-hand torsion bars are different – the right one is identified by one painted ring whereas the left one has two painted rings.
11 If the original torsion bar is being refitted and the ride height is correct, check that the dimension recorded in paragraph 4 is still correct. If the ride height is being adjusted refer to Section 12 and set the dimension accordingly. If a new torsion bar is being fitted, set the dimension by raising or lowering the trailing arm to 347.5 mm (13.681 in).
12 Screw in the shouldered stud fully into the 24.2 mm diameter end of the torsion bar.
13 Coat the torsion bar splines with Esso Norva 275 grease, then insert the small end through the arm and engage it with the splines on the suspension tube bracket. It will be necessary to try the bar in several positions, if the original is not being refitted, and the bar will initially only enter by approximately 10.0 mm (0.4 in) as the splines at each end are not in the same plane. When the correct splines are engaged, drive the bar fully into position using the slide hammer and adaptor, or a suitable drift.
14 Pack the recess in the arm with grease then fit the thrust washer, a new seal and the bolt. Tighten the bolt.
15 Using a feeler gauge, check that the gap between the trailing arm and suspension tube is 0.05 mm (0.002 in). If it is greater strike the outer surface of the arm with a wooden mallet.

Fig. 9.12 Peugeot tool 0908 for use as a dummy rear shock absorber (Sec 11)

Fig. 9.13 Rear suspension ride height measurement points (arrowed) (Sec 12)

16 Unscrew the shouldered stud at the opposite end of the bar until it just contacts the cup. Recheck the gap, as in paragraph 15, then fit the washer and nut and tighten the nut. To prevent the stud moving hold it with a screwdriver while tightening the nut.
17 Refit the shock absorber (Section 10) and anti-roll bar (Section 9).
18 Refit the rear wheels and lower the car to the ground.

12 Rear suspension ride height – adjustment

1 The rear suspension ride height must be checked with the car on a level surface with the correct tyre pressures and unladen, but with a full fuel tank. The height dimension is given in the Specifications and is taken from the points indicated in Fig. 9.13. The difference between the dimension on each side must not exceed 10.0 mm (0.4 in).
2 It is recommended that the rear of the car is bounced before taking a measurement, and that the average of three successive measurements be taken as the final reading.
3 Note that an adjustment on one side will slightly alter the ride height on the opposite side.
4 To adjust the ride height the torsion bar must be removed and repositioned after setting the trailing arm. A change in the dimension between the shock absorber mounting bolt centres of 2.0 mm (0.08 in) is equivalent to a change in ride height of 3.0 mm (0.12 in). Therefore it is essential to record the existing shock absorber and ride height dimensions before making an adjustment. The torsion bar removal and refitting procedure is given in Section 11.
5 After ride height adjustment has been made, the headlight beam adjustments should be checked and if necessary readjusted (see Chapter 12).

13 Rear suspension assembly – removal and refitting

1 Disconnect the handbrake cables at the lever end and withdraw them through the floor. Refer to Chapter 8 for details. Each cable can be left attached to the drums during removal/refitting.
2 Remove the exhaust system, with reference to Chapter 3.
3 Disconnect the flexible brake hoses from the rear suspension assembly, with reference to Chapter 8.
4 Unscrew the left-hand rear mounting nut, remove the exhaust bracket then temporarily refit the nut.
5 Unbolt and remove the front clamp and bracket, but do not unscrew the seat belt anchorage.

6 Support the suspension crossmember with a trolley jack (centrally located) or a safety stand each side. A trolley jack is preferable if a couple of assistants are available to help steady the suspension unit as it is detached and lowered.
7 Working in the luggage compartment, unscrew the front and rear mounting nuts (photo).
8 Lower the trolley jack supporting the suspension unit and, as it is lowered, check that the handbrake cables and the hydraulic brake lines are free. As previously mentioned, an assistant will be required on each side to help in steadying the suspension assembly as it is lowered and withdrawn (photo).
9 Refitting is a reversal of removal, but tighten all nuts and bolts to the specified torque. When tightening the front clamp make sure that the ring is centred in the seat belt anchorage bracket. Refer to Chapter 8 for information on reconnecting the brake hydraulic lines and the handbrake cables. Bleed the brake hydraulic system as described in that Chapter.
10 Refer to Chapter 3 for information on reconnecting the exhaust system.

13.7 Rear suspension mounting (front) within the luggage compartment

13.8 Rear suspension assembly removed from the car

14.3 Rear hub bearing retaining circlip (arrowed)

14.5 Oil seal (arrowed) in the rear hub/drum

14 Rear hub/drum – servicing

1   The removal and refitting of the rear hub/drum is described in Chapter 8, together with the inspection of the drum for wear.
2   If the bearing is to be removed from the hub/drum, a new bearing must be used on reassembly. Do not, therefore, remove the bearing unless absolutely necessary.
3   It is not possible to obtain replacement hub bearings from Peugeot although they do in fact supply a bearing retaining circlip separately (photo). If the bearings are worn excessively it will therefore be necessary to renew the complete hub/drum unless non-genuine bearings become available.
4   The bearings can be driven out using a suitable tube drift. Before fitting new bearings, the hub bearing housings must be cleaned and lubricated with Molykote 321R slip compound. The new bearing must be fitted with its lettered face towards the circlip. If pressing the bearing into position do not apply a pressure in excess of five tonnes. Fit a new circlip and carefully drive a new thrust cup into the opposing end of the hub (if removed).
5   If the hub/drum oil seal is worn or damaged it can be renewed by prising it out with a screwdriver and pressing in the new one with a metal tube (photo). Clean and grease the seal contact surface on the trailing arm before refitting the hub/drum.

15 Rear suspension trailing arm and bearings – removal and refitting

1   Jack up the rear of the car and support on axle stands. Chock the front wheels and remove the rear wheels.
2   Remove the handbrake cable and brake shoes on the side being worked on, with reference to Chapter 8.
3   Remove the anti-roll bar, as described in Section 9 (where applicable).
4   Remove the torsion bar, as described in Section 11.
5   Disconnect the hydraulic brake pipes from the wheel cylinder (with reference to Chapter 8).
6   Slide the trailing arm from the suspension tube.
7   Prise the oil seal from the end of the tube and remove the seal sleeve.
8   An extractor is required to remove both the inner and outer bearings and it is recommended that Peugeot tool 0526 is used. The tool comprises a rod and tilting washer which locates behind the bearing – the outer bearing is removed using a slide hammer attachment and the inner bearing is removed using a threaded rod, spacer and nut. If the inner bearing is very tight, a length of rod can be inserted from the opposite end of the tube to release it. Note that the inner bearing may be either plain or needle roller type.

H145852

Fig. 9.14 Peugeot tool 0526 for removing the rear suspension trailing arm bearings (Sec 15)

9   If necessary the shaft may be removed from the trailing arm using a press, but first note the fitted position of the shaft, it is recessed by 2.0 mm (0.08 in) from the outer surface. Always refit the shaft in its original position. This can be achieved by inserting a 2 mm thick washer in the bore of the arm to act as a temporary distance spacer when fitting the shaft into the arm. With the shaft fitted, remove the washer.

10 To fit the bearings, first pack them with multi-purpose grease then use the special tool to pull or drive them into position. When fitting the needle bearings the side with the manufacturer's name on it must face towards the relevant open end of the tube.

11 Drive the seal sleeve into the end of the tube.

12 Locate the new seal over the trailing arm shaft, having first filled the spacers between the lips with grease.

13 Insert the trailing arm in the tube until the seal contacts the sleeve, then position a 0.05 mm (0.002 in) feeler gauge between the arm and tube and use a wooden mallet to drive the arm into position.

14 Refit the hydraulic brake pipe to the wheel cylinder and tighten the union.

15 Refit the torsion bar (Section 11) and anti-roll bar (Section 9) as applicable.

16 Refit the handbrake cable and brake shoes then bleed the brakes as described in Chapter 8 (photo).

17 Refit the wheels and lower the car to the ground.

15.16 Rear suspension arm showing handbrake cable and brake hydraulic line attachment

16 Rear suspension mountings and bushes – renewal

1   Remove the rear suspension assembly, as described in Section 13.

2   Unbolt the rear mountings from the side-members.

3   Identify the front mounting brackets for position then unscrew the bolts and remove the brackets.

4   Saw off the ends of the front mounting bushes then drive them out with a metal bar.

5   Dip the new bushes in soapy water and press them into position using a long bolt, nut and spacers. Note that the notch in the flange must be in the vertical plane (ie facing up or down when fitted).

6   Refit the front mounting bracket, insert the bolts from the rear and tighten the nuts with the brackets horizontal.

7   Fit the new rear mountings with the studs towards the wheel side and tighten the nuts.

8   Refit the suspension assembly, with reference to Section 13.

Fig. 9.15 The notch in the rear suspension mounting bushes (arrowed) must be fitted in the vertical plane (Sec 16)

17 Wheels and tyres – general care and maintenance

Wheels and tyres should give no real problems in use provided that a close eye is kept on them with regard to excessive wear or damage. To this end, the following points should be noted.

Ensure that tyre pressures are checked regularly and maintained correctly. Checking should be carried out with the tyres cold and not immediately after the vehicle has been in use. If the pressures are checked with the tyres hot, an apparently high reading will be obtained owing to heat expansion. Under no circumstances should an attempt be made to reduce the pressures to the quoted cold reading in this instance, or effective underinflation will result.

Underinflation will cause overheating of the tyre owing to excessive flexing of the casing, and the tread will not sit correctly on the road surface. This will cause a consequent loss of adhesion and excessive wear, not to mention the danger of sudden tyre failure due to heat build-up.

Overinflation will cause rapid wear of the centre part of the tyre tread coupled with reduced adhesion, harsher ride, and the danger of shock damage occurring in the tyre casing.

Regularly check the tyres for damage in the form of cuts or bulges, especially in the sidewalls. Remove any nails or stones embedded in the tread before they penetrate the tyre to cause deflation. If removal of a nail *does* reveal that the tyre has been punctured, refit the nail so that its point of penetration is marked. Then immediately change the wheel and have the tyre repaired by a tyre dealer. Do *not* drive on a tyre in such a condition. In many cases a puncture can be simply repaired by the use of an inner tube of the correct size and type. If in any doubt as to the possible consequences of any damage found, consult your local tyre dealer for advice.

Periodically remove the wheels and clean any dirt or mud from the inside and outside surfaces. Examine the wheel rims for signs of rusting, corrosion or other damage. Light alloy wheels are easily damaged by 'kerbing' whilst parking, and similarly steel wheels may become dented or buckled. Renewal of the wheel is very often the only course of remedial action possible.

The balance of each wheel and tyre assembly should be maintained to avoid excessive wear, not only to the tyres but also to the steering and suspension components. Wheel imbalance is normally signified by vibration through the vehicle's bodyshell, although in many cases it is particularly noticeable through the steering wheel. Conversely, it should be noted that wear or damage in suspension or steering components may cause excessive tyre wear. Out-of-round or out-of-true tyres, damaged wheels and wheel bearing wear/maladjustment also fall into this category. Balancing will not usually cure vibration caused by such wear.

Wheel balancing may be carried out with the wheel either on or off the vehicle. If balanced on the vehicle, ensure that the wheel-to-hub relationship is marked in some way prior to subsequent wheel removal so that it may be refitted in its original position.

General tyre wear is influenced to a large degree by driving style – harsh braking and acceleration or fast cornering will all produce more rapid tyre wear. Interchanging of tyres may result in more even wear, but this should only be carried out where there is no mix of tyre types on the vehicle. However, it is worth bearing in mind that if this is completely effective, the added expense of replacing a complete set of tyres simultaneously is incurred, which may prove financially restrictive for many owners.

Front tyres may wear unevenly as a result of wheel misalignment. The front wheels should always be correctly aligned according to the settings specified by the vehicle manufacturer.

Legal restrictions apply to the mixing of tyre types on a vehicle. Basically this means that a vehicle must not have tyres of differing construction on the same axle. Although it is not recommended to mix tyre types between front axle and rear axle, the only legally permissible combination is crossply at the front and radial at the rear. When mixing radial ply tyres, textile braced radials must always go on the front axle, with steel braced radials at the rear. An obvious disadvantage of such mixing is the necessity to carry two spare tyres to avoid contravening the law in the event of a puncture.

In the UK, the Motor Vehicles Construction and Use Regulations apply to many aspects of tyre fitting and usage. It is suggested that a copy of these regulations is obtained from your local police if in doubt as to the current legal requirements with regard to tyre condition, minimum tread depth, etc.

18 Fault diagnosis – suspension, hubs, wheels and tyres

Symptom	Reason(s)
Car pulls to one side	Worn front suspension lower balljoint Incorrect tyre pressures
Excessive pitching or rolling	Worn shock absorbers
Wheel wobble or vibration	Unbalanced wheels Damaged wheels Worn wheel bearings Worn shock absorbers
Excessive tyre wear	Incorrect tyre pressures Worn front suspension lower balljoint Unbalanced wheels

Chapter 10 Steering

For information applicable to later models, see Supplement at end of manual

Contents

Specifications

General

Type	Rack and pinion. Steering column with universal joint. Power-assisted steering on some models
Steering wheel turns (lock to lock)	3.8
Turning circle (between kerbs)	10.50 m (34.5 ft)

Front wheel alignment

Toe-in	2 ± 1 mm (0.08 ± 0.04 in)
Castor	0°30' ± 30'
Camber	0° ± 30'
Steering axis inclination	9°30' ± 30'

Power-assisted steering

Fluid type	Dexron II type ATF (Duckhams D-Matic)

Torque wrench settings

	Nm	lbf ft
Steering gear	35	26
Column-to-pinion clamp bolt	15	11
Track rod balljoint nut	35	26
Track rod inner locknut	45	33

1 General description

The steering system is of rack and pinion type with side track rods connected to the hub carriers by balljoints. Further balljoints on the inner ends of the track rods are screwed into the rack.

The steering column incorporates a single universal joint at its lower end connected to an intermediate shaft which also incorporates a universal joint at its connection to the pinions on the steering gear. The steering column is angled to prevent direct movement into the passenger compartment in the event of a front end impact.

Power steering

Fitted to certain models only, the power assistance is derived from a pump which is driven by the alternator drivebelt. At the time of writing, limited information on the power steering system is available and therefore any repairs concerning the power steering system and components should be entrusted to your Peugeot dealer.

2 Routine maintenance

Carry out the following procedures at the intervals given in Routine Maintenance at the beginning of the manual.

1 Jack up the front of the car and support on axle stands. Apply the handbrake. Thoroughly examine the bellows at each end of the steering gear for splitting and deterioration, and renew if necessary.

2 Check the track rod ends for excessive wear by attempting to move them up and down. If there is more than the very slightest movement the track rod end should be renewed. Similarly check the track rod inner joints by gripping the track rod through the bellows and attempting to move them up and down. Track rod ends should also be renewed if the rubber boots are split or damaged.

Power steering

3 Maintenance consists of checking the fluid level in the reservoir and checking the pump drivebelt tension and condition.

4 The power steering pump reservoir is translucent and has level markings on it, these being 'high' and 'low'. The fluid level must not drop below the minimum level mark (fluid cold). If topping-up becomes necessary do not fill beyond the maximum mark.

5 Topping-up should only be done with clean fluid of the correct type (see Specifications). Regular need for topping-up can only be due to a leak, which should be rectified. If the pump is run dry it will be damaged: disconnect the drivebelt rather than let this happen.

6 To check, adjust and/or renew the drivebelt refer to Chapter 12, Section 5.

3 Steering wheel – removal and refitting

1 Set the front wheels in the straight-ahead position.

2 Prise out the centre pad (photo), then use a socket to unscrew the

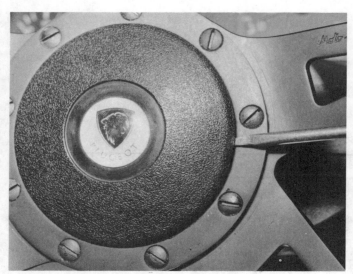

3.2 Prise free the steering wheel centre pad – SRi model shown

4.3 Steering column lower universal joint, clamp bolt and intermediate shaft

retaining nut. On some models the centre pad is secured by retaining screws recessed in the underside of the steering wheel.
3   Mark the hub in relation to the inner column then pull off the steering wheel. If it is tight a rocking action may release it from the splines.
4   Refitting is a reversal of removal, but check that the steering wheel is correctly centred with the front wheels straight-ahead. Tighten the nut while holding the steering wheel rim.

4 Steering column and lock – removal and refitting

Note: *To remove the steering column lock only, proceed as described in paragraphs 1, 2, 8 and 9.*
1   Remove the steering wheel, as described in Section 3.
2   Remove the lower trim panel from under the steering column.
3   Mark the column lower universal joint in relation to the intermediate shaft then unscrew and remove the clamp bolt (photo).
4   Remove the combination switches, as described in Chapter 12.
5   Disconnect the ignition switch wiring multi-plugs.
6   Unscrew the mounting nuts and bolts (photo) disconnect the inner column from the intermediate shaft, and withdraw the steering column from the car. Where shear-bolts are fitted they must be drilled to remove the heads, then unscrewed after removing the column.

7   If necessary, the intermediate shaft can be removed after prising out the grommet and unscrewing the bottom clamp bolt (photo).
8   To remove the steering lock, unscrew the retaining bolt then, with the ignition key in position A, depress the plunger in the housing (photo).
9   Refitting is a reversal of removal. Renew all shear-head bolts and tighten them until the heads break off.

5 Steering gear – removal and refitting

1   Jack up the front of the car and support on axle stands. Apply the handbrake and remove the front wheels.
2   Unscrew the track rod end nuts then use a separator tool to detach the track rod end balljoints from the hub carriers.
3   On models fitted with power steering, disconnect the feed and return hydraulic hoses from the steering gear pinion housing by unscrewing the union connectors. As each hose is detached, allow for a certain amount of fluid spillage. Plug both the hose and pinion hydraulic ports to prevent excessive leakage of fluid and the ingress of dirt. Position the hydraulic lines out of the way.
4   Mark the lower column in relation to the pinion on the steering gear.
5   Unscrew and remove the column-to-pinion clamp bolt.

4.6 Undo the steering column mounting bolt/nuts

4.7 Steering column intermediate shaft, universal joint and clamp bolt. Note clamp tag location in intermediate shaft (arrowed)

4.8 Steering lock retaining bolt (arrowed)

Fig. 10.1 Steering column assembly (Sec 4)

1 Bolt
2 Steering lock and ignition switch
3 Steering column
4 Mounting nut
5 Clamp bolt and nut

Fig. 10.2 Steering column intermediate shaft components (Sec 4)

1 Grommet
2 Intermediate shaft
3 Nut
4 Bolt
5 Steering gear

Fig. 10.3 Manual steering gear unit (Sec 5)

Fig. 10.4 Power steering gear unit (Sec 5)

1 Steering gear unit	3 Hydraulic cylinder	5 and 6 Feed and return pipes	8 Bolt and nut
2 Housing	4 Spacer tube	7 Cylinder bolt	9 Flexible joint

6   Unscrew and remove the two mounting bolts and withdraw the steering gear from one side of the subframe (photo).

7   Refitting is a reversal of removal, but tighten all nuts and bolts to the specified torque and check the front wheel alignment on completion. On power steering models top up and bleed the hydraulic system as described in Section 10.

6   Steering gear – overhaul

The steering gear has a very long life before any wear becomes evident, always provided that the bellows are kept in order to maintain adequate lubrication.

In view of the special tools and gauges required to overhaul the steering gear it is recommended that, when the need for this arises, the assembly should be changed for a new or factory reconditioned one rather than dismantle the worn unit.

7   Track rod end – removal and refitting

1   Jack up the front of the car and support on axle stands. Apply the handbrake and remove the relevant roadwheel.

2   Loosen the locknut on the track rod.

3   Unscrew the balljoint nut and use an extractor tool to separate the taper from the hub carrier (photo).

5.6 Steering gear-to-subframe mounting bolts (arrowed)

7.3 Separating the track rod end from the hub carrier

4 Unscrew the track rod end from the track rod, noting the number of turns necessary to remove it.
5 Screw the new track rod end the same number of turns on the track rod.
6 Clean the taper surfaces then fit the balljoint to the hub carrier and tighten the nut to the specified torque. **Note:** *If difficulty is experienced in loosening or tightening a balljoint taper pin nut due to the taper pin turning in the eye, apply pressure with a jack or long lever to the balljoint socket to force the taper pin into its conical seat.*
7 Tighten the locknut on the track rod end.
8 Refit the roadwheel and lower the car to the ground.
9 Check and if necessary adjust the front wheel toe-in setting, as described in Section 12.

8 Steering rack bellows – renewal

1 Remove the relevant track rod end, as described in Section 7.
2 Release the clips from each end of the bellows then ease the bellows from the steering gear and pull it from the track rod.
3 Clean the track rod and bellows location on the steering gear. If necessary, add molybdenum disulphide grease to the steering gear.
4 Slide the new bellows onto the track rod and steering gear, check that it is not twisted, then fit the clips.
5 Refit the track rod with reference to Section 7.

9 Track rod – renewal

1 Remove the steering rack bellows, as described in Section 8.
2 Using open-ended spanners, hold the rack and loosen the track rod joint socket. Unscrew the socket and withdraw the track rod.
3 Fit the new track rod using a reversal of the removal procedure, but fit a new lock washer and tighten the joint socket to the specified torque.

10 Power-assisted steering – bleeding

1 The power-assisted steering system will normally only need to be bled if (a) the fluid level has dropped below the minimum specified and allowed air to enter the system, (b) part of the system has been disconnected for any reason or (c) if the system is suspected of having air in it.
2 Top the reservoir up with the specified fluid.
3 Start the engine and allow it to idle. Turn the steering wheel from

Fig. 10.5 Track rod components (Sec 7)

1 Bellows   4 Self-locking nut
2 Lock washer   5 Track rod end
3 Track rod

lock to lock two or three times. **Do not** hold the steering wheel on full lock.
4 Stop the engine and check the reservoir fluid level; top up if necessary. Inspect the power steering unions for leaks.

11 Power-assisted steering pump – removal and refitting

1 Remove the alternator/power steering pump drivebelt as described in Chapter 12, Section 5.
2 Syphon as much fluid as possible out of the fluid reservoir using an old poultry baster or similar item.
3 Disconnect and plug the pipe at the steering pump.
4 Unbolt and remove the pump.
5 Refit in the reverse order of removal. Tension the drivebelt (Chapter 12) and bleed the system (Section 10) to complete.

12 Steering angles and front wheel alignment

1   Accurate front wheel alignment is essential to provide good steering and roadholding characteristics and to ensure slow and even tyre wear. Before considering the steering angles, check that the tyres are correctly inflated, that the front wheels are not buckled, the hub bearings are not worn and that the steering linkage is in good order, without slackness or wear at the joints.

2   Wheel alignment consists of four factors:

Camber is the angle at which the roadwheels are set from the vertical when viewed from the front or rear of the vehicle. Positive camber is the angle (in degrees) that the wheels are tilted outwards at the top from the vertical.

Castor is the angle between the steering axis and a vertical line when viewed from each side of the vehicle. Positive castor is indicated when the steering axis is inclined towards the rear of the vehicle at its upper end.

Steering axis inclination is the angle when viewed from the front or rear of the vehicle between vertical and an imaginary line drawn between the upper and lower strut mountings.

Camber, castor and steering axis inclination are set during production of the car and any deviation from specified tolerance must therefore be due to gross wear in the suspension mountings or collision damage.

Toe is the amount by which the distance between the front inside edges of the roadwheel rims differs from that between the rear inside edges. If the distance between the front edges is less than that at the rear, the wheels are said to toe-in. If the distance between the front inside edges is greater than that at the rear, the wheels toe-out.

3   To check the front wheel alignment, first make sure that the lengths of both track rods are equal when the steering is in the straight-ahead position.

4   Obtain a tracking gauge. These are available in various forms from accessory stores or one can be fabricated from a length of steel tubing suitably cranked to clear the sump and bellhousing and having a

Fig. 10.6 Track rod initial setting dimension – measure between points (a). Length of each rod to be equal (Sec 12)

setscrew and locknut at one end.

5   With the gauge, measure the distance between the two wheel inner rims (at hub height) at the rear of the wheel. Push the vehicle forward to rotate the wheels through 180° (half a turn) and measure the distance between the wheel inner rims, again at hub height, at the front of the wheel. This last measurement should differ from the first by the appropriate toe-in according to specification (see Specifications Section).

6   Where the toe-in is found to be incorrect, release the track rod end locknuts and turn the track-rods equally. Only turn them a quarter of a turn at a time before rechecking the alignment, and release the bellows outer clips to prevent the bellows from twisting.

7   On completion tighten the track rod end locknuts, and refit the bellows clips.

13 Fault diagnosis – steering

Symptom	Reason(s)
Stiff action	Lack of rack lubrication Seized track rod end balljoint Seized track rod inner balljoint
Excessive movement at steering wheel	Worn track rod end balljoints Worn rack and pinion
Tyre squeal when cornering and excessive tyre wear	Incorrect wheel alignment

Chapter 11 Bodywork and fittings

For modifications, and information applicable to later models, see Supplement at end of manual

Contents

1 General description

The hatchback style body has a shell which is of one-piece design and safety cell construction, whereby the outer members yield progressively and in a controlled direction in the event of impact, giving maximum protection to the passenger compartment. The body panels are of lightweight high strength steel.

The front wings are bolted to the main body for ease of removal. The complete body is given an extensive anti-corrosion treatment during manufacture; including stone chip protection and wax injection. Peugeot guarantee the body against perforation as a result of corrosion for a period of six years provided the car is given periodic inspections by a Peugeot garage.

Fig. 11.1 Peugeot 309 bodyshell (5-door) (Sec 1)

2 Maintenance – bodywork and underframe

The general condition of a vehicle's bodywork is the one thing that significantly affects its value. Maintenance is easy but needs to be regular. Neglect, particularly after minor damage, can lead quickly to further deterioration and costly repair bills. It is important also to keep watch on those parts of the vehicle not immediately visible, for instance the underside, inside all the wheel arches and the lower part of the engine compartment.

The basic maintenance routine for the bodywork is washing – preferably with a lot of water, from a hose. This will remove all the loose solids which may have stuck to the vehicle. It is important to flush these off in such a way as to prevent grit from scratching the finish. The wheel arches and underframe need washing in the same way to remove any accumulated mud which will retain moisture and tend to encourage rust. Paradoxically enough, the best time to clean the underframe and wheel arches is in wet weather when the mud is thoroughly wet and soft. In very wet weather the underframe is usually cleaned of large accumulations automatically and this is a good time for inspection.

Periodically, except on vehicles with a wax-based underbody protective coating, it is a good idea to have the whole of the underframe of the vehicle steam cleaned, engine compartment included, so that a thorough inspection can be carried out to see what minor repairs and renovations are necessary. Steam cleaning is available at many garages and is necessary for removal of the accumulation of oily grime which sometimes is allowed to become thick in certain areas. If steam cleaning facilities are not available, there are one or two excellent grease solvents available which can be brush applied. The dirt can then be simply hosed off. Note that these methods should not be used on vehicles with wax-based underbody protective coating or the coating will be removed. Such vehicles should be inspected annually, preferably just prior to winter, when the underbody should be washed down and any damage to the wax coating repaired. Ideally, a completely fresh coat should be applied. It would also be worth considering the use of such wax-based protection for injection into door panels, sills, box sections, etc, as an additional safeguard against rust damage where such protection is not provided by the vehicle manufacturer.

After washing paintwork, wipe off with a chamois leather to give an unspotted clear finish. A coat of clear protective wax polish will give added protection against chemical pollutants in the air. If the paintwork sheen has dulled or oxidised, use a cleaner/polisher combination to restore the brilliance of the shine. This requires a little effort, but such dulling is usually caused because regular washing has been neglected. Care needs to be taken with metallic paintwork, as special non-abrasive cleaner/polisher is required to avoid damage to the finish. Always check that the door and ventilator opening drain holes and pipes are completely clear so that water can be drained out. Bright work should be treated in the same way as paint work. Windscreens and windows can be kept clear of the smeary film which often appears by the use of a proprietary glass cleaner. Never use any form of wax or other body or chromium polish on glass.

3 Maintenance – upholstery and carpets

Mats and carpets should be brushed or vacuum cleaned regularly to keep them free of grit. If they are badly stained remove them from the vehicle for scrubbing or sponging and make quite sure they are dry before refitting. Seats and interior trim panels can be kept clean by wiping with a damp cloth. If they do become stained (which can be more apparent on light coloured upholstery) use a little liquid detergent and a soft nail brush to scour the grime out of the grain of the material. Do not forget to keep the headlining clean in the same way as the upholstery. When using liquid cleaners inside the vehicle do not over-wet the surfaces being cleaned. Excessive damp could get into the seams and padded interior causing stains, offensive odours or even rot. If the inside of the vehicle gets wet accidentally it is worthwhile taking some trouble to dry it out properly, particularly where carpets are involved. *Do not leave oil or electric heaters inside the vehicle for this purpose.*

4 Minor body damage – repair

The photographic sequences on pages 186 and 187 illustrate the operations detailed in the following sub-sections.
Note: *For more detailed information about bodywork repair, the Haynes Publishing Group publish a book by Lindsay Porter called The Car Bodywork Repair Manual. This incorporates information on such aspects as rust treatment, painting and glass fibre repairs, as well as details on more ambitious repairs involving welding and panel beating.*

Repair of minor scratches in bodywork

If the scratch is very superficial, and does not penetrate to the metal of the bodywork, repair is very simple. Lightly rub the area of the scratch with a paintwork renovator, or a very fine cutting paste, to remove loose paint from the scratch and to clear the surrounding bodywork of wax polish. Rinse the area with clean water.

Apply touch-up paint to the scratch using a fine paint brush; continue to apply fine layers of paint until the surface of the paint in the scratch is level with the surrounding paintwork. Allow the new paint at least two weeks to harden: then blend it into the surrounding paintwork by rubbing the scratch area with a paintwork renovator or a very fine cutting paste. Finally, apply wax polish.

2.4A Check the sill drain points for blockage

2.4B Check the door drain points for blockage

Where the scratch has penetrated right through to the metal of the bodywork, causing the metal to rust, a different repair technique is required. Remove any loose rust from the bottom of the scratch with a penknife, then apply rust inhibiting paint to prevent the formation of rust in the future. Using a rubber or nylon applicator fill the scratch with bodystopper paste. If required, this paste can be mixed with cellulose thinners to provide a very thin paste which is ideal for filling narrow scratches. Before the stopper-paste in the scratch hardens, wrap a piece of smooth cotton rag around the top of a finger. Dip the finger in cellulose thinners and then quickly sweep it across the surface of the stopper-paste in the scratch; this will ensure that the surface of the stopper-paste is slightly hollowed. The scratch can now be painted over as described earlier in this Section.

Repair of dents in bodywork

When deep denting of the vehicle's bodywork has taken place, the first task is to pull the dent out, until the affected bodywork almost attains its original shape. There is little point in trying to restore the original shape completely, as the metal in the damaged area will have stretched on impact and cannot be reshaped fully to its original contour. It is better to bring the level of the dent up to a point which is about 1/8 in (3 mm) below the level of the surrounding bodywork. In cases where the dent is very shallow anyway, it is not worth trying to pull it out at all. If the underside of the dent is accessible, it can be hammered out gently from behind, using a mallet with a wooden or plastic head. Whilst doing this, hold a suitable block of wood firmly against the outside of the panel to absorb the impact from the hammer blows and thus prevent a large area of the bodywork from being 'belled-out'.

Should the dent be in a section of the bodywork which has a double skin or some other factor making it inaccessible from behind, a different technique is called for. Drill several small holes through the metal inside the area – particularly in the deeper section. Then screw long self-tapping screws into the holes just sufficiently for them to gain a good purchase in the metal. Now the dent can be pulled out by pulling on the protruding heads of the screws with a pair of pliers.

The next stage of the repair is the removal of the paint from the damaged area, and from an inch or so of the surrounding 'sound' bodywork. This is accomplished most easily by using a wire brush or abrasive pad on a power drill, although it can be done just as effectively by hand using sheets of abrasive paper. To complete the preparation for filling, score the surface of the bare metal with a screwdriver or the tang of a file, or alternatively, drill small holes in the affected area. This will provide a really good 'key' for the filler paste.

To complete the repair see the Section on filling and re-spraying.

Repair of rust holes or gashes in bodywork

Remove all paint from the affected area and from an inch or so of the surrounding 'sound' bodywork, using an abrasive pad or a wire brush on a power drill. If these are not available a few sheets of abrasive paper will do the job just as effectively. With the paint removed you will be able to gauge the severity of the corrosion and therefore decide whether to renew the whole panel (if this is possible) or to rejoin the affected area. New body panels are not as expensive as most people think and it is often quicker and more satisfactory to fit a new panel than to attempt to repair large areas of corrosion.

Remove all fittings from the affected area except those which will act as a guide to the original shape of the damaged bodywork (eg headlamp shells etc). Then, using tin snips or a hacksaw blade, remove all loose metal and any other metal badly affected by corrosion. Hammer the edges of the hole inwards in order to create a slight depression for the filler paste.

Wire brush the affected area to remove the powdery rust from the surface of the remaining metal. Paint the affected area with rust inhibiting paint; if the back of the rusted area is accessible treat this also.

Before filling can take place it will be necessary to block the hole in some way. This can be achieved by the use of aluminium or plastic mesh, or aluminium tape.

Aluminium or plastic mesh is probably the best material to use for a large hole. Cut a piece to the approximate size and shape of the hole to be filled, then position it in the hole so that its edges are below the level of the surrounding bodywork. It can be retained in position by several blobs of filler paste around its periphery.

Aluminium tape should be used for small or very narrow holes. Pull a piece off the roll and trim it to the approximate size and shape required, then pull off the backing paper (if used) and stick the tape over the hole; it can be overlapped if the thickness of one piece is insufficient. Burnish down the edges of the tape with the handle of a screwdriver or similar, to ensure that the tape is securely attached to the metal underneath.

Bodywork repairs – filling and re-spraying

Before using this Section, see the Sections on dent, deep scratch, rust holes and gash repairs.

Many types of bodyfiller are available, but generally speaking those proprietary kits which contain a tin of filler paste and a tube of resin hardener are best for this type of repair. A wide, flexible plastic or nylon applicator will be found invaluable for imparting a smooth and well contoured finish to the surface of the filler.

Mix up a little filler on a clean piece of card or board – measure the hardener carefully (follow the maker's instructions on the pack) otherwise the filler will set too rapidly or too slowly. Using the applicator apply the filler paste to the prepared area; draw the applicator across the surface of the filler to achieve the correct contour and to level the filler surface. As soon as a contour that approximates to the correct one is achieved, stop working the paste – if you carry on too long the paste will become sticky and begin to 'pick up' on the applicator. Continue to add thin layers of filler paste at twenty-minute intervals until the level of the filler is just proud of the surrounding bodywork.

Once the filler has hardened, excess can be removed using a metal plane or file. From then on, progressively finer grades of abrasive paper should be used, starting with a 40 grade production paper and finishing with 400 grade wet-and-dry paper. Always wrap the abrasive paper around a flat rubber, cork, or wooden block – otherwise the surface of the filler will not be completely flat. During the smoothing of the filler surface the wet-and-dry paper should be periodically rinsed in water. This will ensure that a very smooth finish is imparted to the filler at the final stage.

At this stage the 'dent' should be surrounded by a ring of bare metal, which in turn should be encircled by the finely 'feathered' edge of the good paintwork. Rinse the repair area with clean water, until all of the dust produced by the rubbing-down operation has gone.

Spray the whole repair area with a light coat of primer – this will show up any imperfections in the surface of the filler. Repair these imperfections with fresh filler paste or bodystopper, and once more smooth the surface with abrasive paper. If bodystopper is used, it can be mixed with cellulose thinners to form a really thin paste which is ideal for filling small holes. Repeat this spray and repair procedure until you are satisfied that the surface of the filler, and the feathered edge of the paintwork are perfect. Clean the repair area with clean water and allow to dry fully.

The repair area is now ready for final spraying. Paint spraying must be carried out in a warm, dry, windless and dust free atmosphere. This condition can be created artificially if you have access to a large indoor working area, but if you are forced to work in the open, you will have to pick your day very carefully. If you are working indoors, dousing the floor in the work area with water will help to settle the dust which would otherwise be in the atmosphere. If the repair area is confined to one body panel, mask off the surrounding panels; this will help to minimise the effects of a slight mis-match in paint colours. Bodywork fittings (eg chrome strips, door handles etc) will also need to be masked off. Use genuine masking tape and several thicknesses of newspaper for the masking operations.

Before commencing to spray, agitate the aerosol can thoroughly, then spray a test area (an old tin, or similar) until the technique is mastered. Cover the repair area with a thick coat of primer; the thickness should be built up using several thin layers of paint rather than one thick one. Using 400 grade wet-and-dry paper, rub down the surface of the primer until it is really smooth. While doing this, the work area should be thoroughly doused with water, and the wet-and-dry paper periodically rinsed in water. Allow to dry before spraying on more paint.

Spray on the top coat, again building up the thickness by using several thin layers of paint. Start spraying in the centre of the repair area and then, using a circular motion, work outwards until the whole repair area and about 2 inches of the surrounding original paintwork is covered. Remove all masking material 10 to 15 minutes after spraying on the final coat of paint.

Allow the new paint at least two weeks to harden, then, using a paintwork renovator or a very fine cutting paste, blend the edges of the paint into the existing paintwork. Finally, apply wax polish.

Plastic components

With the use of more and more plastic body components by the vehicle manufacturers (eg bumpers, spoilers, and in some cases major body panels), rectification of more serious damage to such items has become a matter of either entrusting repair work to a specialist in this field, or renewing complete components. Repair of such damage by the DIY owner is not really feasible owing to the cost of the equipment and materials required for effecting such repairs. The basic technique involves making a groove along the line of the crack in the plastic using a rotary burr in a power drill. The damaged part is then welded back together by using a hot air gun to heat up and fuse a plastic filler rod into the groove. Any excess plastic is then removed and the area rubbed down to a smooth finish. It is important that a filler rod of the correct plastic is used, as body components can be made of a variety of different types (eg polycarbonate, ABS, polypropylene).

Damage of a less serious nature (abrasions, minor cracks etc) can be repaired by the DIY owner using a two-part epoxy filler repair material. Once mixed in equal proportions, this is used in similar fashion to the bodywork filler used on metal panels. The filler is usually cured in twenty to thirty minutes, ready for sanding and painting.

If the owner is renewing a complete component himself, or if he has repaired it with epoxy filler, he will be left with the problem of finding a suitable paint for finishing which is compatible with the type of plastic used. At one time the use of a universal paint was not possible owing to the complex range of plastics encountered in body component applications. Standard paints, generally speaking, will not bond to plastic or rubber satisfactorily. However, it is now possible to obtain a plastic body parts finishing kit which consists of a pre-primer treatment, a primer and coloured top coat. Full instructions are normally supplied with a kit, but basically the method of use is to first apply the pre-primer to the component concerned and allow it to dry for up to 30 minutes. Then the primer is applied and left to dry for about an hour before finally applying the special coloured top coat. The result is a correctly coloured component where the paint will flex with the plastic or rubber, a property that standard paint does not normally possess.

5 Major body damage – repair

The construction of the body is such that great care must be taken when making cuts, or when renewing major members, to preserve the basic safety characteristics of the structure. In addition, the heating of certain areas is not advisable.

In view of the specialised knowledge necessary for this work, and the alignment jigs and special tools frequently required, the owner is advised to consult a specialist body repairer or Peugeot dealer.

6 Bonnet – removal and refitting

1 Open the bonnet and support with the stay.
2 Using a pencil, mark the position of the hinges on the bonnet.
3 Disconnect the windscreen washer tubing.
4 Enlist the aid of an assistant to support the weight and help balance the bonnet on one side, then release the bonnet support stay.
5 Place some cloth beneath the rear corners of the bonnet, unscrew the hinge bolts and withdraw it from the car (photos).
6 Refitting is a reversal of removal, but check that the bonnet is central within its aperture and flush with the front wings. If necessary loosen the hinge bolts and move it within the elongated holes to reposition it, then adjust the bonnet lock and striker, as described in Section 7.

7 Bonnet lock and remote control cable – removal, refitting and adjustment

1 If the cable is broken, the bonnet lock will have to be released by deflecting the lock lever with a rod inserted through the grille slats – refer to Chapter 13.
2 Remove the front grille, as described in Section 8.
3 Unbolt the lock from the crossmember and disconnect the control cable (Fig. 11.2).
4 Working inside the car, remove the inner trim panel forward of the nearside front door for access to the cable at the release handle end.
5 Detach the inner cable from the release handle and the outer cable from the retaining clip. Push the cable through the bulkhead and remove it from the engine compartment (photo).
6 If necessary, the bonnet striker may be unscrewed from the bonnet and the safety spring unclipped.
7 Refitting is a reversal of removal, but check that the striker enters the lock centrally and holds the front of the bonnet level with the front wings. If necessary loosen the lock bolts and move the lock within the elongated holes. Adjust the bonnet height by screwing the striker pin in or out. Adjust the rubber buffers to support the front corners of the bonnet.

8 Front grille – removal and refitting

1 Open the bonnet and support it with the stay.
2 Carefully prise free the plastic retaining clips from the top edge then lift the grille clear of its location peg grommets at the bottom edge.
3 Refitting is a reversal of the removal procedure.

6.5 Bonnet hinge bolts

7.4 Bonnet release cable and retaining clip within the car

Fig. 11.2 Bonnet lock and release cable components (Sec 7)

1	Bonnet lock (upper)	4	Cable	7	Cable location clip
2	Bonnet lock (lower)	5	Clip	8	Striker
3	Release handle	6	Grommet	9	Safety catch

10	Pivot
11	Spring

9 Front wing – removal and refitting

1 Remove the front indicator lamp and repeater lamp, as described in Chapters 12 and 13.
2 Remove the front bumper, as described in Section 10.
3 Unscrew the mounting bolts located on the top flange, rear flange and inner rear lower edge of the wheel arch. Access to the rear flange is

gained by opening the front door (Fig. 11.3).
4 Prise the wing from the mastic bead and remove it from the car. Where applicable, detach the side indicator lamp wire as the wing is withdrawn.
5 Refitting is a reversal of removal, but apply mastic to the inner surface of the flanges. If a new wing is being fitted, paint the inside surfaces and apply an anti-corrosion sealant.

Fig. 11.3 Front wing panel and fittings (Sec 9)

10 Bumpers – removal and refitting

Front
1 Disconnect the battery earth lead.
2 Working under each front wheel arch in turn, unscrew and remove the bumper-to-chassis retaining bolts and the corner retaining bolt on each wing (photo).
3 Undo the bumper-to-front skirt bolts working on the front underside of the car (photo).
4 Partially withdraw the front bumper, detach the horn wire, then fully remove the bumper.
5 Refitting is a reversal of the removal procedure.

Rear
6 Disconnect the battery earth lead.
7 Undo the three retaining bolts from the underside of the bumper along the body rear edge and the single bolt from the corner section each side. Withdraw the outer bumper (photo).
8 To remove the inner rear bumper, undo the two retaining bolts within the luggage compartment (one each side), withdraw the inner bumper and detach the rear number plate wiring (photo).
9 Refit in the reverse order of removal. Check that the rear number plate lights are fully operational.

10.2 Front bumper retaining bolts under the wing panel

Fig. 11.4 Front bumper and associated fittings (Sec 10)

1	Bumper moulding	3	Bumper counterleaf	5 to 7 Retaining bolts
2	Counterleaf support bracket	4	Crossmember	8	Moulding inset

10.3 Front bumper-to-skirt retaining bolt

10.7 Rear bumper and underside support bracket

10.8 Rear inner bumper removal

**Fig. 11.5 Rear bumper and associated fittings
(Sec 10)**

1   Bumper   4   Screw
2   Support   5   Moulding (inset)
3   Seal

11 Door – removal and refitting

1   The door hinges are welded to the body pillar and bolted to the door (photo).
2   Remove the plastic caps from the hinge pivot pins.
3   Drive out the roll pin from the door check strap.
4   Where applicable, remove the trim panel (Section 12) and disconnect the loudspeaker wiring from the door.
5   Support the door in the fully open position by placing blocks, or a jack and a pad of rag, under its lower edge.
6   Drive out the hinge pivot pins and remove the door.
7   Refit by reversing the removal operations.
8   Where necessary, the striker on the body pillar may be adjusted to ensure correct closure of the door (photo).

12 Door trim panel – removal and refitting

Front door
Note: *Procedure given here is for 5-door models. 3-door models similar.*
1   Remove the door speaker grille, undo the retaining screws and remove the door speaker unit. Disconnect the speaker wires at the in-line connectors as it is withdrawn.
2   Prise free and remove the interior door handle surround (photo).
3   Fully close the window, note the position of the winder handle with the window in the fully shut position and then pull the handle from the spindle (photo).
4   Prise free and lift clear the inner lock button surround (photo).
5   Prise free the finisher strip from the armrest, undo the two retaining

11.1 Door hinge

11.8 Front door striker

12.2 Removing the door interior handle surround

12.3 Removing the door window regulator handle

12.4 Removing the inner lock cover

12.5 Removing the armrest finisher strip

screws and remove the armrest (photo).

6   Undo the door glovebox retaining screws, if applicable (photo).

7   Using a wide-bladed screwdriver, or similar tool, prise the trim panel from the door – working progressively from the bottom upwards and inserting the screwdriver adjacent to each clip.

8   Refitting is a reversal of removal, but first make sure that the clips are correctly located in the panel.

Rear door

9   The procedure is basically as given for a front door, but there will be some slight trim differences.

Models with electric windows

10 The procedure is basically the same as given previously, but there will be no regular handle to remove. Be sure to disconnect the battery before releasing the motor switch wiring.

13 Door – dismantling and reassembly

1   Remove the trim panel, as described in Section 12.

Window regulator

2   To remove the window regulator, unscrew the mounting nuts, slide the two lifting arms from the channels, and withdraw the regulator through the access aperture (photos). Support the glass during this operation.

Door lock

3   To remove the door lock and inner remote handle, disconnect the link rods as necessary and, unscrew the Torx screws retaining the lock (photos).

12.6 Door panel glovebox and retaining screws

13.2A Window regulator mounting nuts (arrowed) – front door

13.2B Window lift arms and glass channel

13.2C Window regulator mounting nuts – rear door

13.3A Door lock and mounting screws

13.3B Door inner remote control handle

This sequence of photographs deals with the repair of the dent and paintwork damage shown in this photo. The procedure will be similar for the repair of a hole. It should be noted that the procedures given here are simplified — more explicit instructions will be found in the text

In the case of a dent the first job — after removing surrounding trim — is to hammer out the dent where access is possible. This will minimise filling. Here, the large dent having been hammered out, the damaged area is being made slightly concave

Now all paint must be removed from the damaged area, by rubbing with coarse abrasive paper. Alternatively, a wire brush or abrasive pad can be used in a power drill. Where the repair area meets good paintwork, the edge of the paintwork should be 'feathered', using a finer grade of abrasive paper

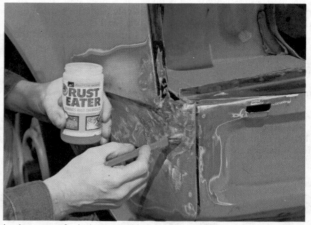

In the case of a hole caused by rusting, all damaged sheet-metal should be cut away before proceeding to this stage. Here, the damaged area is being treated with rust remover and inhibitor before being filled

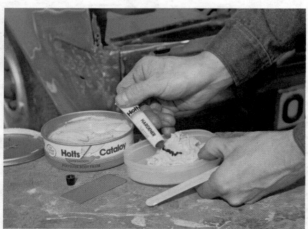

Mix the body filler according to its manufacturer's instructions. In the case of corrosion damage, it will be necessary to block off any large holes before filling — this can be done with aluminium or plastic mesh, or aluminium tape. Make sure the area is absolutely clean before ...

... applying the filler. Filler should be applied with a flexible applicator, as shown, for best results; the wooden spatula being used for confined areas. Apply thin layers of filler at 20-minute intervals, until the surface of the filler is slightly proud of the surrounding bodywork

Initial shaping can be done with a Surform plane or Dreadnought file. Then, using progressively finer grades of wet-and-dry paper, wrapped around a sanding block, and copious amounts of clean water, rub down the filler until really smooth and flat. Again, feather the edges of adjoining paintwork

The whole repair area can now be sprayed or brush-painted with primer. If spraying, ensure adjoining areas are protected from over-spray. Note that at least one inch of the surrounding sound paintwork should be coated with primer. Primer has a 'thick' consistency, so will find small imperfections

Again, using plenty of water, rub down the primer with a fine grade wet-and-dry paper (400 grade is probably best) until it is really smooth and well blended into the surrounding paintwork. Any remaining imperfections can now be filled by carefully applied knifing stopper paste

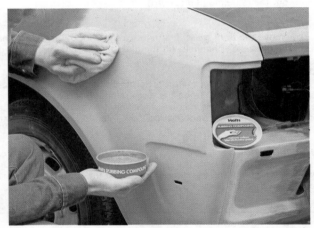

When the stopper has hardened, rub down the repair area again before applying the final coat of primer. Before rubbing down this last coat of primer, ensure the repair area is blemish-free – use more stopper if necessary. To ensure that the surface of the primer is really smooth use some finishing compound

The top coat can now be applied. When working out of doors, pick a dry, warm and wind-free day. Ensure surrounding areas are protected from over-spray. Agitate the aerosol thoroughly, then spray the centre of the repair area, working outwards with a circular motion. Apply the paint as several thin coats

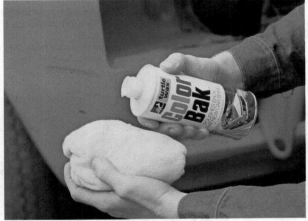

After a period of about two weeks, which the paint needs to harden fully, the surface of the repaired area can be 'cut' with a mild cutting compound prior to wax polishing. When carrying out bodywork repairs, remember that the quality of the finished job is proportional to the time and effort expended

13.4 View of the private lock from inside the door

13.6A Prise free the mirror inner cover ...

13.6B ... for access to the retaining screws

Exterior handle

4   To remove the exterior handle, disconnect the link rod and unscrew the bolts. The private lock is removed by disconnecting the link rod and pulling out the retaining clip (photo).

Door glass

5   To remove the door glass, first remove the window regulator then unbolt the glass side channels, tilt the glass and withdraw it upwards.

Exterior mirror

6   To remove the exterior mirror, prise off the inner cover, prise back the rubber grommet then undo the three retaining screws and remove the mirror. If required the manual adjustment lever can be detached from the mirror unit by undoing the Torx retaining screw above the handle (photos).

General assembly

7   Reassembly of the door is a reversal of the dismantling procedure. However, when refitting the door glass, adjust the position of the side channels so that the glass moves smoothly without excessive play.

14 Tailgate – removal and refitting

1   Open the tailgate and have an assistant support it.
2   Detach the wiring connector from the strut (photo), then prise out the plastic clip and detach the strut socket (photo).
3   Disconnect the wiring for the heated rear window and tailgate wiper motor. Also disconnect the washer tube (photo).
4   Prise free the hinge pin retaining clips and then withdraw the hinge pin each side (photo). Lift the tailgate clear. New pin retaining clips must be used when refitting the tailgate (Fig. 11.6).
5   Refit in the reverse order of removal. On completion, check that the tailgate is positioned centrally in the body aperture, and make any

Fig. 11.6 Hinge pin removal method using slip joint pliers (a) (Sec 14)

adjustments to the lock and striker as described in Section 15. To adjust the tailgate at the hinges, loosen the retaining nuts and move the tailgate as required, then retighten the nuts.

15 Tailgate lock – removal and refitting

1   Undo the two retaining screws and remove the rear outer trim panel. Prise free the inner rear trim panel for access (photo).
2   The lock unit and its retaining rivets are now accessible. Drill out

14.2A Detach the wiring connector from the strut ...

14.2B ... and prise free the retaining clip

14.3 Detach the heated rear window wire connector

14.4 Tailgate hinge showing the pin retaining clip

15.1 Rear outer trim retainer nut

15.2 Tailgate lock showing three retainer rivets

15.3A Tailgate lock unit (shown with inner trim removed)

15.3B Tailgate striker plate showing recessed retaining screws

Fig. 11.7 Tailgate lock and associated components (Sec 15)

1 Lock
2 Striker
3 Actuator rod
4 Transverse rod
5 Lock barrel

the three pop rivets, withdraw the lock and detach the connecting rod through the inner rear panel aperture. Undo the rod-to-lock barrel retaining screw (photo).

3 Refit in the reverse order to removal. Use aluminium stem rivets to secure the lock unit. Check that the latch engages the striker correctly and, if necessary, adjust the striker position within the elongated bolt holes. Adjust the rubber stops so that the tailgate is supported firmly at the corners when shut (photos).

16 Windscreen and tailgate glass – general

The renewal of both the windscreen and the tailgate glass are tasks which are best entrusted to a professional fitter. In each case some specialised tools and knowledge of the safe and successful fitting of these glass panels are essential. Unless they are correctly fitted, they may well leak and at worst prove dangerous, therefore entrust renewal to a specialist.

17 Seats – removal and refitting

Front
1   Move the seat fully forward, then undo the retaining screws and remove the outer trim (photo).
2   Adjust the seat on the runners as required for access and remove the runner retaining bolts (Torx screws) (photos), then remove the seat.
3   Refit in the reverse order of removal. Check that the seat adjustment is satisfactory on completion.

Rear
4   To remove the cushion(s), tilt it forward and lift it clear, pulling at an angle of 45° from the retainers.
5   To remove the rear seat backrest(s), tilt the backrest forwards for access to the hinge retaining nuts at the side (photo). Unscrew the retaining nuts.
6   Where applicable, unscrew the retaining bolt and remove the central hinge. Remove the seat backrest.
7   Refit in the reverse order of removal. Pass the fixed part of the rear seat belts between the backrest and cushion so that they are accessible for use.

18 Grab handles – removal and refitting

1   Prise up the cover plates for access to the screws.
2   Remove the screws and the grab handles.
3   Refitting is a reversal of removal.

19 Fuel filler flap cable – removal and refitting

1   Remove the driver's seat as described in Section 17.
2   Pull free the filler flap release handle from its shaft, then undo the retaining screws and lift clear the handbrake cover (photo).
3   Prise free the release cable retaining clip and disengage the inner cable nipple from the lever clevis (photo).
4   Remove the rear seat and fold back the rear passenger compartment floor covering on the driver's side.
5   Referring to Fig. 11.8, remove the hinges, bolts and finisher panel indicated.
6   Prise free the rear wheel arch seal and unclip the release cable (Fig. 11.9).
7   Remove the side trim panel in the luggage compartment or at least fold it back at the forward upper corner to gain access to the inner body panel apertures. Reach through the inspection aperture and disengage the release cable from the flap, then withdraw the cable (photo).
8   Refit in the reverse order to removal. Check the flap for satisfactory locking and release operation before refitting the inner panels and associated items. If required, adjust the cable control at the sleeve nut (Fig. 11.10).

17.1 Remove the outer trim panel from the front seat ...

17.2A ... for access to the retaining bolts at the front ...

17.2B ... and rear of the seat runners

17.2C Torx screws are used, together with lock washers

17.5 Rear seat backrest retaining nuts at the side hinge

19.2 Withdraw the flap release handle from its shaft

19.3 Cable connection at the release handle

19.7 Disconnecting the cable from the petrol filler flap

Fig. 11.8 Fuel filler flap cable removal. Detach hinges (b), bolts (c) and finisher (d) (Sec 19)

Fig. 11.9 From the rear wheel arch remove the seal (e) and cable (3) (Sec 19)

Fig. 11.10 Fuel filler flap cable control sleeve adjuster nut (h) (Sec 19)

20 Fuel filler flap – removal and refitting

1   Disconnect the battery earth lead.
2   Disconnect the filler flap release cable from the filler flap as described in paragraph 7 of the previous Section.
3   Jack up and support the car at the rear on safety stands. Remove the right-hand rear roadwheel.
4   Lower but do not remove the fuel tank by undoing the tank retaining nuts down to the end of their threads – do not completely unscrew them. (Leave the bottom faces of the nuts and threads flush).
5   Unscrew and remove the three filler neck retaining screws and the two flap securing screws (photo).
6   Working under the wheel arch, release the filler pipe (photos) and then remove the filler pipe and its protective hose. Pull free the filler flap.
7   Refitting is a reversal of the removal procedure. Ensure that the breather pipe is connected to the hose at the top. If necessary adjust the control cable as described in the previous Section.

20.5 Fuel filler flap and retaining screws
1   *Filler neck screws*
2   *Flap retaining screws*

20.6A Fuel filler pipe – detach at points indicated (arrowed)

20.6B Filler pipe retaining nut (arrowed) – unscrew to remove pipe

21 Facia panels – removal and refitting

1   The extent to which the various facia panels and their associated components are removed or detached is obviously dependent on the accessibility requirements of the component concerned. The following sequence describes the removal of the various panels and associated fittings which are necessary when gaining full access to the heater unit. The main items are sub-headed for ease of reference when it is only necessary to remove one or a limited number of items.
2   Before removing any facia panels or associated items, first detach the battery earth lead.
3   As the various panels are removed, note carefully the routing of the wiring harnesses. This is particularly important if removing all of the facia panels since if the harnesses are incorrectly routed when reassembling, they will not reach their various destinations for reconnection. If possible label the various wiring connections for ease of refitting.

Fig. 11.11 Attach breather pipe to hose at top (Sec 20)

Radio/cassette console
4   Withdraw the ashtray for access to the front retaining screws. Undo the two retaining screws from the front face and one screw each side. Withdraw the console unit and disconnect the wiring and antenna lead from the radio/cassette (photo). Refer to Fig. 11.12 for an alternative console.

Gloveboxes
5   To remove the glovebox on the passenger side, first unclip and lower the fuse/relay box unit. Unscrew and remove the upper and lower retaining screws. Disengage the glovebox lid check strap for access to the retaining screws on the right-hand side. Lift the unit at the rear edge and disengage it from the peg at the front lower edge and remove the glovebox.
6   Removal of the driver's side glovebox is similar to that described for the passenger's but prise free the surround section for access to the retaining screws.

Steering column and shrouds
7   Undo the four retaining screws and remove the lower steering column shroud. Undo the upper column mounting nuts and lower the column. Remove the upper column shroud.

Instrument panel and surround facia
8   Using a suitable length of 2 mm diameter rod, release the instrument facia side mouldings by inserting the rod through the holes and press on the retaining clip in each hole in turn to remove the mouldings. Each moulding is held by two clips (photo).

21.4 Radio/cassette console retaining screw positions (arrowed)

Fig. 11.12 Floor-mounted console assembly fitted to some models (Sec 21)

1 Console
2 Side face flange
3 Console trim moulding
4 Gear lever moulding
5 Gear lever gaiter

Fig. 11.13 Facia gloveboxes and trim fittings (Sec 21)

1 Central glovebox
2 Passenger glovebox
3 Driver's glovebox
4 Driver's glovebox moulding
5 Passenger glovebox lid
6 Clip
7 Lock unit
8 Striker

H.20137

21.8 Releasing a facia panel side moulding

21.9 Facia panel switches and wiring connectors

21.10 Instrument panel retaining screws (arrowed)

9   Remove the instrument panel surround facia. This facia panel is secured by six screws, two each side and two under the heater control panel. Withdraw the surround facia and disconnect the wiring to the switches (photo).
10 Unscrew the two instrument panel retaining screws (one each side) and tilt the column to partially withdraw it so that the speedometer cable and wiring connections to the instrument panel can be detached (photo).
11 Remove the panel and note how the wires are fed through the facia to it.

Heater controls and main facia panels
12 Withdraw the choke control lever from the facia panel by pulling it sideways. The cable can be left attached if required.
13 Carefully prise free the upper finisher panel from the top edge of the facia (near the windscreen). Do not damage the top of the facia when levering free the finisher panel which is secured by clips (photo).
14 Unscrew and remove the facia retaining screws, three from the top edge under the windscreen (photo), two at the bottom end on the passenger side, one on the lower end on the driver's side and six screws from the centre of the facia near the heater control panel (Fig. 11.15).

Fig. 11.14 Facia panel and side mouldings (Sec 21)

H.20138

Fig. 11.15 Facia panel retaining screw locations (Sec 21)

H.20139

15 Withdraw the facia panel and withdraw/release the respective wiring harnesses. Note the harness routing and retaining clip locations to ensure correct reassembly.

Facia panels refitting

16 In most instances, the refitting procedures for the panels and their associated components are a direct reversal of the removal procedure, but note the following special points:

   (a) *Wiring: Ensure that the wiring harnesses and cables are correctly arranged and routed before fitting the main facia panel. The wires tend to be only just long enough and the correct routing is therefore critical. Where applicable secure the harnesses in retaining clips out of the way of adjacent components (as noted during removal). Ensure that all connections are correct and secure*

   (b) *When reconnecting the steering column, ensure that the upper shroud is located before raising the column and securing the mounting bolts*

   (c) *On completion, reconnect the battery earth lead and check that the various instruments and associated electrical components are fully functional*

22 Heater matrix – removal and refitting

1 Working from the engine compartment side of the bulkhead, clamp each heater hose to prevent leakage of coolant when the hoses are detached at the matrix. Alternatively, if suitable clamps are not available, drain the cooling system as described in Chapter 2.

2 Detach the hose clamp plate from the bulkhead.
3 Remove the glovebox/facia on the driver's side (see Section 21).
4 Protect the carpets and trim with suitable coverings then unclamp the heater feed and return coolant hoses from within the car. Allow for a certain amount of spillage and take care if the coolant is still hot (photos).
5 Detach the hose retaining bracket from the side of the heater, then withdraw the matrix by pulling it out of the heater unit (photo).
6 Refit in reverse. Top up the cooling system and bleed it as described in Chapter 2.

23 Heater assembly – removal and refitting

1 Remove the facia assemblies as described in Section 21, and detach the heater flow and return hoses as described in paragraphs 1 to 5 in the previous Section, but leave the matrix in position in the heater if required.
2 Disconnect the wiring harness connections to the heater control panel (photo).
3 Remove the gear lever knob, undo the retaining screws and remove the gear lever gaiter and central console panel to which it is attached.
4 Unscrew the heater retaining nuts (two each side) and the single nut at the lower rear. Withdraw the heater assembly, but note how the wiring harnesses are routed round it (photo).
5 Refitting is a reversal of the removal procedure. Ensure that the wiring connections are secure to the heater control panel and also that the harnesses are correctly routed as noted during removal. Refer to Section 21 to refit the facia (photo).
6 On completion top up and bleed the cooling system as described in Chapter 2.

21.13 Removing the upper facia finisher panel

21.14 Facia panel upper retaining screws are recessed

22.4A Heater inlet and outlet hoses showing retaining clamp (arrowed)

22.4B Heater inlet and outlet hose connections to the matrix

22.5 Withdrawing the heater matrix

23.2 Wiring connections on rear face of heater control panel

23.4 Heater unit retaining nut location – upper left side (arrowed)

23.5 Wiring loom layout is critical when refitting heater and facias

H.20140

Fig. 11.16 Exploded view of the heater box assembly (Sec 23)

Fig. 11.17 Heater/fresh air fan motor and associated fittings (Sec 23)

1 Fan motor
2 Heater control module
3 Air inlet flap control
4 Air inlet gasket
5 Air valve housing

H 12703

Chapter 12 Electrical system

For modifications, and information applicable to later models, see Supplement at end of manual

Contents

Specifications

System type ....

12 volt, negative earth battery. Alternator and pre-engaged starter motor

Battery
1.1 models .... 30 Ah
1.3 models .... 35 Ah
1.6 models .... 40 Ah

Alternator
Make .... Bosch, Paris-Rhone or Mitsubishi
Rating .... 750 watt
Drivebelt tension (all engines) .... 5.0 mm (0.20 in) deflection on longest run
Drivebelt tension using Seem C Tronic tensioner tool:
    Used belt .... 300 to 400 N
    New belt .... 500 to 600 N

Starter motor

Make .... Bosch, Ducellier, Paris-Rhone or Mitsubishi
   Type .... Pre-engaged
   Rating .... 850 watt

Fuses

No	Circuit protected	Rating (amp)
1	Coolant level indicator, reversing lights, tachometer and clock illumination	10
2	Heater, instrument panel supply, direction indicators and cigar lighter	25
3	Windscreen wipers, front/rear washers, stop-lights and heated rear window switch	25
4	Front foglights	15
5	Hazard warning system	10
6	Spare	
7	Central door locking, battery condition indicator, radio and clock, luggage/glovebox compartment lights, interior lights ...	10
8	Horns and heated rear windows	25
9	Electric front windows	30
10	Rear fog light	5
11	Tail light (left-hand)	5
12	Tail light (right-hand)	5
13	Front sidelights and number plate light	5
14	Electric fuel pump	15

Bulbs

	Wattage
Headlights	55
Front sidelights	4
Direction indicators (front)	21
Rear (tail) lights	5
Direction indicators (rear)	21
Rear foglight	21
Stop-lights	21
Reversing lights	21

1 General description

The electrical system is of the 12 volt negative earth type and the major components consist of a battery, of which the negative terminal is earthed, an alternator which is belt-driven from the crankshaft pulley, and a starter motor.

The battery supplies a steady amount of current for the ignition, lighting and other electrical circuits and provides a reserve of electricity when the current consumed by the electrical equipment exceeds that being produced by the alternator.

The alternator is controlled by a regulator which ensures a high output if the battery is in a low state of charge or the demand from the electrical equipment is high, and a low output if the battery is fully charged and there is little demand for the electrical equipment.

When fitting electrical accessories it is important, if they contain silicone diodes or transistors, that they are connected correctly, otherwise serious damage may result to the components concerned. Items such as radios, tape players, electronic ignition systems, electronic tachometer, automatic dipping etc, should all be checked for correct polarity.

It is important that both battery leads are always disconnected if the battery is to be boost charged; also if body repairs are to be carried out using electric arc welding equipment, the alternator must be disconnected, otherwise serious damage can be caused to the more delicate instruments.

2 Routine maintenance – electrical system

Carry out the following procedures at the intervals given in Routine Maintenance at the beginning of the manual.

1 Check the condition of the battery and its terminals, as described in Section 3.

2 Check the general condition of the alternator drivebelt. If it shows signs of excessive wear and/or cracking, it must be renewed. Check that the drivebelt tension is as specified. If not, loosen the pivot and adjuster bolts, reposition the alternator then retighten the bolts (see Section 5 for further details).

3 Regularly top up the washer fluid reservoirs.

3 Battery – maintenance and inspection

1 The battery fitted as original equipment is of low maintenance type; however, on some models, it incorporates the standard cell covers for checking the electrolyte level. Under normal conditions it is not necessary to check the level, but if the battery is subject to severe conditions such as taxi work or extreme temperatures, the level should be checked every 10 000 miles (15 000 km).

2 When topping-up is required use only distilled water and cover the battery plates to a depth of 10.0 mm (0.40 in).

3 Acid should never be required if the battery has been correctly filled from new, unless spillage has occurred.

4 Inspect the battery terminals and mounting tray for corrosion. This is the white fluffy deposit which grows at these areas. If evident, clean it away and neutralise it with ammonia or baking soda. Apply petroleum jelly to the terminals and paint the battery tray with a suitable anti-corrosion preparation.

5 Keep the top surface of the battery casing dry.

6 An indication of the state of charge of a battery can be obtained by checking the electrolyte in each cell using a hydrometer. The specific gravity of the electrolyte for fully charged and fully discharged conditions at the electrolyte temperature indicated, is listed below.

Fully discharged	Electrolyte temperature	Fully charged
1.098	38°C (100°F)	1.268
1.102	32°C (90°F)	1.272
1.106	27°C (80°F)	1.276
1.110	21°C (70°F)	1.280
1.114	16°C (60°F)	1.284
1.118	10°C (50°F)	1.288
1.122	4°C (40°F)	1.292
1.126	−1.5°C (30°F)	1.296

7 There should be very little variation in the readings between the different cells, but if a difference is found in excess of 0.025 then it will probably be due to an internal fault indicating impending battery failure. This assumes that electrolyte has not been spilled at some time and the deficiency made up with water only.

8 If electrolyte is accidentally spilled at any time, mop up and

neutralise the spillage at once. Electrolyte attacks and corrodes metal rapidly; it will also burn holes in clothing and skin. Leave the addition of acid to a battery cell to your dealer or service station as the mixing of acid with distilled water can be dangerous.

9   Never smoke or allow naked lights near the battery; the hydrogen gas which it gives off is explosive.

10 With normal motoring, the battery should be kept in a good state of charge by the alternator and never need charging from a mains charger.

11 However, if the daily mileage is low, with much use of starter and electrical accessories, it is possible for the battery to become discharged owing to the fact that the alternator is not in use long enough to replace the current consumed.

12 Also, as the battery ages, it may not be able to hold its charge and some supplementary charging may be needed. Before connecting the charger, disconnect the battery – earth lead first.

13 Specially rapid 'boost' charges which are claimed to restore the power of the battery in 1 to 2 hours are most dangerous as they can cause serious damage to the battery plates through overheating.

14 While charging the battery note that the temperature of the electrolyte should never exceed 38°C (100°F).

15 When charging a low maintenance battery **do not** remove the cell covers; however, on other types of battery, the cell covers should be removed.

4 Battery – removal and refitting

1   The battery is located in the front left-hand corner of the engine compartment.

2   Disconnect the battery leads, negative lead first (photo). On some batteries the negative lead has a wing type terminal nut which, if unscrewed two or three turns, will isolate the battery without the need for complete removal. This is a useful facility when undertaking routine electrical jobs on the car.

3   Release the battery clamp and lift the battery carefully from the engine compartment (photo).

4   Refitting is a reversal of removal, but smear the terminals with petroleum jelly on completion. Ensure that the negative lead is reconnected last.

5 Alternator and drivebelt – general description and maintenance

1   All models covered by this manual are fitted with alternators. The alternator generates alternating current (AC) which is rectified by diodes into direct current (DC) which is the current needed for charging the battery.

2   The main advantage of the alternator lies in its ability to provide a high charge at low revolutions. Driving slowly in heavy traffic with a dynamo invariably means no charge is reaching the battery. In similar conditions, even with the heater, wiper, lights and perhaps radio switched on, the alternator will ensure a charge reaches the battery.

3   The alternator is of the rotating field ventilated design and comprises principally a laminated stator, on which is wound the output winding, a rotor carrying the field winding and a diode rectifier.

4   The rotor is belt-driven from the engine through a pulley keyed to the rotor shaft. A fan adjacent to the pulley draws air through the unit. Rotation is clockwise when viewed from the drive end. On models with power-assisted steering, the drivebelt also operates the power steering hydraulic pump. Drivebelt adjustment and removal are otherwise the same.

5   The voltage regulator is mounted externally on the rear cover of the alternator.

6   The equipment has been designed for the minimum amount of maintenance in service, the only items subject to wear being the brushes and bearings.

7   Brushes should be examined after about 80 000 miles (120 000 km) and renewed if necessary. The bearings are pre-packed with grease for life, and should not require further attention.

8   Regularly check the drivebelt tension.

9   Correct tensioning of the alternator drivebelt will ensure that it has a long and useful life. If the belt is loose, alternator performance will be affected and possibly the battery could be discharged. If the belt is too tight it will cause unnecessary alternator bearing wear. In either case the belt itself will suffer and its life will be shortened.

10 The drivebelt is tensioned by pivoting the alternator out and securing it when the belt is correctly tensioned.

11 To adjust the drivebelt tension, first check that it is correctly located in both pulleys then, with the mounting and adjustment strap bolts loosened, pivot the alternator outwards to tighten the drivebelt (photo). You can use a lever to help achieve this but it must be a wooden one and it must be used only at the pulley end of the alternator. Levering on the case or at the end opposite to the drive pulley can easily cause expensive damage. On some OHC engine models, adjustment can be made by turning the special adjuster screw as required (photo).

12 Tighten the belt as much as possible (but without over stretching it) to take up any play in the belt at its mid point on the longest run between the pulleys (refer to the Specifications for deflection). Whilst a taut tension is required the belt must not be overtightened. Tighten the alternator mounting and adjuster strap bolts to set the tension.

13 If a new belt has been fitted recheck its tension after a nominal mileage has been covered.

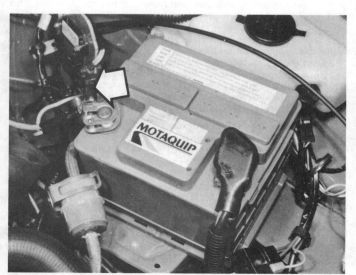

4.2 Battery and terminal lead connections with the earth lead connector securing knob indicated (arrowed)

4.3 Battery retaining clamp

5.11A Alternator and drivebelt – OHV engine. Remove side shield for access

A *Check tension at point indicated*
B *Adjuster*

5.11B Alternator drivebelt tension adjuster – OHC engine models

6.3 Wiring connections to alternator – OHV engine

6 Alternator – removal and refitting

1 Disconnect the battery negative lead.
2 Loosen the pivot and adjustment bolts, swivel the alternator towards the engine then remove the drivebelt.
3 Disconnect the wiring from the alternator (photo).
4 Unscrew the pivot and adjustment bolts and lift the alternator from the engine. On OHC engine models note that the alternator front bracket is slotted to allow the pivot bolt to remain in the bracket on the engine (photos).
5 Refitting is a reversal of removal, but tension the drivebelt, as described in Section 5.

7 Alternator – brush renewal

1 Remove the alternator (Section 6) then remove the rear shield (where fitted).
2 Remove the regulator/brush holder mounting screws and withdraw the assembly. Disconnect the regulator lead, where necessary (photo).
3 With the brush holder removed, check the condition of the slip rings. If they are blackened, clean them with a fuel-moistened rag. If they are deeply scored or grooved then it will probably indicate that the alternator is coming to the end of its life.

4 Unsolder the old brushes and solder in the new ones. Have this done professionally if you lack skill in soldering.
5 Refit the regulator/brush holder and tighten the mounting screws. Reconnect the regulator lead, where necessary.
6 Refit the rear shield (where fitted) then refit the alternator, with reference to Section 6.

6.4A Alternator removal – OHV engine

6.4B Alternator and mounting bolts – OHC engine

7.2 Regulator/brush holder removal

Fig. 12.1 Exploded diagram
of a Bosch alternator
(Sec 7)

1 Pulley
2 Fan
3 Drive end housing
4 Bearing
5 Rotor
6 Bearing
7 Stator
8 Diode plate
9 Brush end housing
10 Brush holder/regulator
11 Condenser

Fig. 12.2 Exploded diagram
of a Paris-Rhone alternator
(Sec 7)

1 Pulley
2 Fan
3 Drive end housing
4 Stator
5 Rotor
6 Bearing
7 Brush end housing
8 Brush holder/regulator
9 Diode plate
10 Cover

8 Starter motor – description and testing

1 The starter motor is mounted on the front of the engine and is of the pre-engaged type, where the drive pinion is brought into mesh with the starter ring gear on the flywheel before the main current is applied.
2 When the starter switch is operated, current flows from the battery to the solenoid which is mounted on the top of the starter motor body. The plunger in the solenoid moves inwards, so causing a centrally pivoted lever to push the drive pinion into mesh with the starter ring gear. When the solenoid plunger reaches the end of its travel, it closes an internal contact and full starting current flows to the starter field coils. The armature is then able to rotate the crankshaft, so starting the engine.
3 A special freewheel clutch is fitted to the starter drive pinion so that as soon as the engine fires and starts to operate on its own it does not drive the starter motor.
4 When the starter switch is released, the solenoid is de-energised and a spring moves the plunger back to its rest position. This operates the pivoted lever to withdraw the drive pinion from engagement with the starter ring.
5 If the starter motor fails to turn the engine when the switch is operated there are four possible reasons why:

(a) The battery is discharged or faulty
(b) The electrical connections between switch, solenoid, battery and starter motor are somewhere failing to pass the necessary current from the battery, through the starter to earth
(c) The solenoid has an internal fault
(d) The starter motor is electrically defective

To check the wiring connections at the starter motor on some models it will be necessary to raise and support the car on axle stands at the front end and remove the engine undershield.
6 To check the battery, switch on the headlights. If they go dim after a few seconds the battery is discharged. If the lamp glows brightly, next operate the ignition/starter switch and see what happens to the lights. If they go dim it is indicative that power is reaching the starter motor but failing to turn it. If the starter should turn very slowly go on to the next check.
7 If, when the ignition/starter switch is operated, the lights stay bright then the power is not reaching the starter motor. Check all connections from the battery to solenoid for cleanliness and tightness. With a good battery fitted this is the most usual cause of starter motor problems. Check that the earth cable between the engine and body is also intact and cleanly connected. This can sometimes be overlooked when the engine is taken out.
8 If no results have yet been achieved turn off the headlights, otherwise the battery will soon be discharged. It may be possible that a clicking noise was heard each time the ignition/starter switch was operated. This is the solenoid switch operating but it does not necessarily follow that the main contact is closing properly. (If no clicking has been heard form the solenoid it is certainly defective.) The solenoid contact can be checked by putting a voltmeter or bulb between the main cable connection on the starter side of the solenoid and earth. When the switch is operated there should be a reading or a lighted bulb. If not, the switch has a fault.

9 Starter motor – removal and refitting

1 Disconnect the battery earth lead.
2 Raise and support the car at the front end, then unclip and remove the engine undershield. This allows the necessary access to the starter motor from underneath the vehicle. The procedures now differ according to engine type as follows:

OHV engine
3 Disconnect the wiring loom from the solenoid connections (photo).
4 Undo the starter motor support bracket bolt at the rear (from the crankcase).
5 Undo the three retaining bolts to the clutch housing, then withdraw the starter motor.

OHC engine
6 Unscrew and remove the oil filter as described in Chapter 1. Allow for oil spillage as it is withdrawn.
7 Detach the crankcase ventilation pipes adjacent to the starter motor.
8 On SRi mdels, undo the two retaining bolts and remove the inlet manifold support arm.
9 Disconnect the wiring to the starter motor solenoid.
10 Undo the starter motor support bracket bolt from the crankcase (at the rear end).
11 Undo the three retaining bolts to the clutch housing. One of these bolts will require the clutch operating lever pivot arm to be unbolted and moved out of the way so that the bolt can be withdrawn. Remove the starter motor.

Refitting (all models)
12 Refitting is a reversal of the removal procedure. Ensure that the wiring connections are correctly and securely made. Where applicable refit the engine oil filter with reference to Chapter 1.

10 Starter solenoid – removal and refitting

1 The procedure for removal of the solenoid is basically the same for all four types of starter motors that may be fitted. In all cases, once the starter motor has been removed from the car the solenoid can be removed without further dismantling of the motor. Consult the relevant illustration for the type of motor you are working on and proceed as follows.
2 First undo the terminal nut and then lift off the wire that connects the solenoid to the motor field coils.
3 Next undo and remove the nuts on the retaining studs, or the screws, that secure the solenoid to the end housing.
4 Now slide the solenoid rearward, taking care not to lose the return spring, shims or washers (where fitted). Note that on the Bosch unit the solenoid armature must be unhooked from the pinion carriage actuating arm as the solenoid is removed.
5 Refitting the solenoid is the reverse sequence to removal. Adjust the drive pinion travel as described in Section 14, before refitting the starter motor to the car.

11 Starter motor brushes – inspection and renewal

1 Begin by removing the starter motor from the car and placing it on a clean uncluttered work bench. Have some containers handy to store the small screws, washers and circlips that may otherwise be easily lost. Refer to the starter motor illustration applicable to your model.

9.3 Starter motor wiring connections and retaining bolts (arrowed) – OHV engine

Paris-Rhone

2 Remove the small cap from the centre of the commutator end cover.

3 Undo and remove the armature end bolt and recover the washer.

4 Undo and remove the two long end cover retaining bolts and carefully withdraw the end cover from the armature and starter motor body. As the end cover is withdrawn, lift up the springs and slide the two field coil brushes out of the end cover.

5 If the brushes are suspect, compare their length against new ones and renew them if worn excessively. To do this, cut off the old brush lead onto the severed end of the old one. Take care to localise the heat during the operation and do not damage the insulation of the field coils.

6 Wipe the starter motor armature and commutator clean with a non-fluffy rag, wetted with carbon tetrachloride, or other similar solvent.

7 Refit the brushes into their holders and then reassemble the starter motor using the reverse sequence to removal.

Ducellier

8 Undo and remove the two nuts and lift off the commutator end cover retaining bracket.

9 Undo and remove the armature end bolt and recover the washers.

10 Undo the second pair of retaining nuts and carefully lift off the end cover followed by the brush holders, taking care not to lose the tension springs.

11 The procedure is now the same as for the Paris-Rhone motor described in paragraphs 5 to 7 inclusive.

Bosch

12 Undo and remove the two small screws and lift off the armature end cap.

13 Extract the circlip from the end of the armature and lift off the washers and rubber sealing ring.

14 Undo and remove the two long bolts which hold the motor assembly together. The commutator end cover can now be withdrawn to reveal the brushes and brush mounting plate.

15 Lift up the springs and slide the field coil brushes out of the mounting plate, then remove the mounting plate from the motor. Retrieve the spacer washers from the end of the armature.

16 The procedure is now the same as for the Paris-Rhone motor described in paragraphs 5 to 7 inclusive.

Fig. 12.3 Exploded view of the Paris-Rhone starter motor (Sec 11)

1 Solenoid	6 Thrust washers	11 Pinion carriage operating lever	14 End cover
2 Spacer	7 Armature	12 End cap and washers	15 Brush
3 Return spring	8 Drive pinion	13 Through-bolt	16 Brush spring
4 Eccentric pivot and pin	9 Stop collar		17 Body
5 End housing	10 Stop ring		

Fig. 12.4 Exploded view of the Ducellier starter motor (Sec 11)

1 Solenoid terminals
2 Solenoid
3 Return spring
4 Plunger
5 Pinion carriage operating lever
6 Dust pad
7 Stop ring
8 Stop collar
9 Thrust washer
10 Armature
11 Drive pinion
12 Retaining stud
13 End housing
14 Pivot pin
15 End cover assembly
16 Brush assembly
17 Body

Fig. 12.5 Exploded view of the Bosch starter motor (Sec 11)

1 Armature
2 Solenoid
3 Pinion carriage operating lever
4 Dust cover
5 End housing
6 Solenoid retaining screw
7 Pivot pin
8 Retaining stud
9 Stop ring
10 Stop collar
11 Drive pinion
12 Bracket
13 End cap assembly
14 End cover
15 Brush holder
16 Brush spring
17 Field coils and body

11.17 Mitsubishi starter motor through bolts (arrowed) and support bracket

11.18 Removing the end cover

11.19 Brush removed from holder for inspection

Fig. 12.6 Exploded view of the Mitsubushi starter motor (Sec 11)

1 End housing	6 Pinion carriage operating	10 Solenoid	14 Brush and holder
2 Thrust washer	lever	11 Thrust washers	15 End cover
3 Stop ring	7 Return springs	12 Body	16 End bracket
4 Stop collar	8 Armature	13 Brush spring	17 Retaining bolt
5 Drive pinion	9 Solenoid shims		

Mitsubishi

17 Undo and remove the two long bolts which hold the motor assembly together (photo).
18 Lift of the rear support bracket and the commutator end cover (photo).
19 Release the springs on the two field coil brushes and slip these brushes out of their holders. Now lift off the brush holder assembly (photo).
20 The procedure is now the same as for the Paris-Rhone motor described in paragraphs 5 to 7 inclusive.

12 Starter motor pinion carriage mechanism – removal and refitting

1 With the starter motor removed from the car begin by removing the solenoid as described in Section 10. Next remove the end cover and brush gear as described in Section 11, according to starter motor type.
2 Having carried out these operations the starter motor body can now be carefully slid rearwards off the armature.
3 The procedure now varies slightly according to motor type as described below.

Paris-Rhone

4 Drive out the expansion pin and then withdraw the pin from the end housing.

5 Slide the armature and pinion carriage operating lever out of the end housing and then lift the lever off the armature.

Ducellier

6 Drive out the pinion carriage operating lever pivot pin from the end housing and then slide the armature and operating lever out of the housing. Lift the lever off the armature.

Bosch

7 Undo and remove the nut from the pinion carriage operating lever pivot bolt. Now withdraw the bolt from the end housing.
8 Withdraw the armature and operating lever from the housing and separate the two components.

Mitsubishi

9 On these motors the pinion carriage operating lever is retained by a spring and clip. Extract the clip and spring and then slide the operating lever and armature out of the end housing (photo).

All starter motors

10 Support the armature in a vice, vertically, taking care not to damage the commutator.
11 Using a hammer and tube of suitable diameter, tap the stop collar on the end of the armature shaft down just far enough to reveal the stop ring.
12 Hook out the stop ring, slide off the stop collar and then withdraw the pinion carriage mechanism.

12.9 Pinion carriage and operating lever in end housing of Mitsubishi starter motor

13 The pinion carriage cannot be dismantled and if deemed faulty should be renewed. The armature shaft and spiral spline on which the pinion runs should be thoroughly cleaned and then lubricated with a light grade of engine oil.
14 Reassemble the pinion carriage to the armature shaft, followed by the stop collar. Refit the stop ring, ensuring that it fits tightly in its groove, and then pull the stop collar up over it to lock it in position.
15 The remainder of reassembly is a direct reversal of the dismantling sequence. **Note**: *Before refitting the starter motor to the car, check and if necessary adjust the drive pinion travel as described in Section 14.*

13 Starter motor – checking armature and static field windings

1 Follow the instructions given in Section 12 of this Chapter and dismantle the motor to gain access to the armature and the motor casing with the static field windings attached.
2 The armature windings may be checked for a short onto the motor shaft/armature core, and for an open-circuit in the windings.

3 Using a test circuit comprising two probes, a bulb and 12v battery, touch the commutator bars with one probe, whilst holding the other against the armature metal. The test bulb should not light up.
4 To check the armature windings for open circuit, replace the bulb with an ammeter (0 to 10 amp). Touch commutator bars (90° spaced) with the probes and note the ammeter reading. The readings should all be the same; considerable deviation (25%) indicates open-circuits or windings insulation breakdown.
5 The battery and bulb circuit is used to check the static field windings. Touch one probe onto each winding termination and hold the other against the metal motor casing. The test bulb must not light up. Remember to touch the positive brushes to check for short-circuits properly.
6 Faulty armatures or field windings should be renewed, though individual new spares may be difficult to obtain, and it will be possibly be necessary to purchase an exchange motor unit.

14 Starter motor – drive pinion travel adjustment

1 Whenever the starter motor has been dismantled, or if a new or reconditioned unit is being fitted, it is necessary to adjust the drive pinion travel to obtain the correct mesh and clearance between the pinion teeth and the teeth on the flywheel ring gear.
2 With the starter solenoid at rest, the dimension from the end housing flange to the outer edge of the pinion must be 14 mm (0.55 in).
3 With the solenoid energised, the clearance between the end of the pinion and the pinion stop must be 0.5 to 1.5 mm (0.019 to 0.059 in). To energise the solenoid and enable this check to be carried out, connect one lead from a 12 volt battery to a small spade terminal on the solenoid. Using a switch in the circuit, connect the other battery terminal lead to one of the solenoid fixing studs.
4 If the pinion travel is incorrect, the adjustment procedure is as follows.

Paris-Rhone
5 Drive out the steel locking pin and rotate the plastic pivot pin until the 'at rest' dimension is obtained. Check that the clearance with the solenoid energised is satisfactory and then refit the locking pin.

Ducellier
6 Remove the plastic dust cover located between the solenoid mounting bolts in the end housing.
7 Using a suitable socket turn the adjusting bolt in the required direction, clockwise to decrease the 'at rest' dimension, anti-clockwise to increase it.
8 Check the clearance with the solenoid energised and if satisfactory refit the dust cover.

Fig. 12.7 Drive pinion meshing and clearance dimensions (Sec 14)

A   Dimension with solenoid at rest = 14 mm (0.55 in)
B   Straight-edge
C   Pinion stop
D   Clearance with solenoid energised = 0.5 to 1.5 mm (0.019 to 0.059 in)

Fig. 12.8 Pinion mesh adjustment – Paris-Rhone starter motor (Sec 14)

1   Expansion pin   3   End housing
2   Eccentric pin

Fig. 12.9 Pinion mesh adjustment – Ducellier starter motor (Sec 14)

| 1 | Pivot pin | 3 | Socket spanner |
| 2 | Adjusting bolt and locknut | 4 | Dust cap |

Bosch and Mitsubishi

9   If the dimensions are outside the tolerance given, adjustment is by removing the solenoid (see Section 10), and adding or subtracting shims between the solenoid and end housing until the 'at rest' and 'energised' positions of the drive pinion are correct.

15 Fuses and relays – general

1   The main fuse/relay box is located under the lower trim panel on the passenger side. Other relays such as the fuel injection system tachymetric relay are located in the engine compartment (photo), or elsewhere.

2   The circuits protected by the fuses, together with their rating, are given in the Specifications at the start of this Chapter.
3   Access to the fuses is gained by pulling the release handle and swinging the box down (photo).
4   Always renew a fuse with one of similar rating and never renew it more than once without finding the source of trouble. If necessary, refer to the wiring diagrams at the end of this Chapter.
5   Relay units rarely give problems, but they can easily be renewed by pulling them from their location in the box. The relay units and their functions are also shown in the wiring diagrams at the end of this Chapter. Some relay units are connected in-line and are separate from the main fuse/relay box unit.
6   The direction indicator/hazard warning flasher unit is located on the fuse board and controls both the direction indicator and hazard warning functions.
7   In the event of either system not operating, or one lamp flashing very quickly, carry out the following checks before renewing the flasher unit itself.
8   Inspect the circuit fuse and renew it if it is blown.
9   Check the condition of all wiring and the security of the connections.
10 Check the lamp which is malfunctioning for a broken bulb.
11 Make sure that the lamp casing or bulb earth connection is making a good contact.

16 Lights (exterior) – removal, refitting and bulb renewal

Headlight

1   The bulbs are renewed from the rear of the headlamp unit, access being from the engine compartment.
2   Pull free the wiring connector, release the bulb retaining clip and withdraw the bulb (photos).
3   Where halogen bulbs are fitted, do not touch the glass with your

FUSE OK

FUSE BLOWN

Fig. 12.10 Fuse condition check (Sec 15)

15.1 Tachymetric relay unit clipped to underside of the protector box lid in engine compartment

15.3 Fuse/relay box with spare fuse locations (arrowed)

16.2A Pull free the wiring connector and rubber cover ...

16.2B ... release the bulb retaining clips ...

16.2C ... and withdraw the bulb from the headlamp

16.6A Depress the wire retaining clips ...

16.6B ... detach the support (where fitted) ...

16.6C ... and withdraw the headlamp unit

fingers or with a fluffy cloth and, if necessary, allow the bulb to cool before removing it. If the glass is inadvertently touched, clean it with methylated spirit.

4   Refitting is a reversal of the removal procedure. When inserting the bulb into position it must be correctly aligned with the location notches. Check the headlights for satisfactory operation and alignment on completion.

Removal and refitting

5   Raise the bonnet, and pull free the headlamp wiring connector and the sidelight bulbholder.

6   From the front side of the headlamp, depress the retaining wire clip and withdraw the headlamp unit. Access to the inner clip is made easier if the front grille is removed. Detach the support spring (where fitted) from the rear (photos).

7   Refitting is a reversal of removal. Check lamp operation and alignment on completion.

Sidelight

8   This bulb is located in the rear of the headlight unit. Pull free the bulbholder, complete with wiring connections, from the headlamp unit then withdraw the bulb from its holder (photo).

9   Refit in the reverse order to removal and check the operation of the sidelights.

Front indicator

10   Reach down within the front corner of the engine compartment on the side concerned, untwist the bulbholder and withdraw it from the light unit. Remove the bulb from the holder (photo).

11   Renew the bulb if necessary and refit in reverse order of removal.

Removal and refitting

12   Detach the wiring to the bulbholder then release and remove the wire retaining clip from within the engine compartment. Withdraw the indicator light unit (photos).

13   Refit in the reverse order of removal and check that the indicator operates in a satisfactory manner.

Front foglamps

14   Undo the retaining screws and remove the rim and lens. The bulb can now be removed from its holder within the lamp. Renew and refit the bulb as necessary and check for satisfactory operation to complete.

Removal and refitting

15   Detach the wiring connectors to the foglamp, undo the retaining bolts to the rear of the unit and withdraw the foglamp. Refit in the reverse order of removal. Check for satisfactory operation.

Rear combination lights

16   Prise free the black plastic cover from the rear panel directly in front of the rear combination light unit (in the luggage compartment).

17   Unclip and remove the combination bulbholder unit from the aperture (photo). Remove the bulb(s) as required and if necessary detach the wiring harness connector to the unit and remove it.

Removal and refitting

18   If required the lens unit can be unclipped and removed as shown (photo).

19   Refit in the reverse order of removal and check for satisfactory operation on completion.

Rear number plate

20   These units are accessible from the apertures in the underside face of the rear bumper.

21   Undo the two retaining screws, withdraw the unit and remove the lens. Renew the bulb if necessary (photos).

Removal and refitting

22   To fully remove the unit, detach the wiring connections.

23   Refit in the reverse order of removal and check for satisfactory operation.

Side indicator repeater lamp

24   Carefully pull or prise free the lamp unit from the body panel and withdraw it sufficiently to enable the bulb to be removed.

25   Refit in reverse and check operation.

16.8 Sidelight bulb and holder removal

16.10 Front indicator bulb removal

16.12A Front indicator wiring connector and unit retaining clip

16.12B Removing the front indicator light unit

16.17 Rear combination light bulbholder unit

16.18 Rear combination light lens removal

16.21A Undo the retaining screws ...

16.21B ... and remove the number plate lens and unit for bulb renewal

Fig. 12.11 Foglamp assembly components (Sec 16)

1 Light unit (complete)
2 Bulb
3 Lens
4 Rim
5 Housing unit

H.20142

17 Headlamp interior adjustment cable(s) – removal and refitting

1   Access to the adjuster unit can be gained after removing the lower glovebox on the driver's side (see Chapter 11). Pull free the switch control for access to the retaining screws. Undo the screws and withdraw the switch from the instrument panel surround facia (photos).
2   To disconnect the cable from the adjuster at the headlamp, remove the black plastic domed cover, then grip and pull free the flat retainer (photo).
3   If the switch unit or cables are defective, they cannot be repaired and must be renewed as a unit. This unfortunately entails the removal of the facia panels and possibly the heater, as the adjuster cables pass through the bulkhead on the lower left-hand side, and are routed across the bulkhead on the inside to the switch control unit. If removal is necessary, note how the cables are routed and retained both in the engine compartment and car interior as they are removed. This is essential to ensure the correct refitting of the replacements.
4   Refit in the reverse order of removal and check/adjust the alignment of the headlamps if required.

18 Headlamp – beam adjustment

1   Headlamp adjustment can be readily undertaken in one of two ways, depending on the model. With standard models each headlamp has a lever mounted under the bonnet above each headlamp unit and a knurled adjuster to the side of the headlamp (photo). In each case raise and support the bonnet to make the adjustment.
2   An alternative method of adjustment available on some models is the remote control type, with a cable to each headlamp unit from a control unit on the instrument panel facia. This has three basic setting positions: (1) vehicle unladen – normal setting (2) vehicle with average loading and (3) vehicle with full loading at rear.
3   The above setting adjusters are convenient and should be used according to vehicle loading. When the standard beam settings are thought to be incorrect or the headlamp unit(s) have been removed and refitted, a check should be made of the headlamp beam alignment by a garage or Peugeot dealer using optical alignment equipment. They will then make any fine adjustments necessary.

19 Lights (interior) – bulb renewal

Interior lamp and map reading lamp
1   Prise the lamp from the console using a small screwdriver each side (photo).
2   Detach the orange cable connector from the centre pin then withdraw and renew the bulb.
3   Refit in reverse order of removal.

Glovebox lamp (where fitted)
4   This lamp is located in the centre of the top rail. Remove the bulb by pressing it inwards and unscrewing it.
5   Refit in reverse order of removal.

Instrument panel lamps
6   Remove the instrument panel, as described in Section 25.
7   Two types of bulb are fitted. Pull out the square type bulbholder and remove the wedge type holder. Twist the round type bulbholder through 90° to remove it, but on this type the bulb cannot be separated from the holder (photo). Refit in reverse order of removal.

17.1A Prise and remove the headlamp adjuster control knob ...

17.1B ... undo the two retaining screws ...

17.1C ... and remove the control unit

17.2 Remove headlamp adjuster cover and pull free the retainer (arrowed) to release the unit

18.1 Headlamp adjuster knob in engine compartment

19.1 Interior light unit removed to show its wiring connections and the festoon type bulb

19.7 Instrument panel bulbholders – round type holder removed

19.9 Heater control panel rear face bulbholders (arrowed)

19.14 Luggage compartment lamp unit

Heater control panel lamps
8   Remove the facia panel as described in Chapter 11.
9   Untwist and pull the bulbholder from the rear face of the heater control panel and extract the bulb (photo).
10 Refit in reverse order of removal.

Digital clock
11 Remove the facia moulding as described in Chapter 11.
12 Untwist the bulbholder from the rear of the clock and remove the bulb.
13 Refit in the reverse order of removal.

Luggage compartment lamp
14 Prise free the lamp from the trim panel in the luggage compartment, then remove the bulb (photo).
15 Refit in the reverse order.

Facia switch illumination bulbs
16 Remove the instrument facia panel as described in Chapter 11.
17 Untwist and remove the bulbholder from the appropriate switch and renew the bulb.
18 Refit in the reverse order of removal.

Cigar lighter illumination bulb
19 Proceed as described for the facia switches above (photo).

20 Steering column combination switches – removal and refitting

1   Disconnect the battery earth lead.
2   Remove the steering column shrouds as described in Chapter 11.

3   Detach the wiring connector, undo the retaining screws and remove the switch (photo).
4   Refit in the reverse order of removal. Check for satisfactory operation of the switch on completion.

21 Facia panel switches – removal and refitting

1   Disconnect the battery earth lead.
2   Remove the instrument panel surround facia as described in Chapter 11.
3   Disconnect the wiring from the switch concerned then depress the retaining lugs and withdraw the switch from the panel (photo).
4   Refitting is a reversal of the removal procedure. Check for satisfactory operation of the switch(es) on completion.
5   To remove the instrument panel lights rheostat switch, reach behind the panel and compress the retaining lugs whilst simultaneously pushing the switch through its aperture. Disconnect the wiring connectors to remove the unit fully (photo).
6   Refit in the reverse order of removal. Press the unit into the panel so that the retaining lugs engage.

22 Courtesy lamp switch – removal and refitting

1   The switch is secured to the door pillar by a self-tapping screw. Extract the screw and withdraw the switch and leads.
2   If the leads are disconnected, tape them to the pillar to prevent them from slipping inside the pillar cavity.
3   It is recommended that the metal contacts of the switch are smeared with petroleum jelly as a precaution against corrosion.
4   Refit by reversing the removal operation.

19.19 Cigar lighter unit shown with facia panel removed for access

20.3 Steering column switch retaining screws

21.3 Rear view of the facia panel switches

21.5 Instrument lighting rheostat removal

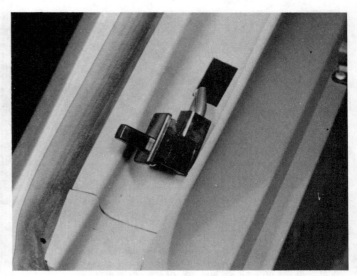

23.1 Luggage compartment switch removed from its aperture

23 Luggage compartment switch – removal and refitting

1   Carefully prise free the switch from the tailgate aperture surround panel on the left-hand side (photo).
2   If the leads are disconnected, tape them and retain them so that they are readily available for reconnection.
3   Refit in the reverse order of removal.

24 Handbrake warning switch – removal and refitting

Refer to Chapter 8, Section 17 for details.

25 Instrument panel – removal and refitting

1   Disconnect the battery earth lead.
2   Refer to Section 21 in Chapter 11 and proceed as described in paragraphs 8 to 11 inclusive to remove the instrument panel.
3   The instrument panel and its wiring connections are shown in the accompanying photos.

4   Refit in the reverse order of removal. Ensure that the wiring connections are securely made.

26 Speedometer cable – renewal

1   Disconnect the speedometer cable from the transmission by removing the retaining bolt or rubber plug.
2   Remove the instrument panel, as described in Section 25.
3   Prise the rubber grommet from the bulkhead beneath the facia.
4   Remove the retaining clips, where fitted, and withdraw the speedometer cable.
5   Refitting is a reversal of removal.

27 Windscreen wiper blades and arms – removal and refitting

1   Whenever the wiper blades fail to clean the screen, the blades or their rubber inserts should be renewed.
2   To remove a blade, pull the arm from the glass, swivel the blade, pinch the two sides of the U-shaped block together and slide the assembly out of the hook of the arm (photo).
3   When refitting, note the pivot pin in the blade is offset to allow the

25.3A Instrument panel and wiring connections

25.3B Instrument panel rear face

27.2 Windscreen wiper arm and blade separated

27.5 Windscreen wiper arm removal from the drive spindle

28.4 Wiper spindle body

28.5 Windscreen wiper motor and wiring multi-plug connector

blade to swivel fully against the glass. Make sure, therefore, that the blade is fitted the right way round so that the 'pip' on the plastic block locates in the cut-out in the hook of the wiper arm.
4   Before removing a wiper arm, note or mark its position on the windscreen using a felt tip pen so that its parked position on the windscreen can be restored when the arm is being refitted to the spindle splines.
5   Flip up the plastic cover, unscrew the nut and pull the arm from the spindle (photo).
6   Refitting is a reversal of removal.

28 Windscreen wiper motor and linkage – removal and refitting

1   Remove the wiper blades and arms, as described in Section 27.
2   Disconnect the battery negative lead.
3   Open the bonnet then remove the air intake grille by removing the screws and easing the grille from the windscreen weatherstrip.
4   Unscrew the nuts from the wiper spindle bodies (photo).
5   Disconnect the wiper motor multi-plug (photo).

Fig. 12.12 Windscreen wiper motor and linkages (Sec 28)

1   *Motor unit*
2   *Crank arm*
3   *Linkages*
4   *Spindle units*

H.12704

6   Unscrew the mounting bolt and disengage the wiper motor from the upper location pins.
7   The motor can be separated from the linkage by removing the nut securing the crank to the spindle (Fig. 12.12).
8   Refitting is a reversal of removal, but use a screwdriver to lift the weatherstrip as the grille is inserted (photo).
9   On completion wet the screen and check the wipers for satisfactory operation and parking.

29 Tailgate wiper motor – removal and refitting

1   Remove the wiper arm and blade, as described for the windscreen in Section 27.
2   Prise free and unclip the tailgate trim panel.
3   Disconnect the battery earth lead.
4   Undo the three motor retaining bolts, prise free the link arm and withdraw the motor. As the motor is being removed detach the wiring connectors and detach the earth lead (photos).
5   Undo the three bolts to remove the wiper motor unit from the mounting cover (photo) (Fig. 12.13).
6   Refit in the reverse order of removal. On completion wet the tailgate window, then check the wiper for satisfactory operation and parking.

28.8 Inserting the intake grille beneath the weatherstrip

29.4A Undo the three retaining bolts ...

29.4B ... withdraw the mounting plate and motor ...

29.4C ... and detach the wiring multi-plug

29.5 Tailgate wiper motor and mounting cover

Fig. 12.13 Tailgate wiper motor and wiper arm assembly (Sec 29)

| 1 Motor support | 3 Connecting link and spindle | 4 Spindle unit retaining nut | 6 Wiper blade |
| 2 Wiper motor | unit | 5 Wiper arm | |

30 Washer system – general

1   The washer fluid reservoir and pump for the windscreen are located in the engine compartment whilst for the tailgate window, the reservoir and pump unit is located in the rear side panel cavity (photos).
2   The washer jets are adjustable by inserting a pin into their nozzles and moving them to give an acceptable pattern on the glass.
3   The use of a good quality screen wash product is recommended. In winter add some methylated spirit to the fluid to prevent freezing. **Never** use cooling system anti-freeze as it will damage the paintwork.

4   Keep the reservoirs topped up with washer fluid and do not operate the washer pump if the reservoir has run dry.

31 Tailgate heated window – general

1   Take great care not to scratch the heater elements with carelessly stacked luggage or rings on the fingers.
2   Avoid sticking labels over the elements, and clean the glass interior surface with warm water and a little detergent, wiping in the same direction as the elements run.

30.1A Windscreen washer reservoir and pump unit (arrowed) – SRi model

30.1B Tailgate washer reservoir located in the luggage compartment

32.5 Electric window regulator switch removal

3 Should an element be scratched, so that the current is interrupted, it can be repaired using one of the silver paint products now available for the purpose.

32 Electrically-operated front windows – general

1 Operation of the front door windows on some models is by electric motors controlled by two switches on the driver's door and a single switch on the passenger door.

2 Access to the motors is gained by dismantling the doors, as described in Chapter 11.

3 Before removing the regulator motor or a switch, first disconnect the battery earth lead.

4 The regulator motor is bolted in position and access to it is obtained through the inner door panel aperture in a similar manner described for the manual regulator type (Chapter 11).

5 To remove a regulator switch, simply prise it free from the location aperture in the door trim then disconnect the wiring (photo).

6 Refitting of the regulator motor and switch is a reversal of the removal procedure.

33 Central door locking system – general

1 On models fitted with the central locking system it is possible to lock all doors, including the tailgate, simply by locking the driver's door. On some models a remote control system is used to lock the doors, whereby an infra red beam transmitter is pointed at the receiver unit above the interior light unit (photo), and when the transmitter button is pressed the door and tailgate locks are activated or released (as applicable).

2 The transmitter unit contains three 1.5 volt batteries and these must be renewed when the warning light in the unit fails to operate when the button is pressed.

3 Whichever system is fitted, electric actuators are used to operate the door/tailgate lock mechanisms. The actuators are accessible for inspection and if necessary removal after removing the door trim and/or the tailgate trim panel(s).

4 If removing an actuator unit, first disconnect the battery earth lead, then disconnect the lock connecting rod from the actuator unit, unbolt the unit and withdraw it. As it is being removed detach the wiring.

5 Refit in reverse order and check for satisfactory operation before refitting the trim panel.

34 Horn – removal and refitting

1 Disconnect the battery earth lead.

2 Remove the relevant headlamp unit for access to the horn (see Section 17). On standard models with a single horn, this is normally on the left-hand side beneath the headlamp (photo).

33.1 Infra red receiver location (central locking system) shown with interior light removed

34.2 Horn and retaining bracket. Note earth lead

3   Disconnect the wiring from the horn, undo the mounting bolt, detach the earth lead and remove the horn.
4   Refitting is a reversal of the removal procedure.

35 Radio – general

1   On some models a radio is fitted as standard equipment, and is located in the central facia. On models where a radio is not fitted during production, an aperture is provided in the central facia, and is blanked off with a finisher panel.
2   Irrespective of whether a radio is fitted from new or not, most cars are fitted with a roof-mounted aerial and coaxial aerial cable, normal interference suppression and radio connection wiring harnesses (including speaker harness on same models). Speaker housings are located in each front door panel and the rear quarter panels on all models (photos).
3   To remove a standard type radio/cassette unit, detach the battery, pull off the radio control knobs and unscrew the mounting nuts. The surround can then be withdrawn and the radio removed after disconnecting the aerial and wiring (photo).

35.2A Door-mounted speaker grille

35.2B Door-mounted speaker with grille removed

35.2C Door-mounted speaker removal showing wiring connections

35.2D Speaker unit location in the rear quarter panel

35.3 Radio and wiring connections

Fig. 12.14 Radio and speaker wiring connections which are accessible with the finisher panel removed (Sec 35)

A3R	+ accessories	B7R	Battery +	211A LH speaker wire	212A RH speaker wire
M3R	− earth	211	LH speaker wire	212 RH speaker wire	

4   If a radio/cassette unit is to be installed where one was not fitted before proceed as follows. First disconnect the battery earth lead.

5   Prise free the radio aperture trim finisher.

6   Withdraw the various radio wiring harness connections and the aerial. Identify and connect the wiring to the radio/cassette unit in accordance with the following and with reference to Fig. 12.14.

(a) *Red connector (wire A3R + accessories and wire M3R − earth). When attached to this connector the radio will be operational when the ignition key is in the A or M position. If required the A3R wire can be repositioned at the main connector board to provide permanent radio operation irrespective of the ignition key position. To do this move the A3R wire to the permanent feed terminal immediately to the right (occupied by wire B7R).*

(b) *Black connector (wire B7R battery +).*
    This wire is used as the main supply when a permanent supply is required – such as for radios with memory functions

(c) *White connector (wire 211 and 211A).*
    This is the left-hand speaker wire

(d) *Yellow connector (wire 212 and 212A).*
    This is the right-hand speaker wire

7   When fitting speaker units to the standard partitions mentioned they should fit the 120 mm (4.7 in) apertures. Ensure that the speakers are connected with the correct polarity in accordance with the manufacturer's instructions.

8   When the radio and speakers are connected, reconnect the battery, switch the radio on and trim the reception in accordance with the manufacturer's instructions. It should be noted that the standard roof-mounted aerial gives the best reception when set rearwards at an angle of 45°.

Fault diagnosis overleaf

36 Fault diagnosis – electrical system

Symptom	Reason(s)
Starter fails to turn engine	Battery discharged Battery defective internally Battery terminal leads loose or earth lead not securely attached to body Loose or broken connections in starter motor circuit Starter motor switch or solenoid faulty Starter brushes badly worn, sticking, or brush wires loose Commutator dirty, worn or burnt Starter motor armature faulty Field coils earthed
Starter turns engine very slowly	Battery in discharged condition Starter brushes badly worn, sticking or brush wires loose Loose wires in starter motor circuit
Starter motor noisy or excessively rough engagement	Pinion or flywheel gearteeth broken or worn Starter motor retaining bolts loose
Battery will not hold charge for more than a few days	Battery defective internally Electrolyte level too low or electrolyte too weak due to leakage Plate separators no longer fully effective Battery plates severely sulphated Drivebelt slipping Battery terminal connections loose or corroded Alternator not charging Short in lighting circuit continual battery drain Regulator unit not working correctly
Ignition light fails to go out, battery runs flat in a few days	Drivebelt loose and slipping or broken Alternator brushes worn, sticking, broken or dirty Alternator brush springs worn or broken Internal fault in alternator Regulator faulty

Failure of individual electrical equipment to function correctly is dealt with alphabetically, item-by-item, under the headings below

Horn

Horn operates all the time	Horn push either earthed or stuck down Horn cable to horn push earthed
Horn fails to operate	Cable or cable connection loose, broken or disconnected Horn has an internal fault Blown fuse
Horn emits intermittent or unsatisfactory noise	Cable connections loose

Lights

Lights do not come on	If engine not running, battery discharged Wire connections loose, disconnected or broken Light switch shorting or otherwise faulty
Lights come on but fade out	If engine not running, battery discharged Wire connections loose Light switch shorting or otherwise faulty

Wipers

Wiper motor fails to work	Blown fuse Wire connections loose, disconnected or broken Brushes badly worn Armature worn or faulty
Wiper motor works very slowly and takes excessive current	Commutator dirty, greasy or burnt Armature bearings dirty or unaligned Armature badly worn or faulty
Wiper motor works slowly and takes little current	Brushes badly worn Commutator dirty, greasy or burnt Armature badly worn or faulty

Key to wiring diagrams

The vehicle is divided into 4 sections. Section codes are given before the component code

Section codes

M Engine H Passenger compartment
P Facia C Luggage area

For connections between harnesses the Section codes, followed by C, are used to indicate where the connection is

eg MC indicates a connector between the engine and facia harnesses which is located in the engine compartment

For earthing points the Section code is followed by M

eg CM indicates an earthing point in the luggage area

Component codes

1	Cigar lighter, front
3	Cigar lighter, rear
5	Distributor, ignition
9	Idling actuator (idling solenoid)
10	Alternator
11	Transistor, heater blower control (power transistor)
13	Strut (earth connection)
14	Ammeter (battery charge)
20	Radio aerial, electric
25	Horn
25A	Horn, low note
25B	Horn, high note
27	Connector, towing attachment
28	Dimmer, dipped beams
30	Radio
35	Actuator, fuel output (VP15)
40	Radio balance control, front
41	Radio balance control, front/rear
45	Battery
47	Diodes unit
48	Unit, electric pump group (EPG)
49	Unit, fuse board group (FBG)
50	Ignition coil
53	Control box, exhaust emission, for pilot carburettor
54	Emission control unit (ignition advance modulator)
55	Emission control unit (idle retard)
56	Control unit, automatic transmission (idle speed)
57	Alarm unit, theft protection
58	Control unit, injection
60	Control unit, air conditioning
61	Electronic unit, brake antilock
65	Control unit, screenwiper
66	Control box, power steering
75	Control unit, ignition, or pick-up amplifier module
76	Detector unit, bulb failure
80	Cruise control unit
85	Indicator unit, oil level
86	Indicator unit, coolant level
90	Control unit, central door locking
95	Infra red signal receiver (PLIP)
96	Control unit, knock detector
97	Thermostat unit (passenger compartment)
110	Control unit, preheater
111	Control unit, fuel cut-off on overrun
112	Control unit, fuel flow (trip computer)
113	Electronic control unit, advance (Diesel)
114	Control box, coolant temperature, air conditioning
115	Preheater plug
120	Terminal connector
121	Buzzer (P4, warning, coolant temperature, oil pressure, charge warning light)
122	Buzzer, direction indicator (P4)
125	Audible warning, seat belt
126	Audible warning (key in the ignition/steering lock with the driver's door open)

127	Audible warning, excessive speed
128	Audible warning (lights on, door open or 'STOP' warning lamp on)
130	TDC sensor
131	Altitude sensor
132	Knock detector
133	Sensor, engine speed
134	Sensor, absolute pressure (Diesel)
135	Sensor, potentiometer (econoscope vacuum)
136	Sensor, demisting the rear glass
137	Pressure sensor, inlet manifold
138	Pressure sensor, speedometer cable
140	Speed sensor, speedometer cable
141	Speed sensor, trip computer
142	Sensor, oil pressure
143	Sensor, No 1 cylinder
144	Sensor, diesel injector needle lifted
145	Direction indicator flasher unit
146	Antilock sensor, LH front wheel
147	Antilock sensor, RH front wheel
148	Antilock sensor, LH rear wheel
149	Antilock sensor, RH rear wheel
150	Air temperature sensor (air conditioning)
151	Load sensor (Diesel)
155	Pilot carburettor
160	Battery isolator
165	Instrument panel
167	Connector, emission control setting
169	Switch, starter/preheater
170	Switch, luggage compartment lamp
171	Switch, enrichment (LPG)
175	Switch, door lock
176	Switch, vacuum (LPG)
177	Switch, LH front lock (door open detector)
178	Switch, RH front lock (door open detector)
179	Switch, LH rear lock (door open detector)
180	Switch, RH rear lock (door open detector)
181	Switch, luggage compartment lock (lid open detector)
182	Switch, bonnet lock (bonnet open detector)
185	Switch, stop lamps
186	Switch, brake pedal travel
190	Switch, handbrake
195	Switch, low pressure (Freon)
196	Switch, mean pressure (Freon)
200	Thermal switch (Freon)
205	Switch, glovebox lamp
210	Switch, seat belt
211	Switch, display (trip computer)
215	Switch, starter inhibitor
216	Switch, reverse lamps
217	Switch, reverse lamp/starter inhibitor
220	Switch, heating/ventilation fan
221	Switch, heating/ventilation fan (rear)
225	Switch, choke warning light

Key to wiring diagrams (continued)

Component codes

229	Switch, ignition/steering lock
230	Door switch, LH front
231	Door switch, RH front
232	Door switch, LH rear
233	Door switch, RH rear
234	Control switch, audible warning (ignition key 'in')
235	Switch, brake fluid pressure drop
236	Switch, brake fluid level
237	Switch, coolant level
238	Switch, water sensing, fuel system
239	Switch, washer bottle level
240	Limit switch, sunroof
241	Switch on accelerator pedal (idle speed)
242	Switch, idle speed
242	Switch, power take-off (P4)
247	Switch, rear differential lock
248	Switch, front differential lock
249	Switch, windscreen wiper lockout (P4)
250	Disengaging switch, cruise control (brake)
250A	Disengaging switch, cruise control (clutch)
251	Throttle switch (idling + full load)
252	Level switch, brake antilock
260	Control, lighting/direction indicators/horn
261	Control, lighting/screen wiper/screen wash
262	Control, lighting/screen wiper/direction indicator/horn
263	Control, screen wiper/wash
264	Control, lighting/horn
265	Control, direction indicator/horn
266	Switch, cruise control
267	Switch, cruise control/direction indicator
268	Switch, flasher unit (P4)
269	Switch, lighting/blackout (P4)
270	Switch, windscreen wiper (P4)
275	Control, driver's seat position
276	Control, rear view mirror LH
277	Control, rear view mirror RH
280	Supplementary air device (cold start)
281	Corrector, fuel reheating
285	Capacitor, coil positive
286	Capacitor, direction indicator flasher unit
290	Tachometer
295	Compressor
296	Compressor, air horn
300	Starter motor
301	Vapour relief valve (LPG)
302	Diode, relay protection
303	Diode, rear foglamps
304	Protection diode, electronic control unit
305	Checking diode, coolant temperature warning light
306	Checking diode, brake warning light
307	Diode, air conditioning control
308	Diode, lighting dimmer
309	Diode, electric fan
310	Diode, compressor
311	Diode, roof lamp
312	Diode, speech synthesizer
313	Flow sensor
329	Solenoid valve, cruise control deceleration
330	Solenoid valve, air conditioning
331	Solenoid valve, EGR (pilot carburettor)
332	Solenoid valve, opening the carburettor throttle valve
333	Solenoid valve, injection cut-off on over-run
334	Solenoid, emission control advance modulator
335	Solenoid, exhaust emission
336	Solenoid, carburettor breather
337	Main solenoid, brake antilock

Component codes

338	Control solenoid, brake antilock
340	Solenoid, pump stop
344	Solenoid, turbine fan
345	Solenoid valve, fast idle stabiliser
346	Solenoid, canister
347	Solenoid, cruise control
348	Advance solenoid, diesel
349	Solenoid valve, temperature control
350	Switches, illumination
351	Illumination, instrument panel
355	Illumination, heating/ventilation control
360	Illumination, console
361	Courtesy lamp
364	Illumination, cigar lighter
365	Illumination, ashtray
370	Illumination, luggage compartment (or tailgate)
375	Illumination, glovebox
380	Illumination, engine compartment
385	Illumination, number plate LH
386	Illumination, number plate RH
390	Illumination, ignition switch/steering lock
395	Floor illumination, driver's side
396	Floor illumination, passenger's side
397	Sill illumination, driver's side
398	Sill illumination, passenger side
400	Illumination, gear selector lever
410	Clutch, compressor
420	Idling cut-off, carburettor
425	Map reading lamp
440	Sidelamp LH
441	Sidelamp RH
445	Tail lamp cluster LH
446	Tail lamp cluster RH
452	Marker lamp, LH rear
453	Marker lamp, RH rear
455	Door marker lamp LH
456	Door marker lamp RH
457	Front foglamp RH
458	Front foglamp LH
460	Rear foglamp LH
461	Rear foglamp RH
462	Reverse lamp
463	Stop-lamp
464	Reverse lamp + foglamp (rear)
465	Suppressor filter, tachometer
466	Fuse holder (+ accessories, brake antilock)
467	Fuse holder (for warning light, brake antilock)
468	Fuse holder (power circuit, brake antilock)
469	Fuse holder Lambda sensor heater
470	Fuses (fusebox)
471	Fuse holder (radio)
472	Fuse holder (locks)
473	Fuse holder (dipped beams)
474	Fuse holder (speech synthesizer)
475	Fuse holder (carburettor heater)
476	Fuse holder (cruise control)
477	Fuse holder, supply pump
478	Flashing lamps, priority
479	Fuse holder (pump, brake antilock)
480	Direction indicator lamp, LH front
481	Direction indicator lamp, RH front
482	Direction indicator lamp, LH rear
483	Direction indicator lamp, RH rear
484	Side lamp/direction indicator, LH front
485	Side lamp/direction indicator, RH front
486	Suppression filter, speech synthesizer
487	Fuse holder (control unit, fuel output VP15)

Key to wiring diagrams (continued)

Component codes

488	Fuse holder (control unit, advance regulator VP15)
489	Fuse holder, cooling fan group (CFG)
490	Impulse generator (speed)
491	Rotating lamp
500	Loudspeaker, LH front
501	Loudspeaker, RH front
502	Loudspeaker, LH rear
503	Loudspeaker, RH rear
505	Hour meter (P4)
510	Switch, front foglamps
511	Switch, rear foglamps
512	Switch, auxiliary driving lamp
513	Switch, siren
514	Switch, rotating lamp
515	Switch, rheostat, instrument panel illumination
516	Switch, parking lights
517	Switch, general (military P4)
518	Test switch, oil, coolant or charging fault (P4)
519	Switch, horn (P4)
520	Switch, window winder (driver's)
521	Switch, window winder (passenger's)
521A	Switch, passenger's window winder
522	Switch, window winder, LH rear
523	Switch, window winder, RH rear
524	Switch, window winder, LH rear (in rear compartment)
525	Switch, window winder, RH rear (in rear compartment)
526	Child safety switch, rear window winders
527	Switch, main/dip beams (P4)
530	Switch, sunroof
532	Switch, heated rear window
535	Switch, driver's seat heating
536	Switch, passenger's seat heating
540	Switch, preheater
545	Switch, central roof lamp
548	Test switch, brake wear warning light
549	Diagnostic switch, diesel
550	Switch, rear screen wiper
552	Switch, headlamp wiper
555	Switch, fuel supply warning light
556	Switch, police horn
557	Switch, rotating lamp
558	Switch, air fan
560	Switch, warning bell
565	Switch, pressure drop
566	Switch, air conditioning control
567	Switch, cruise control
570	Switch, hazard warning
571	Test switch
572	Switch, lamps (police)
574	Injectors
575	Cold start injector
576	Information display, injection control box
580	Fuel tank unit
590	Map reading lamp
591	Indicator, coolant temperature
592	Gauge, turbocharger pressure
593	Fuel gauge
594	Gauge, engine oil temperature
595	Gauge, engine oil pressure
598	Electronic control unit, ignition
600	Motor, screen wiper
601	Motor, window wiper, rear
605	Wiper motor, headlamp LH
606	Wiper motor, headlamp RH
607	Motor, heater control flap

Component codes

610	Motor, sunroof
615	Motor, LH front window winder
616	Motor, RH front window winder
617	Motor, LH rear window winder
618	Motor, RH rear window winder
620	Motor, heating/ventilation fan
625	Actuator, LH front door lock
626	Actuator, RH front door lock
627	Actuator, LH rear door lock
628	Actuator, RH rear door lock
629	Actuator, luggage compartment lock
630	Motor, fuel filler flap lock
635	Motor, engine cooling fan
636	Motor, air conditioning fan
640	Clock
645	Pressure switch, brake servo
646	Pressure switch, power steering
647	Pressure switch, air conditioning cut-out
650	Oil pressure switch
651	Vacuum-pressure switch
652	Pressure switch, turbocharger cut-out
653	Fuel throttle enrichment switch
654	Advance curve selection switch
660	Trip compter
660A	Keyboard, trip computer
660B	Display, trip computer
669	Potentiometer, throttle
669A	Potentiometer, accelerator pedal (Diesel)
670	Headlamp LH
671	Headlamp RH
672	Headlamp blackout (P4)
673	Driving lamp LH
674	Driving lamp RH
675	Brake pads, LH front
676	Brake pads, RH front
677	Brake pads, LH rear
678	Brake pads, RH rear
679	Vacuum pump, cruise control
680	Washer pump, front
681	Washer pump, rear
682	Washer pump, headlamp
683	Fuel supply pump
684	Scavenge pump
685	Coolant pump, heater matrix
686	Hydraulic pump, brake anti-lock
688	Interior lamp, front
689	Interior lamp, rear
690	Interior lamp, centre
691	Interior lamp, LH front
692	Interior lamp, RH front
693	Interior lamp, LH rear
694	Interior lamp, RH rear
697	PLIP
700	Pressure switch
705	Connector board
706	Services connector board
710	Battery supply socket
720	Diagnostic socket
721	Test socket (injection)
723	Front foglamp LH
724	Front foglamp RH
729	Relay, emission control
730	Relay, starter motor
731	Relay, preheater
732	Relay, fan clutch
733	Relay, electric fan motor
734	Relay, hour meter (P4)

Key to wiring diagrams (continued)

Component codes

735	Relay, main beams
736	Relay, auxiliary driving lamps
737	Relay, dipped beams
738	Relay, heating/ventilation fan, fast speed
740	Relay, coil
741	Relay, coil resistance
742	Relay, cold start control
743	Relay, compressor
744	Tachymetric relay or pump control relay
745	Relay, air horn compressor
746	Tachymetric relay (cut-off on over-run)
747	Relay, CLT
748	Relay, ECU, exhaust emission
749	Relay, cold cut-off
750	Relay, front foglamps
751	Relay, rear foglamps
752	Relay, compressor cut-out (105°)
753	Relay, pump, brake antilock
754	Relay, power circuit, brake antilock
755	Relay, headlamp wiper
756	Relay, headlamp wiper timer
757	Relay, advance curve selection
760	Relay, heated rear window
761	Relay, rear electric window
762	Relay, front electric window
763	Relay, sunroof
764	Relay, sunroof tilt + central locking
765	Relay, front screen wiper
766	Relay, rear window wiper
767	Relay, warning light occultation (P4)
770	Relay, accessories
771	Relay, visual warning
772	Relay, two-speed (mixture control)
773	Relay, carburettor heater
775	Relay, starter motor isolator
776	Relay, cruise control disengagement
777	Relay, pilot carburettor supply
778	Relay, scavenge pump
780	Relay, lighting dimmer
781	Relay, excessive speed
782	Relay, ignition supply
783	Relay, injection supply
784	Relay, trip computer/cruise control/speech synthesizer information
785	Relay, brake warning (Australia)
786	Resistor, coil
787	Resistor, heating/ventilation fan
788	Resistor, two-speed cooling fan
789	Resistor, lighting dimmer
790	Heater, diesel fuel
791	Heater, carburettor
793	Resistor, preheater (P4)
794	Resistor, injection matching
795	Rheostat, instrument illumination
800	Regulator, voltage
801	Regulator, control pressure
810	Side repeater flasher LH
811	Side repeater flasher RH
812	Rheostat, temperature display
814	Rear view mirror LH
815	Rear view mirror RH
817	Heated seat, front LH
818	Heated seat, front RH
820	Bell
829	Servo, power steering
830	Servo, cruise control
832	Sensor, evaporator

Component codes

833	Sensor, blown air
834	Sensor, interior air temperature
835	Sensor, oil level
836	Sensor, fuel flow (trip computer)
837	Sensor, coolant level
838	Sensor, mixture regulator
840	Sensor, high temperature
841	Siren
845	Speech synthesizer
846	Sensor, body temperature (exhaust)
847	Sensor, passenger compartment temperature regulation
848	Lambda sensor
849	Sensor, external air temperature
850	Thermal switch, cooling fan (coolant)
852	Thermal switch, transmission oil
853	Thermal switch, 18°C (coolant temperature)
855	Thermal switch, coolant
861	Thermal switch, 40°C (coolant temperature)
862	Thermal switch, 60°C (coolant temperature)
865	Thermostat, electronic (air conditioning)
870	Thermal time switch (cold start opening)
880	Tachograph
885	Timer switch, seat belt
886	Timer switch, interior lamp
887	Timer switch, headlamp wash
888	Sender unit, oil temperature gauge
889	Temperature sender unit, injection
890	Sender unit, coolant temperature gauge
891	Temperature sender unit, electronic (heating/ventilation)
892	Sender unit, engine oil temperature
893	Timer switch, rear screen wiper
893A	Timer switch, windscreen wiper
894	Temperature sender unit, controlling cooling fan motors by ECU (liquid cooling)
895	Sender unit, exhaust emission
896	Thermal resistor, inlet air temperature
897	Tester, anti-lock
898	Sender unit, oil pressure
899	Test unit, variable power steering
929	Proportioning valve, cruise control
930	Fan, electromagnetic clutch
935	Fan, heating/ventilation
936	Fan, heating/ventilation, rear
945	Heated rear window
950	Fan
955	Ram, driver's seat
960	Fan, air conditioning
965	Cold start flap
970	Voltmeter
+AA	Supply from accessories terminal
+AC	Supply from ignition switch
BL	Screened cable
+D	Supply from starter motor
L1	Warning lamp, seat belt
L2	Warning lamps, direction indicator
L3	Warning lamp, low fuel level
L4	Warning lamp, main beams
L5	Warning lamp, hazard warning
L6	Warning lamp, side/tail lamps 'on'
L7	Warning lamp, no battery charge
L8	Warning lamp, preheater
L9	Warning lamp, choke control
L10	Warning lamp, oil pressure
L11	Warning lamp, oil and coolant

Key to wiring diagrams (continued)

L12	Warning lamp, coolant temperature		L30	Warning lamp, rear differential lock
L13	Warning lamp, brake safety		L31	Warning lamp, front differential lock
L14	Warning lamp, rear foglamps		L32	Warning lamp, knock detector
L15	Warning lamp, fuel supply		L33	Warning lamp, diagnosis
L16	Warning lamp, 'stop'		L34	Warning lamp, water in fuel
L17	Warning lamp, brake fluid/stop-lamps		L35	Warning lamp, dipped beams
L18	Warning lamp, sidelamp failure		L36	Warning lamp, trailer direction indicator
L19	Warning lamp, tail lamp failure		L37	Warning light, power take-off (P4)
L20	Warning lamp, screenwash level		L38	Warning lamp, catalytic converter
L21	Warning lamp, coolant level		L39	Warning lamp, Brake anti-lock alert
L22	Warning lamp, engine oil level			
L23	Warning lamp, brake pad wear		M	Earth connections
L24	Manual test switch, instrument panel		+P	Supply from battery
L25	Warning lamp, oil temperature			
L26	Warning lamp, 'door open'			*Not all items are fitted to all models*
L27	Warning lamp, tail lamp or rear foglamp failure			*The wires are not colour-coded*

Fig. 12.15 Wiring socket locations (on fuse/relay board)

The socket code corresponds to the connector suffix in Fig. 12.17

Connector colours

H706	Black	F	White	MR	Brown
A	Yellow	G	White	P	White
B	White	H	Brown	R	Yellow
BA	White	J	White	S	Yellow
C	Brown	K	Brown	T	White
D	Yellow	L	Brown	V	White
E	Blue	M	Yellow	W	Blue

Fig. 12.16 Wiring diagram for all Peugeot 309 models except GTI

Fig. 12.16 Wiring diagram for all Peugeot 309 models except GTI (continued)

Fig. 12.17 Fuse/relay board connections

Fig. 12.17 Fuse/relay board connections (continued)

Fig. 12.18 Wiring diagram for fuel injection system – except GTI

Chapter 13 Supplement:
Revisions and information on later models

Contents

1 Introduction

This Supplement contains information in respect of changes and modifications which have taken place since 1987. The major items include details of the 309 GTI, and of the automatic transmission fitted to some models.

In order to use the Supplement to its best advantage, it is suggested that it is referred to before the main Chapters of the manual; this will ensure that any relevant information can be noted and incorporated within the procedures given in Chapters 1 to 12.

Project vehicle

The vehicle used in the preparation of this Supplement, and appearing in many of the photographic sequences, was a 1989 model 309 GTI.

2 Specifications

The Specifications given below are supplementary to, or revisions of, those given at the beginning of the preceding Chapters.

Engine – 1905 cc (GTI)
Specifications as for XU5-JA engine in Chapter 1, except for the following

General
Engine type	XU9-JA (D6B)
Stroke	88.0 mm
Capacity	1905 cc
Compression ratio	9.6 : 1
Maximum power	93.5 kW (127 bhp) at 6000 rpm
Maximum torque	161 Nm (119 lbf ft) at 4750 rpm

Cylinder block
Material	Light alloy, with cast-iron wet liners and O-ring base seals
Liner protrusion	0.03 to 0.10 mm
Maximum difference between liners	0.05 mm

Valves
Valve head diameter:	
Inlet	41.6 mm
Exhaust	34.05 mm

Valve timing:
  Inlet opens .... 11° 30' BTDC
  Inlet closes .... 43° ATDC
  Exhaust opens .... 46° BBDC
  Exhaust closes .... 2° ATDC

Crankshaft and main bearings
Crankpin diameter (new) .... 49.684 to 50.000 mm

XU type engines – October 1987 on
Torque wrench settings

	Nm	lbf ft
Cylinder head bolts (Torx type):		
Stage 1 (All bolts, in sequence)	60	44
Stage 2: Slacken bolt 1, then	20 + 300°	15 + 300°
Repeat Stage 2 on remaining bolts in sequence		

Fuel system
Carburettor
Type .... Weber 36 TLC
Application .... Models with XU5-1C (1580 cc carburettor) engine and automatic transmission

Calibration and settings:
  Venturi .... 28 mm
  Main jet .... 140 ± ^{2}/3
  Air correction jet .... 150 ± 10
  Emulsion tube F80
  Accelerator pump injector 40
  Needle valve 150
  Idling fuel jet .... 47 ± ^{2}/0
  Idling speed .... 900 ± 50 rpm
  CO% .... 1.0 ± 0.5
  Float level .... 28.0 mm (1.102 in)

Ignition system
Spark plugs (October 1987 on)
XU5-1C:
  Type .... Champion C9YC, or equivalent
  Electrode gap .... 0.8 mm (0.032 in)
XU5-JA:
  Type .... Champion C7YC, or equivalent
  Electrode gap .... 0.8 mm (0.032 in)
XU9-JA:
  Type .... Champion C7YC, or equivalent
  Electrode gap .... 0.9 mm (0.035 in)

Ignition timing
XU9-JA .... 5° BTDC @ 700 rpm

Manual gearbox
BE1 gearbox (January 1987 on)
Gear ratio (except GTI):
  1st .... 3.25 : 1
  2nd .... 1.85 : 1
Gear ratios (GTI):
  1st .... 2.92 : 1
  2nd .... 1.85 : 1
  3rd .... 1.36 : 1
  4th .... 1.07 : 1
  5th .... 0.87 : 1
  Reverse .... 3.33 : 1
  Final drive .... 3.69 : 1
Lubrication (October 1987 on):
  Oil type/specification .... Gear oil, viscosity 75W/80 (Duckhams Hypoid PT 75W/80)

Automatic transmission
General
Transmission type .... ZF 4 HP 14
Gear ratios:
  1st .... 0.398 : 1
  2nd .... 0.701 : 1
  3rd .... 0.960 : 1
  4th .... 1.300 : 1
  Reverse .... 0.339 : 1
  Final drive .... 3.82 : 1
Fluid type/specification .... Dexron II type ATF (Duckhams D-Matic)

Fluid capacity:
    From dry .... 6.2 litres (10.9 pints)
    At service refill .... 2.4 litres (4.2 pints)

Torque wrench settings	Nm	lbf ft
Inhibitor switch	41	30
Fluid cooler centre bolt	50	37
Dipstick tube union nut	45	33
Selector cable bracket	30	22
Torque converter-to-driveplate bolts	35	26
Torque converter housing to engine	45	33
Transmission mounting bracket to body	18	13
Mounting bracket to transmission	35	26

Braking system – GTI
Front disc brakes
Type .... Ventilated
Disc thickness (new) .... 20.4 mm
Minimum disc thickness (refinished) .... 18.5 mm
Caliper piston diameter .... 48.0 mm

Rear disc brakes
Type .... Solid
Disc thickness (new) .... 8.0 mm
Minimum disc thickness (refinished) .... 7.0 mm
Caliper piston diameter .... 30.0 mm

Master cylinder diameter .... 20.6 mm

Servo diameter .... 228.6 mm

Torque wrench setting	Nm	lbf ft
Rear caliper mounting bolts	120	88

Suspension, wheels and tyres (GTI)
Rear suspension geometry
Toe-in .... 0.6 to 3.6 mm
Camber .... 0° 20' to 1° 20' negative

Roadwheels and tyres
Roadwheel type 6J 15
Tyre size .... 185/55 VR 15
Inflation pressure – front and rear (185/55 VR 15) ... 29 lbf/in² (2.0 bar)

Steering
Power-assisted steering
Steering rack ratio .... 18.6 : 1
Steering wheel turns (lock-to-lock) 3.26
Turning circle (between kerbs) .... 10.4 m (34.1 ft)

Front wheel alignment (automatic transmission models)
Toe-in .... 2.8 to 4.8 mm
Castor .... 0° 25' to 1° 25' positive
Camber .... 0° 30' negative to 0° 30' positive
Steering axis inclination .... 8° 50' to 9° 50'

Front wheel alignment (GTI)
Toe-in .... 2.3 to 3.3 mm
Castor .... 1° to 2° positive
Camber .... 1° negative to 0°
Steering axis inclination .... 9° 40' to 10° 40'

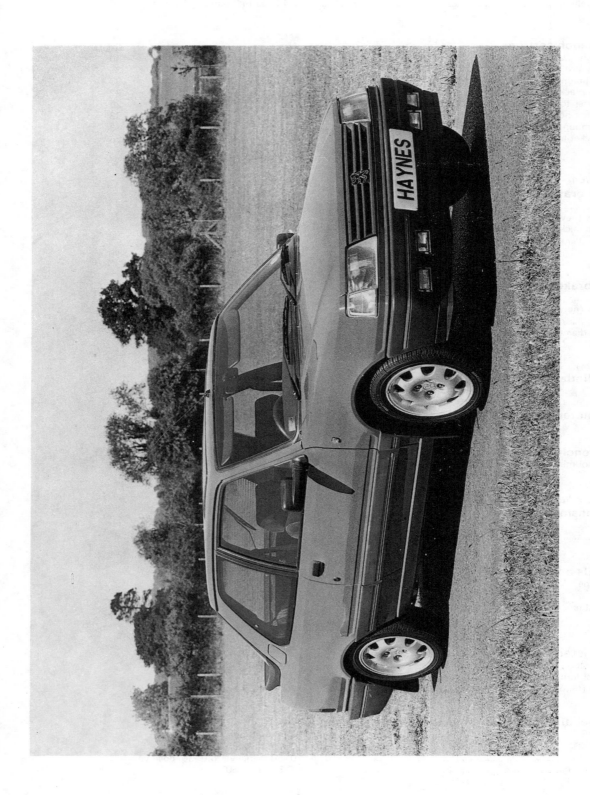

Peugeot 309 GTI

3 Routine maintenance

Manual gearbox oil – renewal
1   As from the beginning of 1988, the service interval for changing the oil in pre-October 1987 BE1 gearboxes has been extended to 36 000 miles (57 000 km)..
2   On cars manufactured after October 1987, the BE1 gearbox is 'sealed for life', and renewing the oil is no longer required. It is essential to use only the specified type of oil when topping-up.

4 Engine

Oil consumption – general
1   The emission of blue smoke frtom the exhaust may be due to bore wear if the engine has covered a high mileage. More likely, smoke emission on a low-mileage engine will be due to one of the following causes.

> Blockage in crankcase ventilation system components
> Worn valve stem oil seals
> Second piston ring fitted upside-down (refer to Figs. 1.17 or 1.31)

2   If worn valve stem oil seals are to be renewed, fit new polyacrylate ones (part number 0956.18).
3   An engine oil consumption figure of 700 miles per pint (1000 miles per 0.5 litre) is acceptable.

Engine right-hand mounting (XU engine)
4   In order to eliminate a knock, which may occur in the right-hand flexible mounting on XU engines, a spring plate has been fitted between the rubber snubber and the mounting bracket on later models.
5   The spring may be fitted to earlier cars, noting that the notch in the spring must be towards the right-hand side of the car.

Fig. 13.1 Right-hand engine mounting anti-knock spring (Sec 4)

Oil filler cap (XU engine)
6   Due to the likelihood of corrosion occurring in the steel mesh within the engine oil filler cap, it is recommended that the mesh is removed and discarded.

Camshaft lubrication pipe (XU engine)
7   A modified camshaft bearing lubrication pipe has been introduced, in order to reduce tappet noise.
8   The pipe incorporates O-ring seals, and may be fitted to earlier models.

Inlet manifold gasket (XU engine)
9   Two inlet manifold gaskets are supplied in the Peugeot decoke set, one for carburettor engines, and the other for fuel injection engines.
10   It is most important that the correct gasket is fitted, otherwise loss of power will occur in the lower engine speed range.

Cylinder head modifications (XU engine)
11   As from October 1987, the cylinder head bolts are of Torx (T55) socket-headed type, with thicker washers.
12   The cylinder liner height has been reduced by 0.05 mm, and in consequence, the liner protrusion has also been reduced – see Specifications, noting that the revised values for all XU engines are given in the 1.9 litre engine section.
13   The final tightening angle for the cylinder head bolts has been revised (see Specifications), and once the tightening has been carried out, subsequent re-tightening is not required.
14   Lightly grease the bolt threads, and the undersides of their heads before tightening, following the sequence shown in Fig. 1.27.

Engine (XU9-JA) – GTI
15   This engine is fitted to the GTI model introduced in February 1987.
16   The engine is essentially an increased-capacity version of the XU5-JA power unit, but refer to the Specifications for differences.

Engine undertray (all engines)
17   The engine undertray is secured by quick-fit plastic fasteners. Remove them using a pair of pliers, and refit them using thumb pressure (photo).
18   The rear edge of the undertray is secured by clips.

4.1 An engine undertray pin removed

Fig. 13.2 Engine right-hand mounting tightening tool (Sec 4)

Engine right-hand mounting (all engines)
19 The section of the right-hand engine mounting which is attached to the bodyshell incorporates a notched tubular-shaped body. It is essential that it is tightened to 40 Nm (30 lbf ft).
20 Although a special tool is available (Fig. 13.2) to enable a torque wrench to be used, it should be possible to fabricate something similar. Alternatively use an oil filter strap wrench to obtain the correct tightness.

5 Cooling system

Cooling system pressure
1 As from April 1987, the cooling system pressure in all engines is increased to 14 lbf/in^2 (1 bar). In consequence, a higher-rated expansion tank cap is used. A higher-rated temperature coolant temperature switch and radiator fan thermal switch are also fitted.
2 A guide tube type of level indicator is fitted in the neck of the expansion tank.
3 The top of the slot in the tube is the maximum coolant level (photo).

6 Fuel system

Unleaded fuel
1 Unleaded 95 RON fuel may be used in all Peugeot 309 models except the GTI, subject to the possibility of adjusting the ignition timing where stated in the following table.

Engine	Ignition timing
1118 cc (E1A)	*Unchanged*
1294 cc (G1A)	*Unchanged*
1580 cc (XU5-1C) manual	*Retard by 4°*
1580 cc (XU5-1C) automatic	*Unchanged*
1580 cc (XU5-JA)	*Retard by 2°*

Note: *GTI models require an unacceptably large ignition timing retardation to run on 95 RON unleaded fuel – this leads to a substantial loss of engine performance, so its use is not recommended.*

Weber 36 TLC carburettor – description
2 The Weber 36 TLC carburettor is fitted to the XU5-1C (1580 cc) engine on automatic transmission models. It is of single-barrel downdraught type, incorporating an automatic choke, and a temperature-controlled air cleaner is fitted.

Weber 36 TLC carburettor – idle speed and mixture adjustment
3 Where fitted remove the tamperproof cap from the mixture screw.
4 Select the Park (P) position with the transmission selector lever, then run the engine to normally operating temperature. Do not remove the air cleaner.
5 Connect a tachometer to the engine.
Without an exhaust gas analyser
6 With the engine idling, adjust the idle speed screw so that the engine speed is 950 rpm.
7 Adjust the mixture screw to obtain the highest engine speed.
8 Repeat the procedure given in paragraphs 6 and 7 until the highest engine speed is 950 rpm.
9 Screw in the **mixture** screw until the engine idling speed is as specified.
With an exhaust gas analyser
10 With the engine idling adjust the idle speed screw until the engine speed is 900 rpm.
11 Adjust the mixture screw to obtain the specified CO reading.
12 Repeat the procedure given in paragraphs 10 and 11 as necessary.

Weber 36 TLC carburettor – overhaul
13 The procedure is straightforward, but refer to the accompanying illustrations for the positions of the various jets.
14 To check the float level, hold the cover vertically with the gasket in place. Check that the dimension shown in Fig. 13.8 is as specified, and if necessary bend the tongue on the float arm to correct it.
15 To adjust the cold start device choke opening after starting (COAS), the engine must be hot and idling, the air cleaner hose

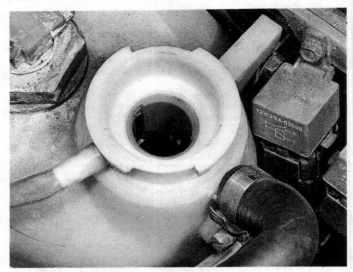

5.3 Coolant expansion tank level guide tube

Fig. 13.3 Idle speed screw (1) on the Weber 36 TLC carburettor (Sec 6)

Fig. 13.4 Mixture screw location (2) on the Weber 36 TLC carburettor (Sec 6)

removed, and the cold start device cover removed. Peugeot tool 0.145 G is essential to make this adjustment.
16 Refer to Fig. 13.10 and fit the tool as shown, then turn screw (4) until the cam (5) contacts the tool peg (6). Using a 9.5 mm drill, check that the choke flap has opened by 9.5 mm – if not adjust screw (1) (Fig. 13.11).
17 Disconnect and plug the hose (1) shown in Fig. 13.14, and check now that the choke flap is open by 5.5 mm – if not, loosen screw (1) (Fig. 13.12), hold the roller (1) (Fig. 13.13) against the top of the cam, and adjust lever (2). Retighten the screw and reconnect the hose afterwards.
18 To adjust the positive throttle opening (PTO), press the roller to open the choke flap and check that the engine speed is 2000 rpm with the electric fan stopped. If necessary, adjust screw (2) (Fig. 13.15).

Fig. 13.5 Top view of Weber 36 TLC carburettor (Sec 6)

1 Air correction jet 3 Emulsion tube
2 Idling jet

Fig. 13.6 Top cover removed from Weber 36 TLC
carburettor (Sec 6)

1 Type number 2 Accelerator pump injector

Fig. 13.7 Top cover inverted – Weber 36 TLC carburettor
(Sec 6)

1 Float   3 Secondary venturi
2 Main jet   4 Fuel inlet needle valve

Fig. 13.8 Float level setting diagram – Weber 36 TLC
carburettor (Sec 6)

1 Gasket X = 28.0 mm (1.1 in)

Fig. 13.9 Peugeot tool 0.145 G (Sec 6)

Fig. 13.10 COAS adjustment on the Weber 36 TLC
carburettor (Sec 6)

1 Locknut   4 Adjusting screw
2 Hole   5 Cam
3 Roller   6 Peg on tool

Fig. 13.11 COAS adjusting screw (1) on the Weber 36 TLC carburettor (Sec 6)

Fig. 13.12 COAS adjustment on the Weber 36 TLC carburettor (Sec 6)

1   Screw

Fig. 13.13 COAS adjustment (second stage) on the Weber 36 TLC carburettor (Sec 6)

1   Roller   2   Lever

Fig. 13.14 COAS adjustment (third stage) on the Weber 36 TLC carburettor (Sec 6)

1   Hose

Fig. 13.15 PTO adjustment on the Weber 36 TLC carburettor (Sec 6)

1   Roller   2   Adjusting screw

19 To adjust the choke cam, fit the tool 0.145 G as shown in Fig. 13.16 and adjust screw (3) until the cam (4) contacts peg (5). Tighten the locknut (6).
20 Stop the engine and refit the cold start device cover and air cleaner hose.

Fuel pump – electrically-operated type
21 This type of pump is fitted to GTI and automatic transmission models. The pump is submerged in the fuel tank.
22 A filter is incorporated in the pump. The two relays which supply the pump are located on the side of the heater. One relay incorporates a safety feature, in that its primary windings are short-circuited to earth via the engine oil pressure switch. When the engine is stationary, this relay will not operate the fuel pump, but as soon as the engine is running it will supply current to the pump. The other relay operates in conjunction with the starter motor to operate the starter motor for starting.
23 If the pump is to be removed, disconnect the battery and take out the fuel tank as described in Chapter 3. In theory, it should be possible to remove the pump and the sender unit after taking out the cover

panels from under the front seats, but as the holes in the floor panel are usually out of alignment, the securing rings cannot be rotated. Tools similar to the ones shown in Fig. 13.18 will be required to unscrew the rings (photo).

6.23 Fuel pump and sender unit location

Fig. 13.16 Choke cam adjustment on the Weber 36 TLC carburettor (Sec 6)

1   Hole
2   Roller
3   Adjusting screw
4   Cam
5   Peg on tool
6   Locknut

Fig. 13.17 Electrically-operated submerged type fuel pump (Sec 6)

1   Pump   3   Fuel filter
2   Cover

Fig. 13.18 Typical tools for removing fuel tank pump and sender unit ring nuts (Sec 6)

A   For sender unit (dimensions   B   For fuel pump – roll pin
    in mm)   arrowed

7 Ignition system

Spark plugs – later models
1 Up until October 1987, taper-seat spark plugs were fitted to XU5-JA and XU5-1C engines. After this date conventional plugs with sealing washers were fitted.
2 Refer to the Specifications for spark plug types and electrode gaps.

8 Manual gearbox

Gearchange linkage – modification
1 As from early 1987, the selector and engagement levers are secured to their shafts by roll pins, instead of the splines and nuts used previously.

Gearbox oil – renewal
2 Refer to Section 3 of this Supplement for details of revisions to the routine maintenance requirements.

9 Automatic transmission

Description
1 Automatic transmission became available in June 1987 and further details are given in the Specifications in this Supplement.
2 Vehicles equipped with this type of transmission are fitted with an automatic choke Weber 36 TLC carburettor, an automatic temperature-controlled air cleaner, and an electric fuel pump located within the fuel tank.
3 Apart from modified front suspension coil springs, all other mechanical details are similar to other models using the XU5-1C engine.
4 In the interests of fuel economy the torque converter is completely bypassed in top (4th) gear and partially bypassed in 3rd; this reduces losses due to torque converter slip.
5 Gearchange is automatic in use, the transmission responding to changes in speed and load. The usual kickdown facility is provided for enhanced acceleration when the throttle is depressed fully.
6 Instead of the customary oil cooler mounted in the radiator, cooling is by means of a coolant/oil heat exchanger mounted on the side of the transmission.

Safety precautions
7 The following safety precautions must be adhered to where an automatic transmission is fitted. Whenever the vehicle is parked, or is being serviced or repaired, ensure that the handbrake is fully applied and the selector lever is in 'P'.
8 If it is necessary to tow a vehicle with automatic transmission, the towing speed must be restricted to 30 mph and the distance to 30 miles. If these conditions cannot be met, or if transmission damage is the reason for seeking a tow, the vehicle must be transported on a trailer.

Fluid level – checking
9 This check should be made directly after the vehicle has been used so that the transmission oil is at its normal operating temperature.
10 With the vehicle parked on level ground and the engine running, move the selector lever through all positons a number of times then finally leave it in 'P'. The handbrake must be fully applied throughout the check procedure.
11 With the engine still running, remove the transmission fluid dipstick, wipe it clean, reinsert it fully then withdraw it again and check the fluid level. The fluid level must be between 'Min' and 'Max' levels.
12 If required, top up the fluid level (but do not overfill) through the dipstick guide tube.
13 Stop the engine and refit the dipstick on completion.

Fluid – draining and refilling
14 Position a suitable container with a minimum capacity of three litres under the transmission (hot). There are two drain plugs to be removed, these being shown in Fig. 13.21. Remove the plugs and drain the fluid, then refit the plugs.

Fig. 13.19 Later type gear selector lever (Sec 8)

1 *Selector lever*	4 *O-ring*
2 *Spring*	5 *Selector finger and pivot*
3 *Washer*	

Fig. 13.20 Later type gear engagement lever – roll pin arrowed (Sec 8)

1 *Lever*	3 *Finger*
2 *Shaft*	

15 Refill through the dipstick guide tube.
16 Recheck the fluid level after a nominal mileage has been covered and, if necessary, top up the fluid, as described in paragraphs 9 to 13 inclusive.

Selector control – adjustment
17 Remove the air cleaner, then using a spanner as shown in Fig. 13.22, disconnect the control rod balljoint from the lever on the transmission.
18 Move the lever on the transmission fully forwards to the 'P' position.
19 Inside the car, move the selector lever fully forwards to the 'P' position.
20 The control rod balljoint should align exactly with the coupling ball on the selector lever, so that when reconnected, neither the selector lever within the vehicle nor the selector lever on the gearbox move. Adjust the position of the balljoint on the connecting rod if necessary.

Fig. 13.21 External components of the ZF 4 HP 14 automatic transmission (Sec 9)

1 Converter housing
2 Main casing
3 End cover
4 Sump
5 Dipstick tube
6 Dipstick
7 Fluid cooler
8 Kickdown cable
9 Breather
10 Inhibitor switch
11 Selector lever
12 Lifting eye
13 Speedometer drive adaptor
14 Final drive left-hand output
15 Final drive right-hand output
16 Final drive drain plug
17 Torque converter
18 Output shaft bearing bolts
19 Brake band adjuster
20 Pressure test points
21 Transmission drain plug

Fig. 13.22 Disconnecting the selector control rod balljoint (1) from the transmission lever (2) (Sec 9)

21 If the selector control was adjusted, check the setting by starting the engine and, when it has reached its normal operating temperature move the selector lever within the vehicle to 'P'. The vehicle should be stationary, and the gearbox parking pawl fully engaged.

22 Now move the lever to 'R' with the handbrake off. The vehicle should move rearwards, the pawl having been released.

23 If either of the checks in paragraphs 21 and 22 is unsatisfactory, unscrew the control rod balljoint one complete turn and repeat the checks until satisfactory.

24 Refit the air cleaner.

Kickdown cable – adjustment

25 Check the adjustment of the accelerator cable as described in Chapter 3, Section 14.

26 Check that there is a small clearance between the crimped stop and the end fitting of the kickdown cable. The clearance should not exceed 0.5 mm (0.020 in). Adjust if necessary, using the nuts on the threaded fitting at the support bracket.

27 Kickdown cable renewal is best left to your Peugeot dealer, as it involves removal of the valve block.

Brake band – adjustment

28 This is not a routine operation, and should only be required if the transmission appears to be malfunctioning.

29 Slacken the locknut (1) (Fig. 13.24) on the side of the transmission casing, and unscrew the nut and the bolt (2) two turns.

30 Tighten the bolt to a torque of 10 Nm (7 lbf ft), and then unscrew it through two complete turns.

31 Tighten the locknut without disturbing the setting of the bolt.

Transmission unit – removal and refitting

32 The transmission is removed downwards and out from under the car.

33 Open the bonnet.

34 Drain the transmission fluid through both the drain plugs provided.

35 Disconnect the air intake hose.

36 Disconnect the battery and remove it.

37 Disconnect the earth strap (transmission-to-body).

38 Using self-locking pliers or brake hose clamps, clamp the coolant hoses at the fluid cooler, and disconnect them from the cooler.

39 Disconnect the selector cable from the lever on the transmission by releasing the balljoint with an open-ended spanner, and then free the cable from its support bracket.

40 Disconnect the leads from the reversing lamp switch.

41 Disconnect the kickdown cable from the throttle spindle quadrant and the support bracket.

42 Remove the socket-headed bolts (1) (Fig. 13.26).

43 With the vehicle raised and securely supported, remove the front roadwheels, and then withdraw both driveshafts as described in Chapter 7.

44 Disconnect the speedometer drive cable from the transmission by pulling out the rubber tapered cotter pin.

45 Remove the TDC sensor bracket (Fig. 13.27).

46 Unscrew the dipstick guide tube nut and remove the tube.

47 Remove the cover plate from the lower part of the torque converter housing.

48 Unscrew the torque converter-to-driveplate connecting bolts. The crankshaft will have to be turned in order to bring each bolt into view.

49 Support the weight of the engine on a crossbeam, with its hook engaged in the left-hand engine lifting eye, as shown in Fig. 13.28.

50 Remove the flexible mounting (1) (Fig. 13.29).

51 Remove the battery tray.

52 Unscrew and remove the three engine-to-transmission connecting bolts.

53 Working under the car, unscrew and remove the socket-headed bolt (1) (Fig. 13.31).

54 Withdraw the transmission from the engine, supporting its weight on a trolley jack, or on a hoist.

55 Fit a suitable retainer to prevent the torque converter being displaced.

56 Remove the transmission from under the car. The car may have to be raised in order to clear the transmission under the left-hand body member.

57 Lower the transmission to the floor, and remove it from under the car.

58 Before refitting the transmission, check the condition of the spigot bush in the rear of the crankshaft, and apply a little grease to aid entry of the torque converter. Also check that the two locating dowels are in place on the engine. Apply a little grease to the differential/driveshaft seals.

59 Make sure that the torque converter is fully engaged by checking the dimension shown in Fig. 13.34. If necessary, rotate the torque converter until it is correctly engaged.

60 Refitting is a reversal of removal, but tighten all nuts and bolts to the specified torque, and adjust the kickdown cable and selector control as previously described. Fill the transmission as previously described and bleed the cooling system.

Fault diagnosis – automatic transmission

61 Faults not due to incorrect fluid level or adjustment of the selector and kickdown cables must be diagnosed by a Peugeot dealer or automatic transmission specialist.

62 Do not remove the transmission for specialist repair without allowing the specialist to test it *in situ*. Some faults cannot be diagnosed with the transmission removed.

Fig. 13.23 Kickdown cable (1) showing crimped stop and clearance (Sec 9)

Fig. 13.24 Brake band adjuster locknut (1) and bolt (2) (Sec 9)

Fig. 13.25 Kickdown cable (1), nipple (a) and end fitting locknut (b) (Sec 9)

Fig. 13.26 Socket-headed starter motor fixing bolts (1) (Sec 9)

Fig. 13.27 Speedometer drive cable (1) at transmission, and TDC sensor bracket bolt (2) (Sec 9)

Fig. 13.28 Engine support crossbeam (Sec 9)

Fig. 13.29 Transmission flexible mounting (1) and battery tray bolts (2) (Sec 9)

Fig. 13.30 Transmission converter housing-to-engine connecting bolts (1) (Sec 9)

Fig. 13.31 Stiffener bolt (1) (Sec 9)

Fig. 13.32 Home-made retainer and bolt (1) for keeping
torque converter fully engaged in housing (Sec 9)

Fig. 13.33 Transmission-to-engine locating dowels (1)
(Sec 9)

10 Driveshafts

Driveshaft rubber bellows – renewal

1   With the driveshaft removed (refer to Chapter 7), loosen the clips
on the outer rubber bellows. If plastic straps are fitted, cut them free
with snips (photo).
2   Prise the bellows large diameter end from the outer joint housing
(photo), then tap the centre hub outwards using a soft metal drift in
order to release it from the retaining circlip. Slide the outer joint from
the driveshaft splines.
3   Extract the circlip from the groove in the driveshaft (photo).
4   Prise off the rubber bellows. If necessary, remove the plastic
seating from the recess in the driveshaft (photos).
5   Loosen the clips on the inner rubber bellows. If plastic straps are
fitted, cut them free.
6   Prise the bellows large diameter end from the inner joint housing,
and slide the rubber bellows off the outer end of the driveshaft
(photo).
7   Mark the driveshaft and inner joint housing in relation to each
other, then separate them, keeping the rollers engaged with their
respective spigots (photo).
8   Clean away the grease, then retain the rollers using adhesive tape
(photo).
9   Remove the pressure pad and spring from inside the inner joint
housing (photo).
10   Clean away the grease, then commence reassembly by inserting

Fig. 13.34 Torque converter is fully engaged if dimension 'x'
is more than 7.0 mm (0.28 in) (Sec 9)

1   Home-made retainer and bolt

the pressure pad and spring into the inner joint housing, with the
housing mounted upright in a soft-jawed vice.
11   Inject half the required amount of grease into the inner joint
housing (photo).
12   Locate the new inner rubber bellows halfway along the driveshaft
(photo).
13   Remove the adhesive tape and insert the driveshaft into the
housing.
14   Inject the remaining amount of grease in the joint.
15   Keeping the driveshaft pressed against the internal spring, refit the
rubber bellows and tighten the clips. Metal type clips can be tightened
using two pliers, by holding the buckle and pulling the clip through.
Cut off the excess, and bend the clip back under the buckle (photos).
16   Fit the plastic seating in the driveshaft recess, and refit the new
rubber bellows small diameter end on it.
17   Refit the circlip in the driveshaft groove.
18   Inject the required amount of grease in the outer joint, then insert
the driveshaft, engage the splines, and press in until the circlip snaps
into the groove.
19   Ease the rubber bellows onto the outer joint, and fit the two clips,
tightening them as previously described.

10.1 Plastic straps on the driveshaft bellows

10.2 Removing the rubber bellows from the outer joint housing

10.3 Driveshaft outerjoint circlip (arrowed)

10.4A Removing outer joint bellows

10.4B Plastic seating (arrowed) for the outer joint bellows

10.6 Removing the inner joint bellows

10.7 Separating driveshaft and rollers from the inner joint housing

10.8 Left-hand driveshaft with rollers retained with adhesive tape

10.9 Removing the pressure pad and spring from the inner joint

10.11 Injecting grease into the inner joint housing

10.12 Inner joint bellows located on the driveshaft

10.15A Tightening metal type bellows clip

10.15B Bellows clip correctly fitted

Fig. 13.35 Modified Girling type brake caliper (Sec 11)

A   Reinforced support plate   B   Welded thrust stop

11 Braking system

Girling front disc caliper – modification

1   In order to eliminate brake knock when parking, a welded thrust stop and a reinforced support plate have been incorporated in the caliper.
2   On earlier vehicles, the caliper lower guide pin can be changed for one of larger diameter, which should cure the problem.
3   The guide pin kit (part number 443909) will service both front calipers.

Rear disc pads – renewal

4   Raise the rear of the car and remove the roadwheels.
5   Extract the spring clip and tap out the locking key (photos).
6   Withdraw the pads, and brush away all dust and dirt, taking care not to inhale it.
7   The pads will be due for renewal if the groove across the friction material has all but disappeared.
8   Using a suitable square-section rod (or the shaft of a screwdriver) engaged in the piston cut-outs, turn the piston in a clockwise direction, at the same time applying pressure to force the piston into its cylinder.
9   This operation is designed to widen the caliper gap in order to accommodate the new thicker pads, and it will cause the fluid level in the master cylinder reservoir to rise. Anticipate this by syphoning some fluid out.
10 The piston should be set with its raised groove horizontal, and either just above or below the notch in the caliper.
11 Apply brake grease to the backs of the pads, and insert the inboard pad, then the outboard pad. Note the alignment lug (photos).
12 Tap in the locking key, and fit the spring clip.
13 Renew the pads on the opposite brake, and then apply the footbrake two or three times.
14 Fit the roadwheels and lower the car.
15 Top up the fluid in the master cylinder reservoir.

Rear brake caliper – removal and refitting

16 Unless an inspection pit or hoist is available, raise the car, support securely and remove the roadwheel.
17 Unscrew the union nut at the rigid brake pipe-to-flexible hose connection, and then pull out the spring clip from the support bracket.
18 Cap the end of the brake pipe to reduce fluid loss.
19 Unscrew the hose from the caliper.
20 Unscrew and remove the two caliper mounting bolts, and manoeuvre the caliper so that the handbrake cable can be released from the lever. Tap out the outer cable sleeve from the caliper (photos).
21 Refitting is a reversal of removal, but observe the following points.

22 Apply thread-locking fluid to the caliper mounting bolts, and tighten them to the specified torque.
23 Bleed the system on completion.
24 Check the handbrake adjustment.

Rear brake disc – removal and refitting

25 Remove the pads as described earlier.
26 Unbolt the caliper and tie it up out of the way, but do not disconnect the hydraulic hose or the handbrake cable (photo).
27 Extract the single countersunk screw, and tilt and remove the disc (photos).
28 Refitting is a reversal of removal.

Rear brake caliper – overhaul

29 The overhaul operations are similar to those described for the front caliper in Chapter 8, Section 5, but the piston must be rotated in an anti-clockwise direction (using a lever engaged in its rim notches) as it is being forced out of its cylinder.
30 If the handbrake operating mechanism in the caliper must be dismantled, carry out the following procedure.
31 Peel back the rubber boot.
32 Using a pair of pliers, release the angled end of the spring (photo).
33 Extract the circlip using circlip pliers, and push out the handbrake lever shaft (photo).

11.5A Removing caliper sliding key spring clip

11.5B Sliding key (arrowed) partially extracted

11.10 Rear caliper – raised groove in piston (A) and notch in caliper (B)

11.11A Fitting an inboard disc pad – note locating lug (arrowed)

11.11B Fitting an outboard disc pad

11.20A Unscrewing caliper fixing bolts

11.20B Disconnecting handbrake cable from caliper lever

11.20C Driving out handbrake cable bush from caliper

11.26 Supporting rear brake caliper

11.27A Extracting rear disc countersunk fixing screw

11.27B Removing rear brake disc

11.32 Releasing spring at handbrake lever shaft in caliper

11.33 Handbrake lever shaft circlip (arrowed)

12 Bodywork and fittings

Rear door quarterlight (5-door models) – removal and refitting

1   Remove the main glass from the door, as described in Chapter 11, Section 13.
2   Extract the fixing screw from the top of the quarterlight divider channel, and press the quarterlight glass, weatherseal and channel away from the door edge.
3   The quarterlight can then be withdrawn from the door. Refit by reversing the removal operations.

Rear side window (3-door models) – cable adjustment

4   The rear side window on the 3-door versions is controlled by a cable.
5   To ensure proper operation, the adjuster should be set to 18.0 mm (0.711 in) as shown in Fig. 13.36.
6   Access to the adjuster can be obtained in the following way.
7   Remove the rear parcel shelf, and fold the seat back down.
8   Unscrew the rear seat release knob from its rod.
9   Extract the six fixing screws from the rear side interior trim panel, and withdraw the panel.
10 Open the rear side window.
11 Turn the cable adjuster to provide the specified setting.
12 Close the window, and check that it seals all round. If necessary, turn the adjuster a little more until a good seal is obtained.

Rear side window (3-door models) – removal and refitting

13 Working inside the car, prise the plastic cover from the toggle-type latch (photo).
14 Disconnect the control cable from the toggle lever, and unhook the tension spring (photo).
15 Slide the latch arm off the ball-stud on the glass.
16 Using the fingers, prise off the plastic hinge cover from the forward edge of the window, to expose the hinges (photo).
17 Drill out the pop-rivets, remove the glass, and unscrew the nuts which hold the hinges to the glass.
18 Fit the hinges to the rear glass, but do not tighten the nuts excessively.
19 Pop-rivet the hinges to the body pillar.
20 Reconnect all the disconnected items, and then check the adjustment of the control cable as described earlier (photo).

Bonnet lock cable renewal – emergency opening of bonnet

21 In the event of the bonnet lock cable breaking, the bonnet can be opened if a large hole, diameter 12.5 mm (0.5 in) is drilled in the plate behind the radiator grille slats as shown. Take care not to damage the radiator (photo).
22 Insert a long screwdriver at the angle shown, and deflect the lever on the bonnet lock to release the lock (photo).
23 Fitting a new cable is described in Chapter 11, Section 7.

Body side rubbing strip – removal and refitting

24 The side rubbing strip can be removed by prising with a flat blade. Be prepared for some clips to break, and take care to protect the paintwork from damage when using the blade.

Exterior mirrors – removal and refitting

25 To remove the mirror, extract the grub screw and take off the control handle.
26 Prise out the triangular trim plate.
27 Extract the mirror fixing screws, and remove the mirror. Refitting is a reversal of removal.
28 Some later models have heated mirrors, and the wiring will have to be disconnected before removal. This will require removal of the door trim panel (see Chapter 11).

Interior mirror – removal and refitting

29 This is bonded directly to the windscreen.
30 The mirror can be removed by using a hot-air gun while an assistant applies a cutting action with a piece of nylon or terylene cord between the glass and the mirror base.

Fig. 13.36 Rear side window cable adjustment diagram (Sec 12)

31 Adhesive patches and special glues are available to bond the new mirror to the glass.

Seat belts – maintenance, removal and refitting

32 Periodically examine the belts for signs of fraying or other damage.
33 Any cleaning required should be done using warm water and liquid detergent. Do not use solvents of any kind.
34 Retain the belt in its extended position until dry before allowing it to retract into its reel housing.
35 Never attempt to modify or alter the location of a belt mounting, and if a belt anchorage is disconnected, always refit the mounting components in their original sequence (photos).
36 Access to the front seat belt reels is obtained after removing the interior quarter trim panel. Access to the rear belts involves removing the trim panel inside the rear corner body pillar (photo).

12.13 Prising off the latch plastic cover

12.14 Disconnecting the window opening control cable

12.16 Plastic hinge cover

12.20 Opening rear side window cable adjuster

12.21 Hole drilling dimensions for emergency opening of bonnet
A = 12.5 mm (0.5 in) diameter
B = 54.0 mm (2.1 in)

12.22 Inserting screwdriver to deflect bonnet lock lever

12.35A Typical seat belt anchorage components

12.35B Lower seat belt anchorage

12.35C Rear seat belt anchorage

12.36 Rear belt inertia reel

13 Electrical system

Alternator (Paris-Rhone) – brush renewal

1 If the brushes have been renewed (see Chapter 12, Section 7) then the action of removing and refitting the regulator/brush holder may prevent the alternator 'self-exciting', to commence charging when the engine is started.

2 Should this happen, carry out the following remedial action.

3 Disconnect the charge warning lamp lead from terminal 'L' on the regulator.

4 Briefly touch the end of a temporary lead from the battery positive terminal to the 'L' terminal on the regulator.

5 Reconnect the charge warning lamp lead to terminal 'L', and remove the temporary lead.

Side repeater lamps

6 The direction indicator side repeater lamps on later models are secured in the wing by twisting (bayonet fitting) instead of the clips used previously (photo).

7 The later type lamps only are supplied as replacements, and their fitting on early models will necessitate filing out the hole in the wing using the template shown in Fig. 13.37.

Fig. 13.37 Template for later type side repeater lamp front wing hole (Sec 13)

Headlamp dim-dip system

8   This is fitted to all later models, and prevents the car being driven on parking lamps only.

9   The headlamp beam intensity is reduced by means of the relay shown (photo), and a power resistor unit, which is normally mounted at the front of the engine compartment, low down beside the radiator. To further aid location of the resistor unit, it will, if working correctly, get very warm when the dim-dip function is in use.

Roof aerial – removal and refitting

10   Using a small screwdriver, prise out the map reading lamp from the roof lining above the windscreen.

11   Extract the fixing screws and lower the lamp housing.

12   The aerial fixing nut is now exposed. An open-ended spanner may be bent at right angles to engage on the two flats of the nut, or a forked tool may be fabricated from a piece of sheet metal (photo).

13   The aerial coaxial lead is fed down the right-hand side windscreen pillar. If it is to be withdrawn, tape a cord or curtain spring to its end, to facilitate installing the new lead.

14   If a new aerial is fitted, trim the aerial in accordance with the radio manufacturer's instructions.

13.6 Later type side repeater lamp

13.9 Headlamp dim-dip system relay (arrowed)

13.12 Roof-mounted aerial securing nut

P 58

309 (XU9JA)

1	14	2	15	3	16	4	17	5	18	6	19	7	20	8	21	9	22	10	23	11	24	12	25	13
112J	2	3	46J	M5.	7	8	9	10	12	MI3

M300

M313

8	8
7	7
E	
9	18A
5	M18

M889

M49
10

M280

20
46A

M251

3
18B
2

M744

1	46B
2	BB 11
3	M 4
4	112A
5	76
6	CC 7
7	
8	18
9	

37
15

38
33

M574

32
40

M50

E2 **E1**

14
41

F14

c683

M45

P 229

+ P
+ ACC
+ CON
+ DEM

Fig. 13.38 Wiring diagram for fuel injection system – GTI models

PARTICULARITE GTI

Fig. 13.39 Wiring diagram for all 1988-on Peugeot 309 models, including GTI

For key, refer to pages 221 to 225

CE PLAN REALISE EN CAD NE PEUT ETRE MODIFIE QU'EN CAD

Fig. 13.39 Wiring diagram for all 1988-on Peugeot 309 models, including GTI (continued)

For key, refer to pages 221 to 225

F1 – 10 A
F2 – 25 A
F3 – 25 A
F4 – 15 A
F5 – 10 A
F6 –
F7 – 15 A
F8 – 25 A
F9 – 30 A
F10 – 5 A
F11 – 5 A
F12 – 5 A
F13 – 5 A
F14 – 15 A

Fig. 13.40 Fuse/relay board connections – 1988-on models

For connector colours, refer to page 225

Fig. 13.40 Fuse/relay board connections – 1988-on models (continued)

For connector colours, refer to page 225

Fig. 13.41 Wiring diagram for dim-dip lighting

Fig. 13.42 Wiring diagram for electrically-operated fuel pump

Fig. 13.43 Wiring diagram for automatic transmission

Fig. 13.44 Wiring diagram for direction indicator side repeater lights

Index